The Italian American Experience

The ITALIANS IN CHICAGO

A STUDY IN AMERICANIZATION

Giovanni E[rmenegildo] Schiavo

ARNO PRESS

A New York Times Company

New York — 1975

Reprint Edition 1975 by Arno Press Inc.

Reprinted from a copy in
  The Princeton University Library

The Italian American Experience
ISBN for complete set: 0-405-06390-3
See last pages of this volume for titles.

Manufactured in the United States of America

Library of Congress Cataloging in Publication Data

Schiavo, Giovanni Ermenegildo, 1898–
    The Italians in Chicago.

    (The Italian American experience)
    Reprint of the 1928 ed. published by Italian
American Pub. Co., Chicago.
        1. Italian Americans--Illinois--Chicago.
2. Chicago--Biography. 3. Americanization.
I. Title. II. Series.
F548.9.I8S3 1975   917.73'11'0651   74-17950
ISBN 0-405-06420-9

The ITALIANS IN CHICAGO

The dream of the Italian immigrant.

The ITALIANS IN CHICAGO

A STUDY IN AMERICANIZATION

BY

Giovanni E. Schiavo

Fellow, Department of Sociology, New York University

WITH A PREFACE BY

JANE ADDAMS

ILLUSTRATIONS BY

ROCCO D. NAVIGATO

ITALIAN AMERICAN PUBLISHING CO.
8 SO. DEARBORN STREET
CHICAGO, ILL.
1928

PREFACE

THE following pages are a study of the Italians in Chicago made by a student born in Italy. The author, Giovanni Schiavo, left the Liceo in Palermo to come to the United States in 1916 when he was eighteen years old. Three years later he took his bachelor's degree at Johns Hopkins University and in the years following was a graduate student in political science and political economy at Johns Hopkins University and Columbia University. His occupation as a journalist and as a special traveling representative since then has led him to all parts of the United States and although long since an American citizen he has had, of course, unusual opportunities to see Italians everywhere and has been equally interested in the immigrant newly arrived from Italy and in the prosperous second and third generation Italians who form so goodly a portion of our population. In recognition of this wide spread interest, Mr. Schiavo has lately received a three years' fellowship from the University of New York for research into social conditions in New York City. We may, therefore, consider him well equipped from the academic standpoint for a study of a selected group such as the Italians in Chicago.

Mr. Schiavo tells me that in presenting the results of his study he has made a "constant effort against Chauvinism" although it must be at once apparent to the reader of this book that as an Italian he resents the estimate placed upon his fellow countrymen by many American students who have preceded him in a study of Italians in the United States. It is further obvious that with many another Latin and Slav, he considers that determining the quota to be admitted under the Selective Immigration Act, by the census of 1890, was both unfair and unwarranted.

His effort to connect the history of Italy with the Immigrant population is perhaps more determined because such history has been so persistently ignored by the American students of Italian immigration; that he says so little of recent events in Chicago connected with a group of Italian lawbreakers may also be due to what psychologists call "compensation" for the prolonged and damaging publicity in the American press. May we not say, however, that a great value of this study inheres the fact that it has been made by a man of Italian origin and while careful of his facts and figures, his presentation of the entire situation inevitably reveals a wide spread state of mind among immigrants living in America.

Having resided for nearly forty years in the midst of foreign born citizens I have long been familiar with this state of mind, and I have long hoped that it might be met with a more courageous understanding and good will.

It is perhaps needless to add that writing a preface to a book does not commit one to all the conclusions therein, but I should like to make clear my gratitude for this fine contribution towards the understanding of our fellow-citizens.

JANE ADDAMS.

Hull House
Chicago

FOREWORD

The photographs appearing in this book are not all the photographs of successful Italians in the city who should have been represented in a work of this kind.

It is hoped, however, that once the character of this work is better understood, a new edition may be printed, richer in photographs and data.

To that end, I shall be grateful to all those people who will kindly make suggestions or furnish informations that may be useful for the next edition.

This book is indebted to Jane Addams and Gertrude Howe Britton for very helpful criticism and suggestions; to Chev. Mastrovalerio for the invaluable assistance rendered; to the superintendent of the Board of Education, Mr. William J. Bogan, and to Mr. Oscar Durante, member of the board, for the data on the Italian children in the high schools of the city; to Prof. John Landesco of Northwestern University and the American Institute of Criminal Law and Criminology, and Prof. Ernest W. Burgess of the University of Chicago for very valuable suggestions; to Mr. Frederick Rex, Municipal Reference Librarian, for the many reports and publications kindly put at my disposal; to the University of Chicago for granting me access to the shelves of its magnificent library; to Dr. Louis Wirth of the University of Chicago, Rev. Manlio Ciufoletti, Dr. S Ingrao, Mr. C. Vitello, Mr. V. Ferrara and Dr. Antonio Lagorio for informations and suggestions, but above all to Mr. Antonio Lombardo, without whose generous assistance this work would never have been made possible.

GIOVANNI SCHIAVO.

As for immigrants we cannot have too many of the right kind; and we should have none at all of the wrong kind; and they are of the right kind if we can be fairly sure that their children and grandchildren can meet on terms of equality our children and grandchildren, so as to try to be decent citizens together for the uplifting of the Republic.

From an address by Theodore Roosevelt to the Executive Council of the American Federation of Labor and other Labor Representatives at the White House, March 21, 1906.

Facta Non Verba
(Facts Not Words)

CONTENTS

WE SHALL *probably have no final answer to this question until the contributions of the various races to American life are better known and compared; and until there is a wider knowledge on the part which each race has played in establishing and maintaining principles of liberty both here and abroad. To what extent immigrants possess the leadership which qualifies them to share in Anglo-Saxon institutions, and to participate in the administration of the form of government already established in America is now a matter of opinion rather than a fact.*

—FRANCES KELLOR, "Immigration and the Future."

❧

NATURALLY, *when men apply the warped categoric judgment to another race, particularly when that race is in political or economic competition with them, they are likely to magnify the evil in the character of the race and rarely even admit the good.*

—E. A. STEINER, "The Immigrant Tide" (page 195).

❧

* * * *those who know the immigrant peoples find that whether they belong to the "old" or the "new" immigration they are all much more alike than they are unlike, and that the really important differences, those that separate the desirable from the undesirable citizen or neighbor, are individual rather than racial.*

—GRACE ABBOTT, "The Immigrant and the Community" (page 290).

INTRODUCTION

THE Italian community of Chicago is typical of the Italian communities in the country. With due considerations for length of residence, number of people and difference of environment what is true of the Italians in Chicago is true of the Italians in any other city in the United States.

Several studies have been made of the Italians in Chicago, but most of them have dealt only with either a particular phase of Italian life in the city or a particular Italian district. All of them are superficial and quite unrepresentative of the community as a whole.

In 1896 Mr. Carroll D. Wright, the then Commissioner of Labor ordered an investigation among the Italians in Chicago. The Italians recorded in that investigation were 6,673 and included the American born of Italian extraction. At that time there were in the city not less than twenty thousand Italians. (According to the U. S. Census in 1900 they amounted to 26,046.) In other words, only 40 per cent of the Italians in the city were investigated.

Previous to that, in 1894, the same Commissioner of Labor ordered an investigation of the slums of the great cities. In that study, the Italians residing in the slums of Chicago are 5,685. According to the Chicago Daily News Almanac for 1895 there were 14,194 Italians in the city in 1895, including those of Italian origin. It follows, therefore, that only about 40 per cent of the Italians in the city were studied.

The reports of the Immigration Commission, made public in 1910, included detailed studies of the Italians throughout the country. The Italian districts of Chicago which were investigated by that commission were the Oakley Avenue section between Twenty-third and Twenty-fifth streets, a block on Ewing Avenue, a block on Gault Court, and a block on Peoria Street. The total number of households studied were 441, with a total of 2,157 Italian born residents. The United States census reports 16,008 Italians in the city in 1900 and 45,169 in 1910. The districts investigated were the poorest Italian districts in Chicago, with the exception of the Oakley Avenue section. Therefore, the Italians who were taken as representative Italians were not representative at all of the Italian people in the city, at that time, although they may have been typical of those in the district. On the other hand, if the Italians in Chicago then were only 35,000, those among whom the investigation of the Immigration Commission was conducted represented not more than 6 per cent of the total number of Italians in the city.

But even if the total population of the districts investigated had been considered, the conclusions could have applied only to the Italians residing in the slums of the city.

How misleading was the method could be visualized from the impression that we would receive of the English people if we were to consider the residents of the Limehouse district of London as representative Englishmen.

Likewise the various investigations that have been made as to housing conditions in the poor sections of the city, are not representative of the various nationalities living there unless the data is viewed in the light of the total number of people of each nationality living in the city.

It is not necessary to stress the fact, on the other hand, that welfare agencies are bound to deal with only those districts with which they have contact or on which they can focus the attention of the city council or the general public for purposes of raising funds.

Those are the official reports and investigations on which the undesirability of the Italians has been proclaimed to the world, and it is on the basis of reports of that kind that the Immigration Act of 1924 was approved.

No congressman or immigration expert has ever taken the trouble to look for the Italians outside the slums and notice the forward march of those that have moved out of the poor districts. Once an Italian makes good, he is no longer an Italian. He remains an Italian, however, as long as he is a failure.

If, besides studying the Italians in the congested districts of the city or those working on railroad gangs, our immigration experts would also study those living in the "strictly" American neighborhoods and the thousands of business and professional successes of Italian birth or extraction, an entirely different picture of the Italians could be presented to the American people.

That is what this book is intended for. It is not complete, by any means. It would be quite a hard task to trace all the Americans of Italian origin in the city. Many of them have Anglicized their names and many others who still retain their original names are not desirous to be associated with anything which does not savor of 100 per cent Americanism.

But as it is, it is hoped that this book may convince our well-intentioned Americans that the Italians in Chicago are not unworthy of the glorious traditions of their race and that they deserve not only a recognition of their contribution to Chicago's greatness but also a more impartial and fair attitude on the part of those who have misunderstood them so far—not as Italians, but as fellow-Americans.

*A man who has never been in Italy is always conscious
of an inferiority from his not having seen what a man is
expected to see. All our religion, almost all our law, almost
all our arts, almost all that sets us above savages, has come
to us from the shores of the Mediterranean.*
— SAMUEL JOHNSON (Boswell's, 1776).

*York—Report of fashions in proud Italy whose manners
still our apish nation limps after in base imitation.*
— SHAKESPEARE (Richard II, Act II).

*Lump the whole thing! Say that the Creator made Italy
from designs by Michael Angelo.*
— MARK TWAIN (Innocents Abroad, page 19).

Italy
*"where the virgins are soft as the roses they twine
and all save the spirit of man is divine."*
— BYRON.

The striking qualities the Italians exhibit are thrift, industry and peaceableness and these qualities in many cases have won the somewhat reluctant admiration of those who originally assumed a hostile attitude.

—Reports Immigration Commission Abstracts, vol. 1, 571.

THE RACE OF COLUMBUS

But in those who made pioneer settlements in Argentina and South Brazil, in those who have gone into the outlying parts of Europe and Asia, as far as the mines of Mysore, in those Sicilian fishermen who, after the Suez Canal was opened, betook themselves to Australia, in those wandering minstrels who have carried their traffic in music into a large part of the cities of the world, in all of these, by way merely of example, the persistence, the tireless verve of the conqueror has been present. They are of the race of Columbus still. In those who have journeyed far or made their journeys repeatedly—like the "swallows" who go to Argentina for the harvest—a certain superiority to circumstance appears, a ripeness and robust self-assurance, an urbanety even, qualities not infrequently encountered among the far-traveled men of leisure or position but till now met rarely among humble folk.

—R. F. FOERSTER, "The Italian Emigration of Our Time," page 419.

The Italians have very little to apologize for.

Ever since the days of Sicily's glorious civilization nearly three thousand years ago, down to our own times, the Italians have been teachers to the world and often masters of its destinies.

There is nothing new under the sun for the Italians. In all fields of human endeavour they have been leaders. From abstract political philosophy to practical experiments in politics, the Italians have tried it all. Imperial and republican with Rome, democratic with the commonwealths of the Middle Ages, under various types of monarchy since the Roman Empire, communist only a few years ago, the Italians are better prepared to absorb the principles that underlie the American Government than many another race in this country. As a matter of fact, political institutions in Sicily have preceded even those of England.

As Macaulay pointed out about one hundred years ago, when "in every other part of Europe a large and powerful privileged class trampled on the people and defied the government, in the most flourishing parts of Italy the feudal nobles were reduced to comparative insignificance."

Italian civilization has never faded out. The nights which have descended upon Italy have been the nights of Arctic summers. The dawn has always reappeared before the last reflection of the preceding sunset had faded from the horizon. (Macaulay, Essay on Machiavelli.)

In commerce as in banking, in the arts as in literature, in medicine as in surgery, in pure philosophy as in pedagogy, in the social sciences as in mathematics, in electricity as in mechanics, the Italians have left an indelible imprint.

That old glories and traditions are not extinct in the Italians is well proved by their revival in Italy today. The corporative state, to mention just one example, is the old "corporazioni" or "guilds" of the times of Florence and Palermo, adapted to present exigencies. Even among the Italians in the United States has the heritage of Rome yielded benefits.

Some of the biggest business men in the country today are of Italian birth or origin. Vaccaro in New Orleans, Cuneo in Chicago, Crespi in Texas, Poli in Connecticut, Bianco in Pennsylvania, Paterno in New York, Giannini in California, Di Giorgio in Maryland are only a few of the phalanx of leading American business men of Italian blood.[1]

Today the Italians in this country are to be found in every field of human activity. In some they have forged ahead, in others they have lagged behind.

Their apparent absence from the high positions in the leading financial and business organizations in the country, however, is to be attributed to the prejudice against them in some quarters, to the lack of confidence in their ability in others, and to the preference that executives have given to members of races more akin to theirs.[2] The leading Italian business men in the country today, with a few exceptions, are heads of their own firms.

Still, if we stop to consider under what conditions the Italians have labored in the New World, the obstacles they had to overcome, and in how short a period of time they have made good, we cannot but admire them.

The Italians do not need any complacency or condescension on the part of their fellow Americans. All they need is time. Time alone will show to the incredulous and the obstinate that the Italians represent just as an important factor in the progress of this nation as the members of all Nordic races, and that under more favorable conditions they are bound to play a leading part in the life of the country.

Apparently they have started to perceive that on the Pacific Coast, where the Italians have achieved tremendous successes, giving to their states leading financiers and educators (Suzzallo was president of the University of Washington for many years) and some of the biggest fruit growers and packers in the country.

It could not be explained otherwise that the fiercest opponents of Italian immigration should hail from the Pacific Coast.

As Dr. Steiner says: ". . . . . when that race is in political or economic competition with them . . . . .."

(1) Vaccaro is one of the leading citizens of New Orleans. He controls vast interests in Central America and owns a fleet for his gigantic fruit trade. He is the owner of the Roosevelt Hotel and many other enterprises in the city. It is said that his fortune is estimated at well over one hundred million dollars. He started years ago as an immigrant boy.

Cuneo is the president of the Cuneo Press, the largest printing establishment in the world.

Crespi is a millionaire cotton grower and merchant of Texas.

Poli owns a chain of high class theatres along the Atlantic Coast, from Washington, D. C., to Boston.

Bianco is one of the leading coal operators and candy manufacturers of Pennsylvania.

Paterno is considered as one of the biggest builders in New York City. He has built many apartment houses on Riverside Drive and other high class residential sections of Gotham. He is several times millionaire.

Giannini, the president of the Bancitaly Corporation, with resources of over one billion dollars (one thousand million dollars), does not need any introduction.

Salvatore Di Giorgio is one of the leading fruit dealers in the country, and controls large interests in Central America. Many other outstanding successes could be mentioned.

(2) Several years of experience with some of the largest financial institutions in the country, from the National City Bank of New York down, have given the writer an unusual opportunity to study the criterion by which executives abide in the promotion of their employees.

THE SICILIANS

"Sicily is the key to the whole. Without Sicily Italy is nothing."—GOETHE.

Siciliani! Voi siete grandi! Voi avete, in pochi giorni, fatto piu' assai per l'Italia, nostra patria comune, che non tutti noi con due anni di agitazione. * * * Per Voi, noi, esuli dell'Italia, passeggiamo con piu' sicura e serena fronte tra gli stranieri, che ieri ci commiseravano ed oggi ci ammirano. Dio Benedica l'armi, le vostre donne, i vostri sacerdoti e voi tutti."—MAZZINI.

On May 24, 1928, the "Chicago Daily Tribune" published on its first page a story about the capture of three members of an extortion ring.

Mr. Rudolph Weiler, wealthy head of H. Weiler & Co., wholesale druggists, had been the victim of blackmailers since March, 1928. According to the "Tribune" Weiler was so frightened by the threats of the gangs who posed as officials of the "Sicilian Society" that he not only made two payments of $250 each but kept his son, Stanley, ten years old, a virtual prisoner in his apartment at the Embassy Hotel for about a week. "The fear instilled in citizens by the ease with which bombs are exploded, leaving no trace of the perpetrators, was used to collect from Weiler, it was said." On Sunday, May 20, a third demand for $250 was made. Mr. Weiler this time decided to turn the matter over to the police, who laid in ambush and captured the three bandits. Their names were: Earl Fraher, Robert E. Kieffer and George David, a taxicab chauffeur. Fraher was an ex-convict who had already served time in Pontiac reformatory on extortion charge. With the arrest of the three men the police believed to have uncovered a gang which had squeezed money from many successful business men.

The Sicilians of Chicago certainly owe a debt of gratitude to Mr. Weiler for his courage to turn the matter over to the police. But unfortunately Mr. Weiler has not been the only person from whom money has been extorted in Chicago by bandits who use the name of "Sicilians" to accomplish their criminal ends. Probably hundreds of people have been paying money and kept quiet about it.

Extortion of money alone is not coupled with Sicilian crimes. Bombings or "pineapples" in the eyes of quite a few people in the city are synonyms of Sicilian vendetta, notwithstanding the fact that most of the bomb throwing in Chicago has been ascribed by people who are in a position to know, to politics, labor feuds, or gambling. (Bombings in Chicago started with the gambling wars of 1907, in which no Italians were involved. See Chapter 22.)

Local newspapers and politicians have created such impressions on the people of Chicago. Politicians, especially, without any self-respect or regard to ethics, have not hesitated to condemn a whole people in order to reach their goal—perverted Machiavellism of candidates for positions of public trust!

It is high time for the people of Chicago to stop believing all the "bunk" that a press without scruples ladles out to them. The fact is, and nobody who is acquainted with actual conditions can deny it, that the SICILIANS OF CHICAGO, AS A WHOLE, ARE JUST AS RESPECTABLE, JUST AS LAW-ABIDING, JUST AS HONEST, JUST AS GOOD CITIZENS AS THE PROUDEST MEMBERS OF THE UNION LEAGUE.

Of course there are Sicilians who go wrong—nobody will deny that—but just as well there is no race in the world that has not its share of criminals.

17

As a matter of fact, the Sicilians of Chicago represent a higher factor of stability in the community than many another race. Those few Sicilians who are associated with illegal or criminal practices, pray, let me say it, would not stay long in "business" without the support of some of our own American officials.

Fifty thousand Sicilians in Chicago are not responsible for the crimes or illegal operations of a few members of their race. It is idiotic and ludicrous to blame thousands of people for the crimes of a few, just as it was idiotic and ludicrous for the people of Europe, before the war, to associate the name of America with drunkards and ruffians or at the most with "marchands de cochons à Chicago" (Chicago pig dealers) just because many Americans who used to go to Europe before 1914 were of the type that would easily get intoxicated or get into a brawl in the streets of Paris or on the Square of St. Mark in Venice.

The ignorance, complacency and prejudice with which some of the people of Chicago regard the Sicilians certainly do not reflect any lustre on their intelligence.

Some high-minded people suggest that the Sicilians should take care of themselves and denounce the members of their race who go wrong.

But how is that possible when the profits of those Sicilians who go wrong are shared by the very people who are supposed to protect the public?

If that were feasible, why is it that over three million Chicagoans have not been able so far to sever the ties that unite criminals and politicians?

To be honest with ourselves, Gentlemen Editors of the Chicago Daily Press, do you not think that the Sicilians are blamed for quite a few crimes that are committed by people of other nationalities? Do you not think that the Sicilians of Chicago are made the scapegoat of police incompetence and corruption?

BUT, WHO ARE THE SICILIANS?

The Sicilians are one of the most glorious and freest people on earth.

Highly civilized long before Rome was born, Sicily reached the highest peak of its glory in the fifth century before Christ. Segesta for eight centuries was under a republican form of government. The Sicilian victories at Imera, in the year 480 B. C., and at Crimiso, in the year 339 B. C. (Nicotri, "Dalla Conca D'Oro al Golden Gate," page 16), probably changed the destinies of the world. As Ettore Pais has stated, to "Sicily fell the glory of being the harbinger of Latin civilization."

From those days to our own, Sicilian civilization has never died out, although at times it has withered and decayed.

The Italian language, for example, was born in Palermo, at the Court of Frederick the Second, Emperor of Germany and King of Sicily, in the thirteenth century. Constitutional liberties were granted to the Sicilians in 1215, or eighty-five years before the English Magna Charta was promulgated. The famous Sicilian Vespers of 1282 attest the unvanquished nature of the proud islanders.

Down to our own times the Sicilians have kept the light of freedom burning. Without the help of the Sicilians the Kingdom of Italy would not have been proclaimed in 1860. Without the aid of the Sicilian "picciotti" Garibaldi could have never conquered the Kingdom of the Two Sicilies. Those are facts that no historian will dispute.

The nature, not the number, of the crimes committed by the Sicilians has weaved around them a myth of weird, awesome dispositions—a ridiculous fear which no doubt originated in the reluctance of the Sicilians to testify so long as they did not feel assured of state protection, thus leaving crimes unsolved.

Those Americans, however, who have come in contact with the Sicilians will tell you that they are as human and as "nice people" as any in the world. Moreover, they happen to be more intelligent than the average person of similar social level, notwithstanding the evidence of the army intelligence tests to the contrary.

Of the generosity of the Sicilians one could write books. In Sicily the low classes entertain with a liberality of a Croesus. In America the home of the Sicilian is always open to the needy and to friends.

In love the Sicilians are rather passionate—likewise in hatred. Under favorable influences, however, they change their "ways" and even dispositions. Although divorce has not invaded the Sicilian home as yet, seldom will the Sicilian in America resort to murder to punish the unfaithfulness of his wife or sweetheart. Circumstances play a very important part in the life of the Sicilians. As Colaianni proved by comparing crimes among the Sicilians in Sicily and the Sicilians in Tunis, the crimes of the Sicilians are not the product of the race, but, to a large extent, the product of environment. (Colaianni, Gli Italiani agli Stati Uniti.)

Friendship the Sicilians hold in very high esteem. As a matter of fact, the Sicilian will never betray a friend under any circumstance.

Easily aroused to a pitch of enthusiasm or anger, the Sicilian soon reverts to his temperate self. Under favorable influences, however, he soon acquires admirable self-control.

Emotional by nature, the Sicilian easily becomes the prey of superstitions, not an inferior trait, by any means, if walking under a ladder or breaking a glass spells misfortune for intelligent Americans. Even D'Annunzio is said to be superstitious.

The staunchness of the Sicilian in friendship finds a counterpart in his strong loyalty to this country. Just as his love for Italy declines, that for America rises in its place. But it is a love all "sui generis". George Washington probably will appeal to him like Garibaldi did in the days of his youth, but Lincoln no doubt he will understand better and admire more. Roosevelt, however, is the type that the Sicilians have loved most. It was reported in the Italian newspapers years ago how some Sicilians were seen one day kneeling before the grave of the great "Teddy" at Oyster Bay. It was an unusual and touching sight for the watchman used to behold silk hatted gentlemen paying their homages to the memory of the great American. But these Sicilians were ordinary workingmen—the same type that we have met so often digging ditches or at menial labors. There was no affectation in their muteness before the grave—no newspaper reporters were on hand, no photographers to record their action. Only a watchman prying out from among the foliage, half astounded and bewildered.

Probably the love of the Sicilian for America may be due to a high sense of duty and gratitude than anything else. Certainly he appreciates what America has done for him and his children and just as he returns the favors that a friend may bestow on him, so he feels that the only way he can pay his debt to America is through unstinted loyalty under any circumstance, for his loyalty is unflinching.

The chief interest of the Sicilian, above all, lies in his family. In his family he centers all his ambitions and activities. For his family he toils, he suffers, he goes through any sacrifice. The honor of his family is the main concern in his life. As Foerster has remarked, the Sicilian's conception of family living is one in which "privacy and intimacy are deemed quite essential." The Sicilian girl's life, for instance, is inseparable from that of her family. She takes over many of her mother's tasks. Her wedding becomes, what her christening was, a great family event. That she should enter a factory at all is a concession to American conventions."

The home of the Sicilian is immaculately clean. Sicilian women, as a matter of fact, are taught since childhood to become good housewives. And, although in the early period of their American life they may neglect all rules of hygiene, on account of the necessity for practically every member of the family to go to work, still as soon as economic conditions allow the Sicilian woman to devote all her attentions to her home, her house becomes a model of cleanliness.

The Sicilian is by nature chivalrous and polite. What in other nationalities is the product of breeding or education, in the Sicilian is innate. It is only when the Sicilian acquires the "manners" of the people he comes in contact at the market or at the factory that the Sicilian loses some of his inborn courtesy.

The spirit of self-denial probably reaches its highest peak in the Sicilian. To reach his goal, whether it is a moneyed return to Italy or the purchase of a fruit store in this country, the Sicilian will go through any privations. Sober by nature, he spends as little as possible even on food and other life necessities. But the moment he can afford it, he entertains with a liberality of a millionaire. It is said that one of the Genna brothers spent about one hundred thousand dollars for entertainment at the wedding of one of his sisters.

In business the Sicilians have been very successful. In Chicago they have done as well as the Genoese who preceded them by at least twenty-five years. Of the ten leading wholesale grocers in the city, seven are Sicilian. The Chicago Macaroni Company, one of the largest in the world, also belongs to Sicilians. Some of the largest wholesalers of fruits in the city are Sicilian. Probably fifty per cent of the Italian retail stores in the city are owned by Sicilians.

As a whole, the Sicilians have made good. Unfortunately, they are still misunderstood, but "as they take American ways they rise in estimation. When they lose their sobriety, habits of economy, devotion to their customs and traditions and attachment to their kind, one student has ironically observed, they tend to come more into favor! It is surely so, for their neighbors then find them less inscrutable." (Foerster, Italian Emigration of Our Times, page 409.)

CHAPTER I

WHY ITALY LEAVES HOME

THE reasons for the exodus of the Italians in the second-half of the nineteenth century and the beginning of the twentieth are to be sought primarily in the economic field.

Although in Italy there never was, at any time, anything like the destitution that was predominant in parts of England and Ireland in the eighteenth and nineteenth centuries, still the latifundium, the ravages of the phyloxera or the olive fly, the malaria or the pellagra, made conditions at times utterly unbearable.[1] The Italians, however, had already learned to make the best of similar situations and were quick to adapt themselves to the new conditions although they were always looking for a way out of the sad plight.

J. H. Bartels, a German traveler of the eighteenth century, describes admirably the spirit that animates the Italians. He wrote of the Calabrians: "I find here people of the brightest intelligence. Under the cruel yoke which hangs upon their necks, it is naturally hard for them to raise their heads. But their means of supporting the yoke and the courage which constantly animates them, is the most eloquent evidence of their intelligence. You will never find a Calabrian giving way to cowardly sobs. He will complain to you of his burden, but he paints you his picture with such exactness that you are forced to admit that he sees to the bottom, and though he bends under his burden because a sword hangs over his head, he tries at the same time to discover ways and means of freeing himself from the burden.[2]

What Bartels wrote about the Calabrians of the eighteenth century applies to people of other Italian regions in the nineteenth century.

The inner motives of Italian migration are revealed by its very fluctuations.

Emigration from Italy, for several decades, was constituted chiefly by groups of people from a few towns, rather than from the whole region. At one time it was the people from Termini Imerese, who emigrated, at another those from Trevigno and still at another time those from Calascibetta and so on.[3]

The explanation is simple. The emigrants followed their relatives or friends who had gone to America and made good—and that explains also why in various cities of the United States we find, although not so noticeably today, little Trevignos, or little Terminis or little Calascibettas.

The Italians did not come to the United States because they were looking for political freedom. They had all they wanted at home. Those who got away to escape military service were few. On the other hand, they did not come in as indentured servants or to escape a famine.

21

The spirit of adventure had something to do with their coming. Before applying for a passport an Italian knew what he was going to find in the new country. He knew that his life in the new world would be one of sorrows, of sacrifices, of humiliations, of self-denials. But the desire to change his economic status was by far much stronger than any obstacle that he was to overcome. The myth of America had already gotten hold of him.

Their port of landing in the majority of cases was New York. Quite a few, however, landed in Boston and New Orleans.

The real influx of the Italians to Chicago came with the building of the railroads and the opening of mines in Illinois. Herded in large numbers by employment agents in the East, they were loaded on freight trains and shipped to camps where they were held more or less in a sort of bondage by their employers.

With the expansion of manufactures in the city a large number of Italians left the railroads and sought work in factories. Many of them, as early as 1880, started in business for themselves, as fruit peddlers and small merchants. Some went back to Italy but in most cases returned to the United States as they could no longer conform themselves to class distinctions and different modes of living.

It was these dissatisfied groups who returned to the United States with the intention of living here permanently that started the movement among the Italians to settle in the country and send for their families.

NOTES TO CHAPTER 1

(1) See R. F. Foerster, The Italian Emigration of Our Times, Chapters 3-5.
(2) In Briefe über Kalabrien and Sizilien, 3 vol. Gottinger, 1787, quoted by Foerster.
(3) Termini Imerese is a good sized town in the Province of Palermo, Sicily; Trevigno is in the Province of Potenza, Basilicata, and Calascibetta in the Province of Caltanissetta, Sicily.

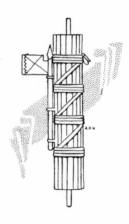

CHAPTER II

THE COMING OF THE ITALIANS

PROBABLY the first Italian to set foot on Chicago Land was Henry de Tonti, the famous Lieutenant of La Salle.

De Tonti's life and exploits are told in all good encyclopaedias. "Tonti, next to La Salle, did more than any other of the early French explorers to make Illinois known to the civilized world.[1]

The assistance Tonti rendered De Nonville, the Governor of Canada, with 170 Frenchmen and 300 Indians from the West, in his attack on the Senecas was very valuable. Says Bancroft, the famous historian, quoting De Nonville: "God alone could have saved Canada in 1688. But for the assistance obtained from the posts of the west, Illinois must have been abandoned, the fort at Mackinaw lost and a general uprising of the nations would have completed the destruction of New France.[2]

Another Italian who rendered invaluable services to Illinois, at the time of the Revolution, was Francis Vigo, a St. Louis merchant of Italian origin who was of great assistance to Gen. George Rogers Clark in connection with his operations in the Illinois Country. Thoroughly committed to the American cause he was intelligent, patriotic, and resourceful, and when General Clarke reached Kaskaskia with his scantily supplied army Vigo furnished him with food and clothing to the value of twenty thousand dollars, taking his pay in Virginia Continental money. By the depreciation of this money and the confiscation of his property by Governor Hamilton, the British Commandant, he was made poor. When Clark determined to capture Hamilton in Vincennes, he sent Vigo accompanied by only one man to reconnoitre the fort. Vigo was arrested as a spy when he was within seven miles of Fort Vincennes but being a Spanish subject was released and returned to St. Louis. He soon rejoined Clark and was with him when he captured Vincennes. Later, he sustained an intimate relationship to Gen. William Henry Harrison for whom he frequently acted as interpreter on important occasions. Born in Sardinia[3] in 1747 he came to America as a private in the Spanish Army quitting the Army in 1772 to come to St. Louis where he engaged in the fur trade. Pierre Menard, who was afterward the first Lieutenant Governor of Illinois was in his employ as a fur trader and together they visited General Washington at Carlisle, Pa., in 1789 to consult with him in reference to the best means of defending the western frontier. Vigo died near Vincennes in 1835."[4] Another Italian who played a very important part in the religious education of the people of Illinois, was the Rt. Rev. Joseph Rosati, 1st Bishop of St. Louis. In 1830 there was not one priest in the whole state of Illinois. Under his energetic administration, however, the various congregations at Kaskaskia, Cahokia, and Prairie du Rocher were soon supplied and many confirmations were reported. It was under him that the

Catholic Church took a firm hold in the state.[5] The first Catholic priest in Chicago, Abbe St. Cyr, was sent by Bishop Rosati.

Another great Italian who probably stopped in Chicago early in the 19th century was G. C. Beltrami, the real discoverer of the sources of the Mississippi River.[6]

Of course, many Italian explorers and missionaries have been through the territory that was to be Chicago ever since the time of La Salle but they were not immigrants in the accepted meaning of the word.

Even before 1850 there were Italian immigrants in Chicago but they were few and apparently they did not remain long. (According to the U. S. Census, less than 100 Italians, on the average, entered the United States each year from 1820 to 1850.)

The Village of Genoa, in Wisconsin, on the other hand, was founded before 1860 by Italians from Piedmont and Lombardy who certainly must have lived in Chicago, even if temporarily, before settling up North. Another village, near Pana, Ill., was settled by Italians around 1865.

The real immigration of Italians in Illinois, however did not start until 1880.

According to the U. S. Census in 1850 Illinois had 43 Italians against over 27,000 Irish, 38,000 Germans, 18,000 English, and 4,000 Scandinavians. In 1860 there were in Chicago 100 Italians, over 22,000 Germans, about 20,000 Irish, and 5,000 English. In 1870 the Italians had increased to 552, in 1880 to 1357, in 1890 to 5591, in 1900 to over 16,000, in 1910 to 45,000, and in 1920 to about 60,000. It is estimated that there are today in Chicago over 80,000 natives of Italy and probably over 180,000 people of Italian stock.

The first Italians to come to Chicago in 1860 were not representative of those who followed in geographic origin and occupation. If we are to judge from the names, as they appear in the Chicago city directory for that year most of them hailed from Genoa and a few from Tuscany. In 1880 we find more or less the same composition, with a sprinkling of South Italians. In 1890 the people from the South of Italy started to come in large numbers. In 1896, according to an investigation conducted by the U. S. Commissioner of Labor,[7] among the Italians in the slum districts of Chicago, out of 1348 families visited, comprising a total population of 6773 persons of whom 4,493 were natives of Italy, we find that 18.28% were from Campania, 17.78% from Basilicata, 12.68% from Calabria, 7.83% from Sicily, 5.18% from Abruzzi and 32.20% born in the United States.

The natives of Italy in Chicago, at that time, probably were around 12,000.

A more definite idea of the composition of the Italian population of Chicago may be had from the annual reports of the Commissioner of Immigration.

According to them we find that from 1899 to 1927, 52,394 people were admitted from North Italy and 140,321 from South Italy.[9] (By South Italy the U. S. Census classifies all regions exclusive of Piedmont, Lombardy and Venetia. So even Genoa is classified as Southern Italy.) The above figures, however, are for the whole State of Illinois so if we consider that over 65% of the Italians in the state reside in Chicago and that the majority of the Italians outside of Cook County hail from North Italy, we can form an approximate idea of the regional origin of the Italians in the city.

Of course, departures are to be considered also. The only figures available are those of the Immigration Commissioner and they date back only to 1908. On the strength of those figures it can be stated that the proportion of North Italians admitted was of 27% to 73% for those from the South, their departures were of 13,961 against 54,135 or about 20% for the North Italians and 80% for the South Italians.

If a census should be taken today, probably we would find that of the Italian stock in Chicago, 15% would trace their origins to Piedmont, Lombardy and Venetia, including Trento and Trieste, 25% to Liguria, Tuscany, Emilia, Marche and Umbria, and 50% to Lazio, Abruzzi, Molise, Campania, Basilicata, Apulia, Calabria, and Sicily. There are very few Sardinians here.

The coming of the Italians coincided with the greatest industrial progress in the history of the United States. In such progress the Italians played a very important part. Says Frank Orman Beck, "The Italians helped to create our national wealth, in fact at one period of our history he was our economic salvation. Today he is our industrial ally."[8]

Any student of the economic history of the United States can testify in regard to that.

As to the economic progress of Chicago, if it be true that Chicago owes its amazing progress to its railroads, then it is indisputable that had it not been for Italian labor the progress of Chicago would have been retarded and probably would have never attained such magnificent proportions. If we consider that railroad mileage in the country from 93,267 miles in 1880 jumped to 240,831 miles in 1910 and that during the same period of time over 2,500,000 Italians entered the country, rising from an average of 25,000 a year for the period 1880-1889 to an average of over 190,000 a year for the period 1900-1909, if we further consider that the great majority of the Italians in America at one period or another of their early life in this country worked as laborers on the railroads, if we consider that had it not been for the railroads the progress of the nation would have been seriously handicapped, then we can properly appreciate how valuable was the contribution of the Italians to the progress of the Republic. (The Italian population of Chicago from 1357 in 1880 increased to over 45,000 in 1910.)

Some adversaries of the newer immigration have remarked that if the Italians had not come, the inventive genius of the Americans would have devised some new machines to take the place of human hands.

It seems the irony of destiny that just a machine of that type should have been invented by an Italian laborer from Chicago, Pasquale Ursino, after 95 years of experimenting by railroad officials and engineers.

NOTES TO CHAPTER 2

(1) Historical Encyclopaedia of Illinois, edited by N. Bateman & P. Selby, Chicago, 1905.
(2) Quoted by A. Davidson and B. Stuve: "A complete history of Illinois," from 1673 to 1873.
(3) The Sardinia referred to probably is the Kingdom of Sardinia, which included the following regions: Piedmont, Lombardy, Sardinia, Nice and Savoy.
(4) Encyclopaedia of the History of St. Louis, vol. 4, 1899.
(5) Illinois, Historical and Statistical, by John Moses, 1895.
(6) Eugenia Masi, G. C. Beltrami.
(7) C. D. Wright, The Italians in Chicago. U. S. Printing Office, Washington, D. C., 1896.
(8) F. O. Beck, The Italians in Chicago, a study made by the Department of Public Welfare of the City of Chicago, 1919.

Regarding the contribution of the immigrants to the development of America, Lippincott says:

> The fear and prejudice that lie at the basis of much of the discussion often obscure the facts. The net addition of something over twenty million able-bodied men and women has made possible a growth that could have not taken place without them and this service has been rendered in every department of industry. There is no question about the value of the skilled immigrant who brings in new and valuable information of some trade, or who adds to the prosperity of the country because of his skill. But the unskilled man, also, has contributed a valuable labor service * * * our natural resources have been largely developed by immigrants. (Page 351, J. Lippincott, Economic Development of the United States, 1927.)

Frederick Haskins has pictured the contribution of the immigrants thus:

> I have shouldered my burden as the American man of all work.
> I contribute eighty-five per cent of all the labor in the slaughtering and meat-packing industry.
> I do seven-tenths of the bituminous coal mining.
> I do seventy-eight per cent of all the work in the woolen mills.
> I contribute nine-tenths of all the labor in the cotton mills.
> I make nineteen-twentieths of all the clothing.
> I manufacture more than half the shoes.
> I build four-fifths of all the furniture.
> I make half of the collars, cuffs and shirts.
> I turn out four-fifths of all the leather.
> I make half the gloves.
> I refine nearly nineteen-twentieths of the sugar.
> I make half of the tobacco and cigars.
> And yet I am the great American Problem.
> When I pour out my blood on your altar of labor, and lay down my life as a sacrifice to your god of toil, men make no more comment than at the fall of a sparrow. * * *
> My children shall be your children and your land shall be my land because my sweat and my blood will cement the foundations of the America of Tomorrow.
> If I can be fused into the body politic the melting pot will have stood the supreme test.
> (Quoted by C. Panunzio, in Immigration Crossroads (1927).
> (9) Figures for the year 1903 are missing.

CHAPTER III

THE HISTORICAL AND CULTURAL BACKGROUND OF THE ITALIAN IMMIGRANT

I T IS outside the province of the present inquiry to dwell on the various ethnical factors that go in the making of the Italian people.

Students of history know that Italy has been the meeting place for the races of the earth and that she still retains the strains of the many people that have occupied her. Among Italians in Chicago such strains are especially noticeable in the Sicilians and the Venetians.

Here I shall simply point out two facts:

One is that the foreign invaders really never conquered Italy. Instead of assimilating the Italians they were assimilated.[1] The Normans for example assimilated the Britons but never succeeded in assimilating the Sicilians. When the invaders attempted to act tyrannically the Italians invariably rebelled.

The other is that foreign domination of Italy with the exception of the Greek and the Norman, and to a certain extent that of the Arabs in Sicily[2] was always disastrous to the country, especially the Southern part. North Italy does not seem, however, to have suffered so much from foreign invasions, aside from the despoliation of her art galleries. As a whole she has fared much better than the South.

Better educational facilities, a fertile soil, a more abundant rainfall, less deforestation, an enlightened clergy and the favor that industrial and commercial people have shown her, have given her many advantages over the South. Even after Italy was united in 1870, the North has been the place where all government contracts have been filled and most improvements made. Moreover, proximity to foreign industrial centers, such as Germany's and France's facilitated the emigration of North Italians to those countries and the consequent learning of industrial trades. Vocational and industrial schools soon flourished throughout the North and that accounts for the larger proportion of skilled laborers among the North Italians.

The South, on the other hand, not only was neglected by its conquerors but was even forced into the darkest conditions especially during the 18th and first half of the 19th century. The South, however had seen civilization before the North. When civilization died out in Athens it flourished again in Sicily and Southern Italy (Magna Graecia). It was from Sicily that it moved northward to Rome. Segesta and Agrigento, Syracuse and Cotrone were civilized before Rome was born.

The kingdom of Sicily, Apulia and Calabria, proclaimed by the great Norman King Rogers, in the 12th century, was the official recognition of the great civilization of the South. Indeed, King Rogers gave to the Sicilian people in 1130, constitutional liberties at that time not enjoyed even by the British. (The

Magna Charta dates back to 1215.)[3] The Italian language was born in Palermo, Sicily, at the court of Frederick II.

But the Spanish domination of Southern Italy followed by that of the Bourbons (Gladstone called their reign "the negation of God erected into a system of government") reduced the country in the most deplorable conditions. It is well over 500 years that have kept Southern Italy in the dark, 500 years of injustices, of sufferings, of abuses.

Misgovernment alone, however, is not responsible for the wretched conditions that have existed in South Italy. Feudalism, the worst type of latifundium (absentee landlordism or large estates owned by one man who spent most of his time in the large cities or abroad and very seldom visiting his estates) slight and for long periods totally absent rainfall, the ravages of malaria, the lack of roads, and other means of transportation, no industrial or commercial opportunities, rampant illiteracy and some ignorant clergy desirous of keeping the people in the dark made South Italy one of the unhappiest regions in the world.[4] Let us add the fact that Italy lacks raw materials, that she has to import her coal and even wheat and cattle and the picture will be clearer.

When Italy became united in 1870 it was thought that the South would have at least been compensated for all the neglect and injustices it had received at the hands of foreign rulers. Far from it. The "questione del mezzogiorno" has not been solved yet. Only recently, thanks to Mussolini, a marked improvement has taken place. In the last few years more than one-half of the total appropriations for the whole country has been allotted to the South.

Out of such misery and squalor two things stand out. The first is the love for the beautiful: art, literature, music. The second is the irrepressible longing for freedom.

Even at times when conditions among the lower classes of society including the bourgeosie, were almost hopeless, the towns and cities of the Peninsula managed to cultivate literature and art. It is from the 13th to the 19th century that Italy has produced its galaxy of great men: poets, painters, architects, sculptors, scientists, musicians—some of them the greatest in their fields that the world has ever produced. Court life had all the pomp and grandeur both of the Romans and the Spaniards. Carnivals, races, celebrations in honor of saints and warriors, poets and artists, statesmen and high officials like those offered to the people of Italy, both North and South, have not been surpassed in any country in the world. They were intended, many times, to divert the attention of the masses from their own problems. Although they succeeded in part, they educated the common people to the love of arts and stirred their imagination.[4] Entertainments offered by land lords during the summer at their estates also served to create among the poor peasants a taste for music and arts. And so what to some people was a luxury to the poor Italians came to be a matter of every day life. In fact, most of Italy's great men were the sons of poor folks.

This tradition has never been broken. In a country like America where opportunities are so plentiful, those atavistic tendencies are coming to the surface more and more every day.

Love for freedom, on the other hand, has always been alive in the hearts of the Italians.

From Dante to Carducci, from Machiavelli to Cavour, from Michelangelo to Verdi, from Vico to Romagnosi, to Mazzini, to Foscolo, to Monti, to Parini, to Alfieri, to Bellini, it is all a firmament of great men who have paved the way to the unification of Italy and the possession of freedom.

But not for Italy's freedom alone have the Italians fought. In the Argentine as in Uruguay, in Mexico as in Cuba, in Greece as in France, the Italians have always fought for the weak and the oppressed.

The genius of the Italians have always revered the struggles of patriotism; when the United States declared its independence Alfieri saw in America the prophet of Italian Unity; and Filangieri was preparing the work in which, with the applause of the best minds, he claimed for reason its rights in the government of men.[5]

The Italian people to some have seemed to be made of a slavish race. But, if they did not regain their liberty before 1860 and 1870 it was not because of lack of courage or because of servile spirit. If the absence of rebellions as De Lapouge tells us is an index of the inferiority of a race[6] then the Italian people are the superior of all peoples.

The Italians by nature are patient and resigned. To a certain extent they are fatalists. They endure as long as they can endure it, but once their patience reaches the breaking point, they break loose regardless of consequences. History proves that. The Vespri in Palermo, Masaniello, in Naples, Cola di Rienzo in Rome, Balilla in Genoa, Micca in Turin, the five days in Milan, the insurrections of 1812, 1820, 1848 and 1860, to cite only the most important, are evidence of the spirit of rebellion in the Italians.

Five centuries of misgovernment and injustices were bound to leave almost indelible traces in a people. Still, the Italians have not lost their old worth. Like old gold that has laid buried for ages under dirt, and cleaned of its earth, regains its old glittering, so the Italians, transplanted in a more favorable environment, are quickly deserving of the best traditions of their race.

NOTES TO CHAPTER 3

(1) Villari, L'Italia e la Civilta'.

(2) Amari, Storia dei Mussulmani in Sicilia.

(3) G. Nicotri, Il Primato della Sicilia nelle liberta' costituzionali. Also "Dalla Conca d'Oro al "Golden Gate" by the same author.

(4) Poor economic conditions, however, did not cause any crime wave. As Garofalo tells us, (Criminology, Criminal science series, Boston, 1914, page 165) "the economic conditions of the proletariat * * * is entirely without influence upon criminality, as a whole; its influence is exerted only upon certain special forms which constitute the specific criminality of the lower classes. * * * Extreme indigence ordinarily results in mendacity, sometimes in vagabondage; the only crimes for which it is clearly accountable are such trivial offenses as the stealing of firewood, articles of food and other articles of insignificant value."

(5) Bancroft, History of United States, vol. 5, page 226.

(6) G. V. De Lapouge, L'Aryen, son role social, Paris, 1899, quoted by Carl C. Brigham in "A Study of American Intelligence," page 184.

CHAPTER IV

THE SOCIAL BACKGROUND OF THE ITALIAN DISTRICTS
OF CHICAGO

TO FULLY understand from what depths of social life the Italians have arisen in the brief period of thirty years, it is necessary to have some knowledge of the conditions existing in the so-called Italian districts of the city before and at the time the Italians settled there.

The wards in which the Italians have lived in large numbers are the twenty-seventh, the forty-second, and the first. The appellatives by which they were known long before the Italians settled there, are significant of their conditions years ago.

The first ward contained the red light district of the city, and as a matter of fact, many of the houses in which the Italians lived had been houses of prostitution.

The forty-second ward, at least that part which was in the old twenty-second ward, had the characteristic name of "Little Hell" and was peopled by Germans and Scandinavians, with a sprinkling of Poles.

The twenty-seventh ward, formerly the nineteenth, had the very significant name of "bloody nineteenth" and was inhabited chiefly by Irish and Germans.

Although before 1890 there was in Chicago a large number of Irish, Germans and Scandinavians who had already become a real asset to the city, there were also some lower elements of the same racial groups, who committed most of the crimes and lived as probably the poorest and thriftiest Italian never lived, not even at the worst time of his life.

Back in the fifties the Irishman was pictured to the people of Illinois "as the noisy, quarrelsome seeker after excitement, who found it in the company of John Barleycorn, in bloody street brawls, and even in the lower depths of crime.[1] The common practice of contemporary journalists was reflected in the point raised by the Chicago Tribune, Dec. 23, 1853, "Why do our police reports always average two representatives from 'Erin, the soft green isle of the ocean', to one from almost any other inhabitable land of the earth? * * * Why are instigators and ringleaders of our riots and tumults in nine cases out of ten Irishmen?" Then followed the report of a riot at La Salle, and of the murder of a contractor by a set of Irishmen. The "Tribune," aroused to the point of approving action under the lynch law, declared, "Had the whole thirty-two prisoners that were taken been marched out and shot on the spot * * * the public judgment would have sanctioned it at once."[2] Some of the Germans of that time were not more peaceable than the Irish. When in 1855 Mayor Boone raised the license fee for saloons from fifty dollars to three hundred dollars a year, a German mob marched to the City Hall and was incited by its ignorant leaders to "pick out the stars and shoot the police". A brisk fire ensued. Many of the rioters were wounded and one was killed. One active German leader of the mob leveled a shotgun at officer Hunt and blew off his left arm.[3]

In 1886 at the time of the Haymarket Massacre, in which seven police officers were killed and sixty wounded by the explosion of a dynamite bomb thrown by German Anarchists, Judge J. E. Gary of the Superior Court in passing on a motion for a new trial, read the following excerpts from the local German paper, "The Arbeiter Zeitung": "Dynamite, of all stuff, this is the stuff," and again, "Have you all prepared yourselves with knives, pistols, guns and dynamite for the unavoidable conflict between labor and capital? * * * Each working man ought to have been armed long ago. Daggers, revolvers and explosives are cheap and can be easily obtained. * * * Those who want to talk to capitalists in earnest must be prepared to attain their object by killing them."[4] The Scandinavians seem to have been less belligerent than either the Irish or the Germans but their mode of living was not any higher. The mortality rate in their wards, especially in the fourteenth, was almost as high as in the stockyard districts.[5] Neither were other statistics before the coming of the Italians in favor of the foreigners. In 1880, when the Italians in Illinois were 1,357, there were in the insane asylums of the State, 2,115 foreign born inmates against 3,019 natives. In 1870 (the Italians in Chicago at that time were 552) out of 10,548 illiterates for the city, 9,200 were foreign born. The reports of the police department, of the Joliet penitentiary and state charitable institutions also show a large proportion of foreign inmates for many years before the Italians were fairly represented in the city.

The standard of living of the immigrants that preceded the Italians was also very low. Conditions existing in the wards later inhabited by the Italians are described in the next chapter. Here I will try to picture conditions existing in districts in which the Italians never settled en masse.

The wretched conditions of the stockyard district have been known throughout the world.

In 1863, "along the south branch of the river were many packing houses where over 100,000 animals were slaughtered every year. The offal and filth from these were discharged into the ditches and waterways flowing into the river and accumulated as semi-solid masses of putrefaction in the sloughs, and the solid refuse was deposited in the fields beyond. During the summer the odor from this was abominable."[7]

In 1901, the stockyards district and portions of South Chicago showed, "outside insanitary conditions as bad as any in the world. Indescribable accumulations of filth and rubbish, together with the absence of sewerage, made the surroundings of every dilapidated frame cottage abominably insanitary. * * * In many parts of the district there were no sewers and the sewage from the houses stood in stagnant pools. The south branch of the Chicago River was a ditch which accumulated a great deal of sewage from the stockyards and filled the air with poisonous odors. The stench from the stockyards was present, the district was overshadowed by heavy clouds from the yards."[8]

"Anyone who rides observantly throughout the stockyards district cannot fail to be struck with the general appearance of squalor, dirt and general dilapidation." At that time there were 500 saloons in the district.[9]

The people living in the stockyards district at that time were:

Americans 19%
Germans 24.6
Irish 31.6
Slavic 10.2
Scandinavians 4.9
All others 3.3

As a whole conditions among immigrant groups in Chicago before the coming of the Italians were as bad as any that our students of immigration have ever observed at the worst period of Italian life in the city. As a matter of fact, if we are to believe the people who have had the opportunity to compare conditions existing at different times in the slums of American cities, "No account of filth in daily surroundings among Italians and Hebrews can outmatch the pictures drawn by observers of immigrant Irish and even Germans.[10]

If we add that the sections in which the Italians settled had been for generations the seat of rampant vice, and of the worst types of political corruption, we may form in our mind a vague picture of the wretched conditions with which the Italians were confronted when they settled in Chicago.

NOTES TO CHAPTER 4

(1) Chicago Democrat, Dec. 17, 1849.
(2) Centennial History of Illinois, vol. 3, page 22.
(3) F. O. Bennett, Politics and politicians of Chicago, etc. (1886). There were times when the Anti-alien movement in Illinois assumed alarming proportions and gave many members to the Know-Nothing party.
(4) Bennett, loc. cit., page 475.
(5) Reports of the Department of health, 1885 and following.
(6) City Housing conditions, South Chicago, in American Journal of Sociology, Sep. 1911.
(7) J. Dill Robertson, Annals of health and Sanitation in Chicago.
(8) City Homes Association Tenement conditions in Chicago, page 3 and 182.
(9) Some Social aspects of the Chicago Stockyards (page 294), Am. Journal of Soc., Nov. 1901.
(10) Report of the Industrial Commission, vol. 15, page 491, quoted by I. A. Hourwich in "Immigration and Labor", page 64. Consult Hourwich for further descriptions of the wretched conditions existing among immigrants of Nordic stock.

CHAPTER V

HOUSING CONDITIONS

S EVERAL surveys have been made at various intervals of conditions existing in the Italian districts of Chicago. They can best give an idea of the
evolution of the Italians.

The first district in which the Italians lived was the one around Clark and
Adams and Plymouth Court. That district was for a long time the red light
district of Chicago. There could be found, as late as 1900, some of "the worst
examples of misery and degradation."[1] "The whole neighborhood was dis-
reputable and old maps show that several of the buildings canvassed where
these Italians are now (1910) were originally houses of prostitution. * * *
On Plymouth Court 66% of the apartments were without sinks. * * * Such
crowded living conditions, setting aside the question of race (Chinese often
lived in the same building) must have a demoralizing influence upon the children, who live much in the streets in a neighborhood where street influences
are dangerous.[2]

The Italians who lived in that district were to a large extent from Southern
Italy, especially from Basilicata and Calabria, but the Genoese had lived there
first. Another Italian district in order of settlement was the one around Illinois
and Wells Street. Apparently conditions in that district never were such as to
require an investigation. The Italians living in that district were mostly from
the provinces of Genoa and Lucca. It is in that district that the first Italian
Church was opened. (Church of the Assunta at 313 W. Illinois.) There still
is a residue of Tuscans living in that district today, although there are more
industrial plants than residences.

From Clark and Polk the Italians kept on moving west until today they
have extended as far as California Ave., along Harrison, Polk and Taylor.
About 1900 the center of the west side "Little Italy" was Halsted and Taylor.
That district has been surveyed on several occasions. One of the first surveys
was that made by the Commissioner of Labor, in 1892-1893, and included the
district from State to Newberry and from Polk to Twelfth. Sanitary conditions
as a whole were fair (table 32) probably due to the fact that as the investigation
was made "in the late spring, people were living with open windows and thus
not subjected to the foul air which might be found in the winter" (page 19).[3]

Social conditions in that district (Halsted to State, Polk to 12th) in 1893
could not have been any worse.

"This third of a square mile east of the river" (most Italians were west of
the river) "includes a criminal district which ranks as one of the most openly
and flagrantly vicious in the civilized world, and west of the same stream the
poorest and probably the most crowded section of Chicago. * * * Enumera-
tion shows eighty-one saloons west of the river. The proportion of wooden

buildings to brick is approximately two to one, throughout this part of the section but on the south side of Polk street it is about four to one and on Ewing more than five to one. (Page 4.) Rear tenements and alleys form the core of the district and it is here that the densest crowds of the most wretched and destitute congregate. Little idea can be given of the filthy and rotten tenements, the dingy courts and tumble-down sheds, the foul stables and dilapidated out-houses, the broken sewer-pipes, the piles of garbage fairly alive with diseased odors and of the number of children filling every nook, working and playing in every room, eating and sleeping in every window-sill, pouring in and out of every door, and seeming literally to pave every scrap of yard. * * * It is customary for the lower floor of the rear houses to be used as a stable and out-house while the upper rooms serve entire families as a place for eating, sleeping, being born and dying. * * * Where there are alleys the refuse and manure are sometimes removed; where there are none it would seem they accumulate undisturbed. Tuberculosis prevails, especially in diseases of the lungs and intestine, and deformity is not unusual. The mortality among children is great and the many babies look starved and wan.[4]

Conditions had not improved much in 1900. In the Italian and Jewish districts, 54.6 per cent of the front houses and 79.9 per cent of the rear houses are frame. * * * A great deal of the tenement-house property is old and in bad state. Aggravated conditions arise from habitual neglect of needed repairs; many of the houses are in a wretched and dangerous state of dilapidation. It is almost impossible to keep such houses clean, and filth and vermin are most common. * * * The rear houses are the worst and many should be classed as unfit for habitation. Bad hygienic conditions, evil associations, and the collapse of home life produce criminals. * * * The Italians, Jews, Poles and Bohemians here lose to criminality many children. * * * The effect upon these people in the first ward for instance, is most pathetic. Coming to us ignorant, but honest and simple minded, they seek out the tenements whose rents have been lowered by vicious inhabitants. Thousands of Jewish, Polish and Italian children are growing up in tenements inhabited by the wretchedly poor, by drunkards, criminals and immoral women. Almost every word these growing children hear and every action they see corrupts their minds and destroys forever their purity of heart. No one who becomes a part of the life of these tenements can escape the contaminated and corrupt atmosphere."[5]

In 1915, Miss Natalie Walker found conditions there deplorable. "Almost one-half of the houses are frame building, many of them apparently disintegrating. * * * Only twenty-one per cent of the buildings were in good repair. * * * Everywhere are rotting clap boards and shingles, walls from which the last flake of paint has long since dropped, rickety porches and stairs, sheds that are literally falling to pieces. The atmosphere is one of general neglect. * * * The narrow space between the front and the rear buildings when it is not obstructed by sheds is also frequently gloomy and sometimes used as a dump. Decaying garbage, thrown there for want of any better place, rubbish of every description, filth from the stables and yard closets fill the so-called yard, which serves as well for the home of various animals and as the playground for many little children."[6]

Improvements in the district, however, were postponed because of the current belief that the whole territory was in the near future to be taken over for commercial and industrial uses.[7]

Today, to a large extent the district has been taken over for industrial purposes as maps at Hull House clearly show. The Italian population has considerably decreased, on account of their moving out to better districts, and Mexicans and Negroes are coming in. Still the number of Italian stores in the district does not seem to have decreased, although here and there we find some Mexican stores.

Between 1910 and 1920 the Italian population in that district (the 19th ward) increased only slightly (from 14,649 to 15,199, U. S. Census). Today probably there are not more than 10,000 Italians (natives of Italy) in that ward. That ward was known long before the Italians settled there as "the bloody 19th." The other section where the Italians settled in large number is the section around Oak and Townsend Sts. Its residents are chiefly Sicilians. In 1910, in that ward, (the old 22nd) there were according to the U. S. Census, 8,216 Italians. The 1920 census recorded, however, only 6,183. That is the section known as "Little Hell" before any Italian ever lived there. Previous to the great fire that district was a network of narrow and unimproved roads crowded with poor cottages. The population was chiefly German and Irish (page 510). It was after the great fire that the neighborhood was first called "Little Hell" owing to the lawlessness of its residents in the years immediately following the fire. As life again became normal the Germans and the Irish, especially those of the better class, began to move east into cleaner streets and more solidly built homes. Room was thus provided for Danish and Swedish immigrants and a little later for the Italians who were beginning to find their way to Chicago. In 1910 the population of that district was 53% Italian, 21% Scandinavian, the rest German and Irish. One of the worst features of the conditions of the houses in that district was the damp walls. Frequently the roofs leaked, destroying the ceiling and flooding the floors. In numerous cases the sinks were frozen, and the water supply entirely cut off. * * * In one apartment there had been seven ambulance calls within a year. Some of the cellars were so damp that they could not be used; often they were in a condition which made them dangerous not only to those living in the cellar apartment but to other occupants of the house. * * * With the dilapidation of the buildings goes a general lack of cleanliness in the yards and alleys."

Of the rooms visited, 1,807 were reported as having insufficient light, of those 459 were called dark and 1,348 "gloomy".[8] That was the district described in the reports of the board of health as one in which the water remaining standing with the yearly accretions, is, during the hot months, converted into a cess-pool, seething, boiling and reeking with filth, filled with mephitic gases. (Reports, 1874.)

The Italians in that district are mostly from Sicily, but they, also, are moving away towards the North and the Northwest.

Another large Italian settlement in the city has been the one around the Church of Addolorata on Grand Ave. In that ward (the old 17th) according to the U. S. Census there were 4,910 Italians in 1910, and 5,199 in 1920.

Indeed the Italians are moving from that district just as rapidly as from the other old districts. The books of the Addolorata Church show that whereas the number of funerals from 170 in 1920 had decreased to an average of 105 for the years 1926 and 1927, the number of christenings for the same period decreased from over 500 to an average of 275. (257 in 1927.) Weddings on the other end, from 160 in 1920 decreased to an average of 87 for 1926 and 1927. This district has had a brief but remarkable story. Five waves of nations have swept over it. Five different kinds of immigrants have dwelt in many of its old battered houses. This district has been the shore on which many a group of poor, ambitious pilgrims found a first foot-hold, from whence they gradually fought their way to the comforts of the well to do. It was settled for some time previous to the Civil War by native Americans. In 1852 one of the first west side public schools was built at the northeast corner of Grand Ave. and Sangamon street.

The first immigrants to settle were the Irish, who began coming in the fifties, probably being part of that great wave of emigration from Ireland that took place in 1848. Most of these Irish settlers in the neighborhood went a little west to attend the Church of St. Columbkill, erected in 1859, where the corner of Grand Avenue and Paulina Street now is. By the time of the great fire in '71 there was a large, flourishing Irish colony and it is at this period that there was built St. Stephen's Church at Ohio and Sangamon Sts., which still stands. Many of the now most prominent Irish in Chicago lived in this vicinity.

Just prior to the great conflagration the Norwegians began to come in. In 1871 they laid the corner stone of a large Lutheran Church at Peoria Street and Grand Ave. They grew and prospered. The Irish remained for some time in the same neighborhood with them, perhaps with a tendency to live somewhat more south, nearer Austin Ave. The Northwestern Railroad had car repair shops in the vicinity and employed a large number of Irish. Just after the great fire they were moved west and a goodly portion of the Irish families followed. A few Germans came in about this time, but the Norwegians remained the preponderating element.

Shortly after the Columbian Exposition the Norwegians began to drift away, going to take up new homes in the Logan square and Humboldt park districts, as they bettered their economic conditions and as the transportation facilities increased.

A few Italian families had come into the district as early as thirty years previous, but a general movement of Italians did not begin until the middle and later part of the nineties. This hastened the migration of the Norwegians. The Italians from Northern Italy first came and then in recent years those from Southern Italy and Sicily. In 1899 the Norwegian Lutheran Church at Grand Avenue and Peoria Street was sold to the Italians and converted into an Italian Catholic Church. Within a year or two the Norwegian Methodist Church at Sangamon Street and Grand Ave. was also sold to an Italian, for use as a hall. By about 1905 the Italians became the dominant racial group."[9]

An investigation conducted there in 1915 revealed that about 25 per cent of the population was "composed of adult lodgers and non-family groups consisting of single men. Several of these men, generally Italian, club together and rent an apartment or a whole house and keep bachelor quarters. About 80 per cent of these men are unemployed, but they do not appear to be depressed over the fact. They live very cheaply and seem extremely light-hearted. In general these bachelor quarters are quite clean, and in good order. The chief objection to their mode of life, from a sanitary standpoint, is the excessive crowding in which they indulge. * * *

That the Italians are economical and thrifty is indicated by the fact that only twenty-two of the one hundred houses canvassed are owned by people not resident in these blocks. * * * The section is developing as a manufacturing center. The investigation revealed the fact that twenty per cent of the houses were in a bad state of repair, and forty-seven per cent in only a fair condition. This is partly due to the evolution of the neighborhood from a residential district to a manufacturing district. * * * Family and non-family groups mingle together, using hall, porches and toilets in common, and here it might be said that so far as one could judge from personal observation and report, the non-family groups were moral and law-abiding men.

Twenty-five per cent of the houses were located in the rear. There is little place for the children to play, and it was perhaps this that led the principal of the Montefiore School to say to one of the investigators, "The children come to school long before the hour of opening and stay around the school yard after hours. They are so little home." Perhaps it is just as well. It is somewhat ironical that the public school of this district should be named Montefiore School. The "School of the Mountain of Flowers."

The general conditions in this section were well summed up by one of the investigators in the following characterization, "The majority of the family in the district are enduring physical discomfort of one kind or another, and in addition, in most instances are existing under conditions endangering health and morals. The rooms are dark or gloomy, with no possibilities of ventilation; windows are out of repair and cannot be raised or lowered; walls are filthy and unsanitary. * * * The plumbing was old and of such inferior grade that pipes were constantly freezing or bursting, and many a kitchen floor, which was the only playground of the children was cold, damp and watersoaked."

It is no wonder the Visiting Nurse or Infant Welfare Nurse shakes her head and says, "Such conditions are bound to give us a future generation of alcoholics and neurotics."[10] (Fortunately, the Nurses' prophecy, in regard to the Italians, at least, has not come true.)

The Italians in that district have been to a large extent from Southern Italy, especially Sicily. At the time of the investigation of the Immigration Commission the following distribution prevailed there:

Provinces of both foreign born South Italian heads of households
(North Italians 77, South Italians 364)

Apulia	2	0.6
Basilicata	18	5.0
Calabria	29	8.0
Campania	84	23.2
Sicily	229	63.3 (Reports of Immigration Commission.)

Another Italian section in the city is the one around Oakley Avenue and 25th Street. It is a rather modern district, in which is located one of the largest plants of the International Harvester.

That section was surveyed by the Immigration Commission in 1910. At that time, out of 68 households in that district, 67 were from North Italy. Conditions there were found to be superior to those found in other Italian sections in the city, the reason perhaps being due to the fact that many Italians, employed by the International Harvester, found more convenient to live not far from their place of work. That district was new and consequently the wretched conditions which the Italians found in other parts of the city, were absent there. The Immigration Commission speaks about that section in the following terms: "In some cases there are small gardens. The houses on Oakley Avenue are more modern * * * although buildings in bad conditions are to be found, the repair of houses in the district is fairly good. There are a few rear houses. Households of the North Italian race form 66.3 per cent of total households of the district."[11] Other sections in which the Italians settled before the World War, are:

The Pullman district. Italians there are mostly from Venetia and Lombardy. Houses, on the average, in good conditions, although in some instances, overcrowded.

South Chicago District—92nd and Commercial, Avenue M and Ewing Ave. Italians from all over the Peninsula. Modern district. Frame houses to a large extent, but in good repairs.

Section around 75th to 79th and Drexel Aves. Mostly Southern Italians. Modern district. Houses in good conditions.

Section around the Church of Santa Maria di Monte Carmelo, 6722 Hermitage Avenue. Also modern district. Houses in good repairs. Mostly Southern Italians.

Another section is around the Church of Resurrection, in the Columbus Park District, a section up-to-date in every respect.

Today the Italians are scattered throughout the city, with a tendency to move towards the Northwest. Probably in ten years from now, there will be no more "Little Italies" to speak of. Such phenomenon is very noticeable in other cities, where the Italian communities are even of a more recent date than that of Chicago. In Baltimore, in Detroit, in Buffalo, in St. Louis, in Kansas City such movement is very pronounced. In Texas, for example (Dallas, Houston, Galveston, St. Antonio, etc.) there is practically no Little Italy. The Italians there, to a large extent from Sicily and the rest of the South, are scattered throughout the city. Even in Detroit there has been such a change in the Italian districts of that city, in the last three years, that it seems almost unbelievable.

The same thing is bound to happen here, although not in the same proportion of other cities.

The Italians here have been in the city comparatively longer than the Italians in other cities. They have bought homes in the districts in which they settled. In many cases they have strong interests there, whether business or professional. In most cases they are waiting that the expansion of manufacturing will claim their properties and therefore they are not willing to sell out now. In Milwaukee, Wis., for example, last year there was a plan on foot to sell out whole Italian blocks in the third ward to manufacturing interests. The operation was not transacted, but if it had been, thousands of Italians would have moved out from that ward, all at the same time.

As I have repeated in several instances, the chief interest of the Italian is his family. The devotion of an Italian father towards his children is not surpassed by any other nationality. The future of his boy is his supreme interest. To take him out of a bad environment is his first thought as soon as his economic conditions allow him to move out. Consequently he seeks a better environment not so much for himself as for the welfare of his family.

Statistics on high school attendance by Italian children show very clearly how fast the Italians are moving from the old districts. Today there is very little housing problem among the Italians. When two years ago a survey was made by the Department of Public Welfare of living conditions among small-wage earners in Chicago, it was found that 91 per cent for foreign-born households occupied four rooms or more, as did the native white. (Page 19.) "Of the households of foreign-born nationalities other than Mexican 97 per cent contained but one family; the native white households were 87 per cent one-family, while among Mexicans only 74 per cent and among Negroes only 70 per cent were one-family households. (Page 11.) Fifty-seven per cent of the households with foreign-born heads other than Mexican were Italian, a nationality not much given to lodger keeping. (Over 40 per cent of the Mexican and Negro one-family households contained lodgers. Only 28 per cent of the native white one-family homes and but 17 per cent of all foreign-born nationalities, Mexican excluded, had lodgers.)"[12]

In conclusion, one may say that as housing problems were shifted from the Germans and the Irish and the Scandinavians on to the Italians, so they are being shifted today on the new immigrant groups, the Mexican and the Negroes.

The Italians today have homes as beautiful and as up-to-date as any American. Thousands of Italians live in Oak Park, River Forest, Rogers Park, Wilmette, and all the fashionable districts of the city. There are over one thousand Italian families in the Up-Town section alone (from Montrose Ave. to Peterson Ave., and from the Lake to the Chicago River, as it results from Italian names in the up-town telephone directory).

A decade or two more and the "Little Italies" of Chicago will be a relic of the past.

NOTES TO CHAPTER 5

(1) Tenement Conditions in Chicago, City Homes Association, 1901.
(2) G. P. Norton, Chicago Housing Conditions: Am. Jour. of Soc., January, 1913.
(3) The slums of Baltimore, Chicago, New York and Philadelphia. 7th special report of the Commissioner of Labor, 1894.
(4) Hull House, Maps and papers.
(5) Ten. cond. in Chicago, loc. cit. page 149.
(6) Chicago Housing Conditions: Am. Jour. of Soc., November, 1915.
(7) Chicago Housing Conditions: Am. Jour. of Soc., July, 1911.
(8) Chicago Housing Conditions: Am. Jour. of Soc., January, 1913.
(9) First semi-annual report of the Department of Public Welfare, Chicago, 1915.
(10) Housing survey in the Italian district of the 17th ward in First semi-annual report of Department of Public Welfare, Chicago, 1915.
(11) Immigration Commission.

(12) Elizabeth A. Hughes, Living Conditions for small-wage earners in Chicago, Dep. of Publ. Welfare, 1925, page 13.

Consult also:

Edith C. Quaintance, Rents and housing conditions in the Italian district of the lower North Side of Chicago. Un. of Chicago, 1924.

Gertrude E. Sager, Immigration: Based upon a study of the Italian women and girls of Chicago, 1914. Un. of Chicago.

CHAPTER VI

STANDARD OF LIVING
(A study of motives)

THE STANDARD of living of the Italians, with due exceptions, is the product of economic conditions, rather than of racial characteristics. That is, an Italian will live the life of a poor man as long as he is a poor man, but the moment that he can afford to live a luxurious life he is the first man on earth to take advantage of all the comforts that money can provide. The study of Italian life in the United States proves that conclusively.

Giuseppe Giacosa, the famous playwright, who was in Chicago in 1892 on the occasion of the performance of his "Madame de Challant" by Sarah Bernhardt, described in the "Nuova Antologia" the conditions in which the Italians of the city were living in those days.

"From clothing to food, to housing, the Italian poors of New York and Chicago exhibit such a supine resignation to misery, such a cynic indifference towards the enjoyments of life to be found, in a worse degree, let us say it, only among the Chinese."[1]

Woodrow Wilson shared Giacosa's impressions. In his History of the American People, referring to the immigrants from South Italy, Hungary and Poland, he says: "And yet the Chinese were more to be desired, as workmen if not as citizens, than most of the coarse crew that came crowding in every year at the eastern ports."[2]

In another article in "Nuova Antologia"[3] Giacosa pictures in a poignant style the old Italian women who could be found all day long in the dumping grounds of the city prying out for articles they could use. "Celery, carrots, withered or decayed cauliflowers, rotting apples, whatever the poorest could beg, in dejection, of the sneering streetcleaner, is their daily meal. Old women scratching and cackling like hens. At times they go barefooted to avail themselves of the sense of touch while looking ahead to distant places."

But, adds Giacosa, "theirs is misery and not poverty, because the wretched conditions of those unfortunate ones is not due to insufficiency of means."

Both Giacosa and Wilson, like the rest of the writers on the Italians in America, were simply recording facts which were not, by any means, peculiar of the Italians as a whole. If we look, for instance, to the ward maps of the city of Chicago, by nationality, we find that the Italians have always been well represented in every ward of the city, although possibly 75% of them in the nineties were residents of the slums.

Our immigration experts, apparently, have never cared to analyze whether such dejection was merely transitory or due to innate characteristics of the Italian people. Not even Giacosa stopped to figure out what percentage of the total population of Italians in the city was living in such destitute conditions.

The type of misery that Giacosa found among the Italians of Chicago in 1892 can be found among the poors of any nation in the world today. All peoples have their own share of paupers and destitutes. When the slums of the great cities were investigated by the Commissioner of Labor in 1893, the population of the slums of Chicago was 57.51% foreign born and 42.49% native born. The Italians represented 16.73% of the total.

In 1893, in the charitable institutions of Cook County there were 3,563 foreign born, of whom only 40 were Italians, the others being Irish (1,457), Germans (727), English (299), Swedes (202), Canadians (183), Scotch (135), Norwegians (116) and others.

In 1870 (at that time there were only 761 Italians in Illinois) one-third of the paupers in the state was foreign born, although they represented only one-fourth of the population. In 1860 their percentage was higher (1,149 against 707 for the natives; population in the state 1,387,000 natives and 324,643 foreign born, of whom only 219 were Italian).

The only fact that Woodrow Wilson and other writers have not considered in connection with the low standard of living of the Italians of the nineties was that other immigrant groups had been coming to the United States ever since the Revolution, and even before, whereas the Italians started around the eighties. When the Italians began to come over, other groups were already an important element in the life of the community. They had welfare agencies of their own, were more familiar with the language than the Italians could ever become during the same period of time, but above all the poors of the various nationalities could rely on at least some people of their own race who were interested in them and willing to give them a chance at every turn.

But the Italians did not have anything of the sort.

Neglected by their own government, fleeced by their own would-be leaders, unacquainted with the language, customs and institutions of the country, illiterate (in 1870 there were in Cook County 10,697 illiterate, of whom 9,346 were foreign born; the total Italian population of the city in 1870 was of 552), superstitious, looked askance and despised by the other immigrant groups, exploited instead of being helped, they were bound to rely more on themselves than on the institutions and men of the country.

Their chief desire was, of course, that of making some money and returning to the native village. Mastrovalerio was one of the few writers on the subject to understand the real cause of their low standard of living.

"On arriving in the new country," he tells us, "they swear to impose upon themselves all sorts of sacrifices, by limiting their personal expenses to the minimum in order to hasten the realization of the dream of a happy and moneyed return. Therefore, if their way of living in the crowded tenement houses of the American cities has been found objectionable, it is to be ascribed to this proposed economy, which is carried to the extreme limit or the imaginable."[4]

The moneyed return, however, was not the only cause of their desire to economize. In most cases the immigrant to pay his fare had to mortgage his little farm or otherwise borrow some money. In other cases he was planning to get his whole family on this side[5] so that they could all work and pile up the amount that he had set as his goal before the return to the village. But above all, the nature of the labor itself in which the Italians were occupied forced them to economize. Usually the Italians would not work more than five or six months out of a year, and that accounts to a large extent for the low earning power which they showed in comparison with other nationalities.

Their standard of living, of course, isolated them more and more and made them more despicable before the native Americans. Until the world war, as a matter of fact, one may be safe to assert that the Italians in Chicago to a large extent were foreign to the community. So it was only natural that in their desire for sociability the Italians would look for men of their own race, with whom they could share their troubles and their joys, on whom they could depend in case of need or advice.

The yearning for sociability, innate in the Italians, together with their lack of familiarity with the language and institutions made them an easy prey of the "padroni" and the labor employment agencies.[6] Invariably the "padrone" was a "paesano" and a "compare". In most cases the "compare" was an almost illiterate man, capable of writing only his signature or making the most elementary calculations (au royaume des aveugles, les borgnes sont rois) but shrewd and without scruples. It was the "compare" who secured the job, by charging an exorbitant commission, besides collecting the one paid by the employer; it was the "compare" who provided the food at railroad camps, at prices much higher than those prevailing in the city; it was the "compare" who transmitted the money abroad at a rate of exchange far above the market. The "compare" was all. He saved the money, in many cases even charging interest for safeguarding it and it was he who in nine cases out of ten would run away with the savings of the "paesani." The poor immigrant would then appeal to the consul, who had already advised him to save his money in an American bank. "Who could believe it?" would wail the victim. "He was from my home town, but now I have a real 'compare,' a real honest man."[7]

So the poor Italian gradually lost faith in people who wanted to help him. He became suspicious of everybody. "If I cannot trust my own people," he would reason to himself, "it is out of the question to trust people of other races." That suspicion, coupled with the desire to economize and the contempt of the Americans, drove him to isolate himself still further. A "Little Italy" soon sprang up, self-supporting in almost every detail. Until 15 years ago, they say, one could see in Chicago whole streets where no word of English was ever spoken, where all signs were in more or less Anglicized Italian. Streets were neither Italian nor American, but the product of the Italo-American. Dirty, dingy places, where sanitation and hygiene were entirely foreign, children romping around in the streets, ragged, barefooted, filthy, emaciated, vicious, corrupted in most cases. Of the newsboys of the Ewing Street Italian colony Jane Addams wrote over thirty years ago:

"Lads who leave home at 2:30 a. m. to secure the first edition of the morning paper, selling each edition as it appears and filling the intervals with blacking boots and tossing pennies until, in the winter half of the year, they gather in the Polk street night school to doze in the warmth or torture the teacher with the gamin tricks acquired by day. * * * they are ill-fed, ill-housed, ill-clothed, illiterate and wholly untrained and unfitted for any occupation."[8]

But, little by little, the Italian would grow contact with the American. One of the first lessons in Americanization the Italian received upon passing from the railroad gangs to the factory. It was in the factory that the Italian started to open his eyes. It was in the factory that the Italian became less suspicious and more receptive to American ideas. Welfare agents would be welcomed and trusted, faith would be born in his heart.

Legislation in due time helped him to get rid of his "compares", safeguarded his savings and protected him from shark employment bureaus, although dishonest practices of employment agents are not totally extinct to date.[9]

Intelligent and vivacious by nature, the moment the diffidence that the American had against him was surmounted, the Italian was initiated into American ideas and customs.

Still, down in his heart Italy reigned supreme.

While gathering rags in the street or living in the most squalid basement in the city, the Italian, no matter how illiterate or backward, would dream of the day that he could go back to his native village and put up a house that could be the envy of his old neighbors. A little farm with a beautiful house, with a clinging vine on the front, with American curtains, American linoleum, American cut glassware, American graphophone, American utensils, American silverplate, everything American. And in that dream the illiterate Italian would toil and sweat, until fagged out he would go back to his couch, with his dream still lingering in his mind.

His dream seldom would come true.

The return to the native village probably has been the greatest disappointment in the life of the immigrant. Already drawn in the whirlwind of American life, he could no longer conform himself to the bucolic tranquillity of his village. Even if he was not shunned by his fellow countrymen, he soon came to realize that he was a foreigner in his home town. A great change had taken place in him. He could not adapt himself any more to the ways of his village. And so he would return to the promised land, with a new faith in his heart and a new determination in his mind. His children would grow up as Americans. He would give them the best education they were willing to accept. He would send them to college. Who knows? In a land like America everything is possible. His child could even become the President of the United States some day!

A new life would then begin. Not a life of tribulations and sacrifices, but an American life with all the comforts that his means could afford, with all the conveniences of which he had deprived himself for so many years.

Even those who settled again in a "Little Italy" lived an entirely different life. Their homes would submit to radical transformations. Their mode of living as a whole changed. No boarders were accepted any longer,[10] Italian and American delicacies could now be found at their tables. Their children would dress in the best possible way, however clumsily and awkwardly. They were not to be deprived of anything that their parents could afford.[11]

It was the returning immigrant that brought the change in "Little Italy". Those who had postponed their return to the village were discouraged by the returning immigrant and settled definitely in the city. The change in mode of living, above all, was contagious. Envy and jealousy played a part. But the change came as rapid and as determined as the old standard had been obdurate in the past.

The immigrant now would no longer remit his savings to the "Cassa Postale di Risparmio" in Rome. He would deposit them in an American bank and as soon as enough was saved he would buy a house in an American neighborhood and move from "Little Italy". Many, however, did not adventure very far. A new section, clean and modern in every respect, close to the boundaries of the old district, would suit them. New sections then would be occupied.

The coming up of children, American children in every respect, would accentuate the aloofness from "Little Italy". Native pride would come into play. He would not be a cause of disgrace to his children. And that, as well as the spirit of pomp and pageantry, latent in him, but present in the race for centuries, would make him furnish his home in the best American way. His children could then invite the boys of the neighborhood to his home—they had all and perhaps more than his neighbors could afford. They could be proud of their fathers.

The love for music, on the other hand, as irresistible in the Italians as baseball is for the American boy, made them invest part of their savings in a piano or a graphophone. Even when the Italian could hardly afford it, he would buy a phonograph or even an expensive Caruso record. He probably would save on his meals to go to the opera or to hear a famous Italian singer at a popular concert.

Today their metamorphosis in the mode of living, if the term may be excused, is so complete in many respects that the Italian home is quite unrecognizable from what it was thirty years ago, just as would be the homes of our well-to-do Americans of Nordic blood if their present conditions could be compared with those of their fathers when they, too, were illiterate and backward, when they, too, used to dig ditches and drain sewers.

Today the Italian of the second generation dresses and lives as well as any native American. In many cases even their outward characteristics have changed, so that often one meets young men of Italian extraction whose original nationality is hard to recognize.

I have met hundreds of them, right here in Chicago, not to mention the thousands I have met in my extensive travels throughout the United States.

NOTES ON CHAPTER 6

(1) G. Giacosa, Le colonie Italiane di New York e di Chicago, Nuova Antologia, August 16, 1892.

(2) W. Wilson, A History of the American People, vol. 10, page 98.

(3) G. Giacosa, La Colonia Italiana di Chicago, Nuova Antologia, March 1, 1893.

(4) In Hull House, Maps and Papers.

(5) Professor Ross' statement that the Italians are (or at least were) loath to encumber themselves with their women, and that women are only a little more than one-fifth of the whole, or that they do not come here more freely as time goes on, is not true, especially of the Italians in Chicago. According to the Immigration Commissioner in 1910, in the blocks investigated in Chicago (the poorest in the city and consequently those in which a higher number of males was naturally to be found) out of 1,791 South Italians 980 were males and 811 females—or a proportion of 45.3 per cent of women to 54.7 for men. Among the North Italians the proportion was 38.5 for women and 61.5 for the men. According to the U. S. Census, in 1920 there were in Illinois 94,407 Italians, of whom 56,974 were male and 37,433 female. In other words, the proportion of male to female was of 152.2. The figures for Chicago were bound to show a higher percentage of women than that given for the whole state, as the Italians in lower part of the state were mostly miners and to a large extent single men.

(6) See J. Koren, "The Padrone System and the Padrone Banks," U. S. Bureau of Labor, Special Bulletin No. 9.

(7) Giacosa, art. cit. Jan. 1893.

(8) Hull House, Maps and Papers, page 55.

(9) See article on Labor Employment bureaus in First Semi-annual Report of Department of Public Welfare, cited before.

(10) The Italians, as a whole, have kept few boarders in their homes. "Of recent immigrants the South Italians show the lowest percentage. Among the households in the country, 5 to 9 years, the Italians again show the lowest percentage (Reports of Immigration Commission). Of 1,348 Italian families visited in 1896, 93.84% were private, 5.05 were cooperative and only 1.11 per cent were boarding and lodging houses." (C. D. Wright, The Italians in Chicago.)

(11) In an investigation conducted in 1925 in the near west side, opinions were asked as to the need of ice in a kitchen. One Italian woman who saved elsewhere to give her child the best care possible, expressed her point of view in a nutshell. "No ice—baby die," said she. Another exclaimed, "Got five children and gotta have ice" (page 9). Use and cost of ice in families with children, by E. P. Wolcott, Chicago Department of Public Welfare, 1925.

THE UNSKILLED WORKERS

The other day, in downtown New York, I could not find the building which two months before, I felt sure, had been there, safe and sound and bustling with life. But one does not wonder at things that happen every instant in this vertiginous country with its fever for renovation. Nothing is less stable, nothing more restless than walls in America.

The building was no more. In its stead there was a void, and men were digging foundations for something new to rise and to fill it. It is a familiar spectacle, strenuous phalanxes of labor forming in the heart of the city, marring its physiognomy, diverting its traffic, deafening it with noise; deep excavations cut through by narrow pathways; piles of naked rock; beams, boards, fragments, scattered and in heaps; wild and uprooted land in the very spot where civilization and luxury dwelt but a little while ago. And there are barracks worthy of the pioneers of the old West.

From time to time there resounds the signal of danger. A red flag is waved, commanding a brief retreat. A radius of solitude is formed, of silence and of expectation. A shout is heard. Then profound explosions, showers of dust, mines that go off. As activity is resumed, men plunge anew into the excavations, move in the mud, and, armed with shining implements, renew their attacks on stone, their struggle against the earth. They group themselves about the electric drills sputtering like machine guns, and man the heavy machines that bite the ground and move slowly like engines of war.

This time I stopped to look, and curious thoughts came back to me out of the depths of my memory. It was as if I were seeing the trenches again. Excited men buried in monster caves; disemboweled land filled with human fever; mud, fatigue, sweat, moments of hiding in expectation of an explosion; ruthless machines, crashes, shouts of command; and occasionally cries of pain from a wounded soldier.

It was no longer the war against men but war against the impassive and powerful hostility of stone, of water and subsoil. It was the glow and combative advance of little men who fight their way and keep the field for the foremost human conquest.

These men are the unskilled workers—workers without knowledge. * * * But the general staffs plan battles, the army officers direct them and the unskilled workers fight them. Without them the plan and the command would be but a puny pretense. They supply the strength, the passion, the blood; they march, attack, win, conquer, die!

At the bottom of every bit of human progress is a trench. It is necessary to dig a trench to defend our country, to make a nation, to create civilization, to construct a building, to build a bridge or a railroad. And in the trench there is the unskilled worker, digging, digging and digging—coal, iron, the oil well, foundations. All that is great, art and science not excluded, has begun under the pick, the ax and the shovel, and has had its basic foundation in caves, subterranean galleries, trenches manned by the obscure army of unskilled workers, strong, tenacious, disciplined, ready to fight, to work and to win.

When I hear it said that the Italian immigrants make up the majority of America's unskilled workers or that they are mostly "only" unskilled workers, I feel like raising my hat to them.

—LUIGI BARZINI in "Corriere D'America." Reproduced from "The Interpreter," May, 1928.

CHAPTER VII

OCCUPATIONS

THE occupations at which the Italians plied in the early period of their American life were not, to a large extent, the occupations at which they had been plying in Italy, but in many cases they were the product of conditions they found in the United States.

"Prior to 1880 our marvelous agricultural development determined or controlled the direction of the larger part of the immigration stream; since that year the equally remarkable industrial demands of the country have drawn the current into the mining and manufacturing states. The same thing would have happened if the racial composition of the stream had been reversed in point of time. It is more than probable that if the Slavs and Italians had come to the United States in large numbers prior to 1880, instead of since that year, they would have settled in the North Central states, as did the Germans and Norwegians and Danes and Swedes. One can be almost equally certain that if the so-called English speaking races had migrated to the United States since 1880, instead of more largely before that year, they would now be found principally in the manufacturing and industrial centers of the North Atlantic division."[1]

The Italians who came to the United States, especially from 1880 to 1914, were not from the large cities of the Peninsula. Probably ninety-five per cent of them hailed from rural districts and small towns.

They were not unskilled laborers, as the Immigration Commissioners would classify most of them. In Italy they were peasants, gardeners, vine-grafters, draymen or teamsters, florists or orchardists.[2] In their passports, however, they all got the classification of "laborers" because steamship agents in Italy found it easier to do so. Even college graduates without any professional degrees were given the passports of laborers.

However, upon landing in the United States, they soon deserved of their "laborers" classification.

Unable and unwilling to go to the country, not even as farm hands, because of the lack of familiarity with the language and institutions of America, lack of the opportunities of which other nationalities had been availing themselves, and to a certain extent because of the fear that once away from the city, they would be held in bondage or slavery; all that, coupled with the fact that the Italians were tired of living in the country, having already been allured by city life, but above all the much higher wages that were paid in the city, compared to those paid for farm-hands, were the chief causes why the Italians remained near the manufacturing centers of the country and became plain unskilled laborers.

Pathetic cases of people who were forced to become laborers there were aplenty. Lawyers and clergymen, musicians and tailors, clerks and even physicians, in many cases joined the brigade of "the pick and shovel" in order to avoid starvation or becoming a burden to the community.

Those examples discouraged professional Italians to come to the United States, in the same way that the Irish, or English, or even Germans and Scandinavians had come. If Professor East, of Harvard University, will investigate this particular phase of Italian emigration, he will find one of the reasons why there have been so far few Italian names in America's "Who is Who".

Educated Italians, especially physicians, started to come in when the various Italian communities in the country were large and strong enough to support them. Their residence in America, on that account, is proportionate to the opportunities they found here.

Since 1919 a large number of educated Italians has applied for passports to come to the United States. Many of them have succeeded in doing so. But what happens?

Former college men, who had never worked for a living at home, they find it hard to work in factories in this country. Whatever positions Italian firms could offer them are filled, connections with American firms they cannot secure because they are not acquainted with the language or with American methods, (apart the fact that an American employer naturally would prefer a native born to a foreign-born) and consequently they remain in the large cities, plying at all sorts of occupations, from piano and sewing machines canvassers to insignificant clerks in small offices. Some have already entered the factories. The situation was so acute a few years ago (1922) that the Italian Chamber of Commerce in New York sent warnings to the Press in Italy to discourage the emigration of intellectual Italians in any possible way.

It is only natural therefore that the first occupations of the majority of the Italians in America should have been that of laborers.

Until the world war a large percentage of the railroad and street car laborers were Italians. Little by little, however, they got in almost every field of human activity. All the Italians needed was to get their bearings. Once they got an idea of where they stood, they chose their own paths.

Not all the Italians, however, have been laborers. As early as 1860, according to the Chicago City Directory, the occupations of the Italians then in the city were as follows:

Confectionery and fruit stores	9	Machinists	2
Barbers and hairdressers	5	Pawnbroker	1
Lager beer saloons	4	Shoemaker	1
Lucca statuary	2	Tailor	1
Plasterers	2	Engraver	1
Carpenters	4	Hatter	1
Coopers	2	Clothing store	1

In 1870 they were:

Barbers	14	Plasterers	6
Laborers	30	Painters	7
Physician	1	Carpenters	7
Teacher	1	Tailor	1
Restaurant and saloons	84	Stone cutters	5
Confectioners	19	Clergymen	1

When an investigation was made of the slums of the Great Cities in 1893 the following occupations were reported for the Italians living in the slums of Chicago:

	Male	Female
Agriculture, fisheries, etc. ...	3	
Professional	29	2
Musicians 23		
Organ grinders 4		
Domestic and personal service	1,108	27
Barbers 46		
Bartenders 10		
Bootblacks 45		
Laborers 951		
Saloon keepers 32		
Trade and transportation ...	353	18
Draymen 18		
Merchants, fruits 11		
Merchants, groceries 11		
Newsboys 21		
Peddlers 13		
Peddlers, fruit 33		
Rag pickers 17		
Steam railroad employees. .194		
Female ragpickers 10		
Mnfg. and Mech. Industries..	152	29
Bakers 10		

Shoemakers	7	
Carpenters	11	
Hod carriers	28	
Masons	12	
Stone cutters	6	
Printers	6	
Tailors	19	
Women clothing workers..	9	
Non-productive (Males)		
At home		130
Scholars		123
No occupation ....·..............		73
Non-productive (Females)		
Housewives, no pay		691
Housework, no pay		114
At home		130
Scholars		87
No occupation		87
Housewives and at work		28
Scholars and at work, males		28
Scholars and at work, females		6
Bootblacks, boys		10
Newsboys		8

When the Commissioner of Labor conducted an investigation among the Italians of Chicago in 1896, out of 6,773 Italians whose households were studied the following occupations were reported:

Laborers 797	Newsboys	78
Street sweepers 126	Small merchants	32
Rag pickers 186	Salesmen	20
Small peddlers 154	Teamsters	15
Railroad laborers 119	Wood pickers	14
Musicians and organ grinders 62	Hod carriers	60
Bootblacks 73	Candy makers	38
Barbers 45	Pants makers	26
Sewer diggers 32	Mosaic layers	22
Pavers 23	Tailors and tailoresses	19
Saloon keepers 22	Shoemakers	16
Scissor grinders 18	Tinkers	14

According to the U. S. Census for 1900, the following were the occupations of the Italians living in Chicago at the end of the nineteenth century:

	Males	Females
Males 8,830		
Females 810		
9,640		
Agricultural pursuits	35	
Professional service	340	31
Domestic and personal.........4,583		189
Trade and transportation 2,537		168
Mnfg. and mechanical pursuits...1,335		420
	8,830	810

Actors	8	Packers and shippers	38
Architects, designers	12	Porters and helpers	32
Artists and teachers of art	33	Salesmen	115
Dentist	1	Steam railroad employees	558
Electricians	9	Stenographers	2
Journalists	5	Street railroad employees	15
Lawyers	7	Undertakers	7
Literary men	1	Bakers	48
Musicians and teachers	227	Blacksmiths	15
Government officials	7	Shoemakers	107
Physicians	17	Butchers	82
Teachers	5	Cabinet makers	14
Veterinary surgeons	1	Candle, soap, etc.	13
Barbers	333	Carpenters	48
Bartenders	140	Engineers and firemen	16
Bootblacks	57	Glassmakers	13
Laborers	3,696	Iron and steel workers	110
Saloon keepers	211	Machinists	38
Servants and waiters	55	Manufacturers and officials	27
Bankers and brokers	6	Marble and stone cutters	77
Bookkeepers	20	Masons, brick and stone	76
Clerks	121	Model and pattern makers	11
Commercial travelers	3	Painters	115
Decorators	7	Piano and organ makers	15
Draymen, teamsters	170	Plasterers	14
Hucksters and peddlers	801	Printers	22
Merchants and dealers (retail)	416	Sawmill employees	21
Merchants and dealers (wholesale)	38	Tailors	144
Messenger and office boys	47	Tin plate makers	12
Newsboys	55	Tobacco and cigar operatives	14
Officials of banks and companies	7		

Females

Musicians	10	Hucksters, peddlers	20
Actresses	3	Merchants	16
Artists	1	Packers and shippers	33
Literary persons	1	Saleswomen	35
Teachers	14	Stenographers and typists	8
Hairdressers	5	Bakers	13
Boarding house keepers	15	Confectioners	30
Laborers	29	Dressmakers	46
Laundresses	18	Manufacturers and officials	1
Nurses and midwives	8	Milliners	10
Servants and waitresses	89	Seamstresses	121
Bookkeepers	11	Tailoresses	123
Clerks	27	Tobacco operatives	6

Today the Italians are practically in every field of industry and commerce, occupying in most cases positions above those of unskilled laborers. As a road-master for the Chicago, Milwaukee & St. Paul R. R. stated in answer to a questionaire on the Italians in railroad work, "it is getting harder each year to secure Italians for track work, due to other industries paying a higher wage; especially the building trade. Due to this, we have to rely on Hobo's for extra gangs during the summer season. The rising generation of Italians are not seeking work on railroads especially in the track department. If they seek laborer work they go to work in the building trades or other industries paying higher wages."

The above mentioned railroad, at the time of our inquiry, employed in Chicago only 141 Italians, of whom one was roadmaster, another an assistant roadmaster, 18 were foremen, 2 timekeepers, 4 skilled mechanics and 115 laborers. The only other traction company that replied, the Chicago Surface Lines, stated that they had in their employ nearly 500 Italians.

The list of the Italians in business, published elsewhere in this volume, proves how diversified are the occupations of the Italians today. It may suffice to mention here, that out of 14,000 members in the Hod Carriers Union, over 60% are Italian, that 25% of the members of the Amalgamated Clothing workers are Italian (7,500 out of 30,000), that approximately ten per cent of the members of the Musicians Union are Italian (700 out of 7,000). Of the members of the Boot and Shoe Workers Union, about 35% are Italian (700 out of 2,000). Moreover, there are about twelve hundred carpenters and 1,200 barbers in the city who are of Italian birth or descent.

The Italians are to be found also in large numbers in the mosaic and terrazzo industry, in the terracotta works, in shoe factories, in the furniture manufacturing trades. Girls of Italian descent work in large numbers in the candy and artificial flower industries. A rather large number of men is employed as elevator operators in down-town office buildings.

The Italians today, with a few exceptions, are all affiliated with their own labor unions, and, of course, are drawing the same wages as the native born or the oldest union men. But twenty years ago it was a different story.

Exploited by their own men, and, incidentally, by the native bosses who naturally took advantage of the situation, the Italians accepted any work that was offered to them and at practically any wage they could secure. In several instances they acted as strike breakers.

As a whole the wages of the Italians were lower than those of many another immigrant group, due to the reasons just mentioned as well as to the fact that they worked only from four to six months out of a year, so lowering their yearly average earning power to the lowest in the scale. The extreme cases[3] noted by Miss Auten of the University of Chicago, that, for instance, of an Italian housewife who worked 66 hours a week for 20 cents a week are simply ridiculous. Possibly the Italian woman could not explain correctly, or may have been suspicious and afraid of eventual taxation and consequently reported falsely.

On the other hand, as the Immigration Commission has pointed out in regard to the high earnings of the Swedes, Germans and Irish compared to those of the Italians, "It will be recalled that these are the races longest established in this country and therefore the races most favorably circumstanced with reference to adaptation to their changed environment. They are also the races whose languages are most closely akin to English."

Today the Italian has "adapted himself to his changed environment" just as had the Germans, the Irish and the Swedes, when he first came over. Today the Italian is no longer exploited. Like the members of any older immigrant group he is getting what is due him. He no longer accepts "a lower wage than others would require for equivalent work."[4] He no longer is considered a competitor "because of his numbers and his qualities deemed unwelcome." If today he is held in favor by the employing classes it is no longer because he is willing to accept any sort of work, any sort of wage, or because "he can be dismissed without serious loss." Today the Italian is held in favor by the employing classes because he turns in a good day's work, at times even without any supervision whatsoever. Once an Italian is being trusted, he does not fall behind, under any circumstance. A personal recollection will illustrate the case.

In the high schools and colleges of Italy written examinations are held under the supervision of teachers. Invariably students try to cheat and in many cases succeed in exchanging notes with fellow students whenever circumstances allow it. I used to exchange notes with schoolmates during examinations. No student was ever ashamed of doing it.

When I came to America and I took my first written examinations at Johns Hopkins I was dismayed at the honor system in vogue at the University. But not for a single second did I ever think of cheating. I could assert with equal emphasis that other students of Italian descent at the University respected the honor system as well as I did. American employers know that too. An Italian may cheat as long as he is not trusted, but the moment that he enjoys the confidence of a man he becomes the most reliable individual on earth. One might add here that members of Italian juries are not prohibited from going home while a trial is on or to communicate with anybody they please. They are granted full freedom of movements. The following opinions of American employers were received in answer to a questionaire regarding the good and bad qualities that the Italians display in their work. They speak for themselves.

From Mr. R. H. Olson, Employment Manager, Sears Roebuck & Co. (employs about eight hundred Italians): "Our impression of the Italian worker is good, especially if he is adapted for and interested in his work. In this case he proves loyal, trustworthy and requires very little supervision. On the other hand, if he is misplaced, he is bound to be a little lazy, usually becomes dissatisfied and resigns. This probably would be true of all nationalities. As mentioned before, we are satisfied with our Italian employees."

From Mr. J. A. Woodward, Superintendent of Employment, The Peoples Gas Light and Coke Company (employs approximately 250 Italians): "Their services are generally satisfactory."

From Mr. J. V. Sullivan, Assistant to the Vice President, Chicago Surface Lines (employ nearly 500 Italians in their track department): "I have not been able to get much information about the characteristics of this class of employees except the general statement that they are doing their work well."

From Mr. W. H. Penfield, Engineer Maintenance of Way, Chicago, Milwaukee and St. Paul Railway: "You will note that we have in this city 141 Italian-born men, of whom one is Roadmaster, another an assistant Roadmaster, 18 foremen, 2 timekeepers, 4 skilled mechanics, 115 laborers. I am also pleased to join these men in expressing the high regard in which we hold these Italian employees." Excerpts from enclosed letters follow:

From Mr. H. Wuerth, Division Engineer: "You will observe from the three letters that all of them speak highly of the Italian-born men, not only as laborers and foremen. They all speak of them as conscientious, willing and steady workers. I am quite sure that my contact with Italian-born men has proven to me without doubt that they are all that. It has been my impression that they are very ambitious and seek promotion. This is probably the reason we have at the present time fourteen Italian-born section foremen out of twenty-three sections. Many of them, as stated in the letters I am attaching, own their own property, raise large families and are giving them a good education, which, in my opinion, makes them desirable citizens."

From Mr. Wm. Ranallo, Roadmaster: "It has been my experience in the past twenty-three years as foreman and roadmaster for this Railroad that the Italians as both laborers and foremen are very conscientious, willing and steady workers. Of course we have a few, which I am happy to say is very much in the minority, that are really undesirable and not worthy of the comradeship of their fellow men, but these men are soon weeded out, and their fellow men ignore and will not associate with them."

From Mr. Leo J. Deny, Chief Carpenter: "At the present time we employ seventeen men of Italian birth or descent. We have two carpenter foremen who prove to be capable and conscientious employes. We have one pump repairer who has held that position for ten years. He also is a conscientious worker and a good supervisor of men. We have four carpenters who also prove to be dependable men. We can rely on them for most anything that we put them at even though they are left to do the work without any direct supervision. As a whole we have had very little trouble with the Italians in our employ and we also find that we have never had any trouble with men of that race in so far as their habits are concerned; temperance or otherwise. As you know we are located where it is almost necessary for us to depend on this race for ordinary labor and we frequently find among those that we hire men who prove to be more than ordinary workmen and show themselves capable of performing their duties far above an ordinary laborer. We have never had any trouble nor has it ever been noticed that this race was clannish while working in this department no matter how many of them we had working for they always mix among any of the other men without showing any difference in their work and without making any difference among the rest of the employees so far as they were concerned. As a whole I believe that the Italian race provides a good grade of workmen. (Of the 17 men, 15 are full-fledged citizens and the other two have already received their first papers.)

From Mr. F. Cleary, Roadmaster: "On this district we have nine Italian section foremen, one Italian in charge of an extra gang, 40 Italian section laborers, and 30 Italian extra gang laborers. Most of the Italians employed on this district come from the southern part of Italy or the Island known as Sicily. Some of these men being employed in this department for the past thirty years. The Italian laborers on this district manage to turn in a good day's work and the majority of them are well acquainted with the proper method of track work. The assistant Roadmaster on this district is also Italian. He came to the United States from Naples, Italy, 30 years ago, a poor immigrant and started in to work for railroads in track department. He was soon promoted to assistant foreman due to his unquestionable ability and served as assistant Foreman, Section Foreman, Extra Gang Foreman, General Foreman in charge of construction work and his present position as Assistant Roadmaster. He is a A-1 track man and a capable assistant to the Roadmaster. He has raised a fine large family, giving each a grammar and high school education, owns his own property, is a fine respectable citizen and a credit to the Italian race. The nine section foremen and the one extra gang foreman on this district are also A-1 track men. Each one owns his own property, and has raised his own family and are good respectable citizens."

NOTES TO CHAPTER 7

(1) Dr. F. J. Warne, in "Immigrant Invasion," page 124, quoted by I. E. Canini, in "What Italians have done for U. S." (Manufacturers News, Chicago, April 26, 1924.)

(2) In 1896 out of 849 families reporting, 633 or 74.56% stated that they worked in the fields in Italy. C. D. Wright, loc. cit.

(3) Some phases of the sweating system in the garment trades of Chicago. Am. Journ. of Soc. vol. 6, page 607, March, 1901.

(4) Foerster, loc. cit., page 402.

CHAPTER VIII

SOCIAL ORGANIZATIONS

The present immigrant organizations represent a separateness of the immigrant groups from America, but these organizations exist precisely because they enable the immigrants to overcome this separateness. They are signs, not of the perpetuation of the immigrant groups here, but of their assimilation. We know no type of immigrant organization which is able to live without some feature related to the needs of the immigrant in America.
—Park & Miller, "Old World Traits Transplanted," page 306.

The organization of the immigrant community is necessary as a regulative measure. Any type of organization which succeeds in regulating the lives of its members is beneficial. If you can induce a man to belong to something, to cooperate with any group whatever, where something is expected of him, where he has responsibility, dignity, recognition, economic security, you have at least regulated his life. From this standpoint even the nationalistic societies do more to promote assimilation than to retard it.
—Loc. cit. above, page 289.

The Italian is not an organizer.
—In "Americanization in Chicago," a survey made by authority and under direction of the Chicago Community Trust.

THE ITALIAN is a born organizer. Penniless, almost illiterate, without any training whatsoever, the Italian will put up organizations that will astound the most consummate promoter.

Some of the largest organizations in the world are the product of the Italians: the Catholic Church, the labor guilds of the Middle Ages, the business firms of Venice and Genoa, the banking houses of Florence and Lombardy, the gigantic industrial organizations of modern Italy, from automobiles to pure silk, from rayon to textiles, from hydroelectric power to airplane making. The cooperative movement in Italy and among the Italians in the United States is another of the proof of Italian skill in organization.

The Italian hankering for organization is nowhere better demonstrated than in the field of social previdence.

Although it is only natural in groups of the same nationality abroad to constitute themselves into some sort of an association, either for mutual protection or for social purposes, among the Italians in the United States the desire to form mutual benefit societies turned into a veritable mania, which found a very fertile soil in the so-called "campanilismo," a form of chauvinistic attachment to the native village (from campanile, the village church belfry) existing among the Italians in American cities. The first association that the Italians of Chicago created was a mutual benefit society.

One of the first, and probably the first, was the *Societa' di Unione e Fratellanza Italiana* (Italian Society of Union and Brotherhood)[1] already in existence in 1880. It used to meet every first Monday of each month at 59 West Randolph Street. In 1890 there were three associations of the same type. The one mentioned above, the *Bersaglieri di Savoia* and the *Societa' Cristoforo Colombo.*

Societies of that type had two main purposes, or, rather, were divided in two bodies. One would take care of the mutual benefit end of the organization, the other would attend to the annual celebration in honor of the Patron Saint. Many organizations, however, especially in the last few years, owed their existence exclusively to the necessity of securing assistance to their members in case of need.

Usually a member would pay from 50 cents to $1 a month, according to the amount of benefit he would draw in case of sickness.

The death benefit was levied from among the members each time that a death occurred. Most societies never maintained offices or club rooms of their own. They would meet at public halls once a month for the discussion of current business or for extraordinary meetings on special occasions.

Some of the societies, however, would keep private quarters, usually a suite of rooms or a flat in a section most suitable to the members, preferably in a "Little Italy". There they would meet evenings for a game of cards or to chat with mutual friends. On the occasion of the death of a member a delegation of the society would intervene with American and Italian colors and private standard. In some instances a band would be provided by the society. The funeral cortege invariably would wind up around the block in which the deceased members used to reside, to proceed then to the cemetery.

The "fratellanza" section of the society attended exclusively to the annual festa in honor of the patron saint. The committee in charge would be held responsible for the success of the celebration, although all the members of the association were required to attend and, of course, to contribute financial assistance. Any funds that would exceed the expenses would be added to the general fund of the organization, but all deficits would be borne by the committee in charge of the celebration.

Some of the associations have maintained women's auxiliaries, but apparently women have never had much to do with their own affairs, at least until recently. Their presence, however, has always been required at religious processions.

"The annual feast is the great event of the year, exceeded in importance by Easter only. The group responsible for a feast put up posters announcing the day and the program, and through committees arrange for all the details of the celebration; electric-light festoons are strung across the streets, concessions for street booths are sold, bands are hired, band stands are erected, and the church is paid for a special mass and for the services of the priest who leads the procession. The whole community participates to some extent, but those from the village whose patron is being honored make the most elaborate preparation in their homes. * * * Those who have been ill or suffered physical injury during the year buy wax figures of the part that was affected—legs, hands, breasts, etc.—to carry in procession; others carry long candles with ribbon streamers to which money is affixed by a member of the brotherhood who rides on the shrine and exhorts the crowds to make their offering. The shrine is lowered to the street every hundred feet or so and little children are undressed, their clothes left as an offering, and they are lifted to kiss the lips of the saint. Sometimes a blind or lame child is carried about on the shrine in the hope of a miraculous cure. The climax is the flight of the angels. The shrine is set in the middle of the street in front of the church and two children, dressed as angels and bearing armfuls of flowers, are lowered by strong ropes so that they are suspended just over the figure of the saint, where they sway while chanting a long prayer. The offerings made during the most important of these feasts amount to from four to six thousand dollars.[2]

These processions, however, in most cases are not approved by the priests or by the prominent Italians in the city. The younger generation certainly has discarded them. More than to the religious sentiments of the people they appeal to the superstition of the populace. In some cases, it is said, they have been prohibited by the bishop.

Soon such celebrations, however colorful and interesting from the social standpoint, are bound to disappear. With the passing of the older generation they will become extinct.

Functions other than those of mutual benefit and pleasure clubs these organizations never had. No lofty aims such as those professed by the Order Sons of Italy and the Dante Alighieri for the whole country, or the Italo-American National Union, of late, have ever been their own. Their associations were strictly the product of the poorer classes and to a certain extent a reproduction of the *societa' di mutuo soccorso* existing among the middle class of Italy.

It has been impossible to estimate the correct number of such societies among the Italians in Chicago. In 1927 there were in Chicago over two hundred Italian mutual benefit societies. In 1912, 400 mutual benefit societies were said to exist, although only 10 were reported.[3] Last year (1927) these societies were asked by the Department of Trade and Commerce of Illinois to disband or to incorporate under the new mutual benefit laws of the state. Up to April 17, 1928, none of these Italian associations had completed incorporation, although a number of such associations had received permits to solicit applications in proposed mutual benefit associations. (Letter of Mr. George Huskinson, superintendent of insurance.) In the Italian community it is estimated that probably none of the old associations will be able to comply with the requirements of the State Insurance Department and that these societies either will continue to exist as pleasure clubs or will join well established fraternal insurance organizations. Of the latter type there are only three in existence today, the Italo-American National Union, the Order Sons of Italy in America, Grand Lodge of the State of Illinois, and the Venetian Fraternal Order.

Apart from the strictly Italian mutual benefit societies there are several Italian sections of American organizations, such as the Knights of Columbus, Knights of Pythias, Workers of the World, Woodmen of the World (twelve Italian lodges), and others. Many Italians are members of the Elks and of various country and athletic clubs.

So, of the strictly Italian organizations we have today, three fraternal beneficiary societies in good standing with the State of Illinois, not less than thirty religious sodalities and whatever is left of the old mutual benefit societies.

The Italo-American National Union is by far the most important of the Italian organizations in the Middle West. Organized in 1895 under the name of "Unione Siciliana" (Sicilian Union), it changed its name into the present one in 1925 in order to enlarge its field of action. That is, as long as the old name of Sicilian Union existed, Italians from other regions of Italy felt that only Sicilians could be admitted.

The Italo-American National Union has rigid by-laws. Members who have been convicted of a felony, for example, are expelled from the organization (article 340). All its members carry insurance varying from $300 to $1,500. In case of sickness a member is entitled to free medical assistance and to an average weekly allowance of $15 to start from the first week. The Union has $100,000 (one hundred thousand dollars) deposited with the Insurance Department of the State of Illinois. Members pay from a minimum of $1.40 to a maximum of $4.75 a month, including insurance premium. Expense of management is provided by a per capita monthly due of 20 cents.

On May 1, 1928, the Italo-American National Union had thirty-nine lodges, with over four thousand adult members and over one thousand boys and girls. Its cash assets were $176,169.58. Insurance in force, $5,317,900. Death indemnity paid in 1925 was $46,046.49; in 1926, $54,600; in 1927, $71,674.50. From foundation to May, 1928, the Union had paid over $930,000 in death benefits.

The Italo-American National Union, according to members of its Supreme Council, is planning to erect a building of its own and to establish a home for the aged and an orphan asylum.

The Union publishes a monthly bulletin. The Juvenile Department of the Union is very active in sports and has a basketball team and a football team.

The following were the officers of the Supreme Council and members of the Board of Directors of the Italo-American Union for 1928:

Officers of the Supreme Council

Hon. Bernard P. Barasa, supreme president.
Costantino Vitello, supreme first vice president.
Vincenzo Schicchi, supreme second vice president.
Rag. P. Scaduto, supreme secretary.
Rag. V. E. Ferrara, supreme treasurer.
Giuseppe Lupo, first supreme trustee.
Domenico Tinaglia, second supreme trustee.
Avv. T. H. Landise, third supreme trustee.
Salvatore Lococo, supreme chaplain.
Sigsmondo Gurgone, supreme sentry.
Salvatore Di Blasi, marshal.
Pietro Congiù, standard bearer.
Michele Dugo, Italian color bearer.
Salvatore Di Maria, American color bearer.

Board of Directors

Hon. B. P. Barasa, chairman; C. Vitello, Vincenzo Schicchi, Giuseppe Lupo, Ciro Balzano, Nunzio Anzalone, Leo Bonaventura, Domenico Tinaglia, Rag. V. E. Ferrara, Dr. S. Ingrao, Rag. P. Scaduto, Avv. T. H. Landise, On. R. Guglielmucci, Salvatore Faso, S. Clausi.

Chief medical examiner, Dr. S. Ingrao.

The Order Sons of Italy in America, Grand Lodge of the State of Illinois, is, as the name clearly shows, the Illinois branch of the national organization. In 1928 it had nineteen lodges in the state, with over fourteen hundred members. According to Mr. J. De Bellis, general recording secretary, the insurance in force at that time was about seven hundred thousand dollars. Two of the Chicago lodges maintain a band and orchestra each, and a lodge has a baseball team. The grand lodge is planning to erect a temple. It also publishes a Monthly News. Its officers for 1928 were:

G. Spatuzza, grand venerable.

N. LoFranco, assistant grand venerable.

Dr. F. La Piana, ex-grand venerable.

Vito B. Cuttone, grand orator.

Jos. De Bellis, grand recording secretary.

G. Serafini, grand financial secretary.

L. Caliendo, grand treasurer.

F. Minaldi, grand trustee.

A. Gabriello, grand trustee.

Mrs. Signora Antonietta Vigna, grand trustee.

Mrs. Maria Bacci, grand trustee.

The directors of the Insurance Department were: Mr. G. Spatuzza, Mr. N. Di Lorenzo, Mr. L. Caliendo, Mr. G. Serafini, Mr. I. Cesaro, Mr. G. Maltese; president, Paolo Gottardo; secretary, Salv. Cammarata; chief medical examiner, Dr. Angelo Aurelio.

It has been especially since Mr. Spatuzza was elected grand venerable that the order has acquired a remarkable increment in Illinois.

The Venetian Fraternal Order was incorporated in 1924 under the name of Venetian Union (Unione Veneziana). In May, 1928, it had 962 members, carrying on the average $1,000 each insurance. Like the Italo-American National Union and the Order Sons of Italy, it provides for free medical examination and allowance of $10 a week in case of sickness. According to its vice president, Mr. L. J. Leo, the officers of the Venetian Order in 1928 were:

Giulio Bianciotti, president.

Richard Guastalli, financial secretary.

R. Mattinotti, recording secretary.

M. Sanfini, treasurer.

L. J. Leo, vice president.

Dr. John Eterno, medical director.

Maurice Marchello and L. J. Leo were the attorneys for the order.

Of the Old Societa' di Mututo Soccorso, the most important is the United Italian Benevolent Association, a federation of twenty societies, having a total membership of between five and six thousand members. It owns a hall at 645 North Clark Street (the Italian Hall), which is also used by other organizations in the city. The officers of the association in 1928 were:

Pietro Nanni, president.

Bruno Passaglia, vice president.

Pasquale Lucchesi, secretary.

Alessio Scatena, treasurer.

A very interesting Italian club in Chicago is the "Club Maria Adelaide," presided by Mrs. Teresa Garibaldi. Said club maintains a section which, according to Mr. Mastrovalerio, may be called the "Italian Beneficent Society of Chicago." It is well known for its famous semi-annual dance-bunco and card parties that it gives at some of the most fashionable hotels in the city.

But probably the most promising sign of Italian progress in Chicago is the Columbus Women's Club, affiliated with the Illinois Federation of Women's Clubs and the Chicago and Cook County Federation of Women's Clubs. At present it has only twenty members, all outstanding Italian women. Dues are $2 a year. The officers for 1928 were: Mrs. Lucy Palermo, president; Miss Lillian Pecorari, secretary; Miss Mary Tacchini, treasurer; and Mrs. Clara Pirofalo, social chairman. The club is interested in social service work, educational work, Americanization work and child welfare work. It has already bought a lot in Indiana at Hudson Lake for a cottage for Italian children. It contributes to Wesley Hospital and the Women's Centers Home. Early in 1928 it placed at the Goodrich School, on Taylor and Sangamon streets, a picture of Columbus and it plans to place several more in the different schools of Chicago.

The Italians have also a section of the Chicago Council for civic education, described in Chapter IX, and cooperate with the various social welfare agencies in the Italian districts.

The Italian section of the Chicago Commons at 955 West Grand Avenue has recently evolved into a unique type of organization. Transformed, so to say, into a club called "The Spirit of the Sons of Columbus," it has under the direction of its president, Mr. Nick La Terza, assisted by Mr. Henry Scaccia, its secretary, grown in a rather short period into an association of about two hundred members. Mr. James M. Manfredini, its honorary president, is the soul of the organization. Mr. Glenn Lawrence is one of the chief supporters of the movement.

The club devotes every Friday to an "Italian Evening," in which an elaborate program is rendered, from moving pictures to musical and vocal numbers, and even a brief Italian comedy, winding up with a dance. Such entertainments usually last about three hours, from 7:30 to 10:30 P. M. At times even "boxing bouts" are arranged. Italian folklore songs and dances are given at frequent intervals. The orchestra usually is a fair one, varying from five to fifteen instruments. All entertainers offer their services free of charge.

The real work of the club, however, is that of Americanization and social work. Italians are gladly assisted to secure their naturalization papers and are enlightened as to the principles and workings of American government and democracy. According to Mr. Manfredini, no proselytism has ever been attempted among the Italians who frequent the Commons.

Of both social and educational character are the activities in which have been engaged the Italians at Hull House. According to the year book (40th year) of that great institution, Italians have played an important part in the following organizations:

West Side Sportsmen's Athletic Association (almost all Italians)
A self-supporting club of men, which rents quarters in the Boys' Club building, containing a large social room, a reading room, and a hand ball court. It

is also equipped with showers. They were organized in 1920 and have been active since that time. They have a membership of one hundred and fifty, and are looked upon as a graduate club into which the older boys from the Boys' Club take up membership when they reach the age of eighteen. In the fall of 1927, sixty of these older boys became members of the Sportsmen.

The activities of this club are social, athletic, and educational. Their baseball team in 1927 won the city championship, conducted by the Boys' Club Federation, among the Boys' Clubs of Chicago. Two of their basket ball teams are in the Fellowship and Settlement league. They have an outside speaker in at one of their regular business meetings each month to address them on some subject of current interest. They sponsor two regular dances each year in Bowen Hall, besides a number of informal parties and socials. Their seven-piece dance orchestra plays for the regular Friday night neighborhood dance, and at many of the dances of the other House clubs. Two of their members are professional baseball players on teams of the minor leagues; one of these players is leader of a group of boys in the Boys' Club.

The Italian Woman's Club

The Italian Woman's Club meets every Tuesday in the afternoon; it has a membership of forty-five. The first Tuesday is given over to a business meeting. The second is a social meeting where games, folk dancing and refreshments make a festive afternoon. The third is a sewing bee. Swimming trunks for the boys and garments for small children are made for the Bowen Country Club, Waukegan. The fourth is excursion day or may be varied by lectures. The excursions include a trip to the Art Institute with Miss Starr and a trip through Marshall Fields with guides furnished by the store. This year the tour ended in the Narcissus Tea Room where the club had a delightful tea with Italian music furnished to fit the occasion. Every spring and fall a day is spent at the Bowen Country Club, the time extending for some of the women into a week-end.

Circolo Italiano

The activities of this committee are not very sharply defined, including in its membership the director of the Circolo Italiano (an Italian club for dancing and social enjoyment), the Italians resident in the House, and other residents who speak Italian and have Italian sympathies. Its members are expected to be interested in rendering any reasonable service to Italian neighbors.

Red Cross Chapter

During the period of the war a Red Cross Chapter was established at Hull House, in which an active interest was taken by Italian women, who made knitted articles and hospital supplies. The members still meet occasionally.

Allegros

A club organized out of a group of fourteen and fifteen year old Italian boys in 1925 for the purpose of teaching them to dance. They have all become proficient dancers and continue their club activities, which are largely social. Once a month girls are invited in for a party.

The Rangers

A club of Italian boys from eight to fifteen years of age, who live on Taylor Street east of Halsted. It has a membership of twenty-three. Their activities are largely social, and through these activities an attempt is made to teach them the

In the Hull-House Labor Museum. *Italian Spinning.*
(By Courtesy of Jane Addams)

Hull-House Boys' Band (almost all Italian boys)
(By Courtesy of Jane Addams)

principles of good sportsmanship, and to increase their respect for the customs and ways of their parents. With this in mind Italian games, stories and songs are used. This club was organized in 1926 under the leadership of one of the employed staff of the Central Y. M. C. A., and is still under the same leader.

The Ravens

A club of Italian boys fourteen to seventeen years of age. The members of this club have been associated with various activities of the House for the past six years. This club was organized in 1927. Their interests are athletic and social. They are developing a basket ball team, and every other week meet with a Hull House club of girls for a social evening.

The Hull House Boys' Band

The Hull House Boys' Band, one of the foremost general activities of the Boys' Club, has been under the leadership of Mr. Sylvester since its organization in 1907. There is a playing membership of sixty pieces and beginner's class of about thirty. Lessons are given three afternoons a week and full rehearsals are conducted on Monday and Thursday nights. Some of the former members are now playing with the best known bands and orchestras of the country. Four of them have at various times been members of the Chicago Symphony Orchestra.

Columbian Society

Composed of seventy-five young Italians who meet the first Sunday evening of each month for serious study and discussion. They have occasional lectures on art, literature and science; and are desirous of elevating the intellectual tone of Italian groups in Chicago. Their discussions are carefully prepared.

The Delta Rho Tau Club

This is a club of Italian girls ranging in age from seventeen to twenty-one. The evenings consist mostly in playing games, card games and other types, frequently ending with dancing. The girls are much interested in making handkerchiefs and scarfs, using gypsy dyes.

Golden Age

This is a club of Junior Italian girls who were formerly in afternoon classes. They are organized as a social club. They play games, have folk dances and sing. The girls had a Christmas party for which they made favors and decorations. They entertained a club of boys and may eventually organize as a mixed group since they entertain the boys or are entertained by them about twice a month.

Eleanora Duse Dramatic Club

The "Circolo Filodrammatico Eleanora Duse" is composed of Italian men and women from 18 to 50 years of age. The meetings are held every Wednesday evening and the activities are mainly for "scacciapen, sicri" pleasures. In the weekly program refreshments are served and dancing and games are held. Italian and English plays are given, the proceeds of which are divided between charity and the club expenses. This club was founded by Mr. Hector Toniatti, who directs the activities.

The Italians certainly owe a big debt of gratitude to Jane Addams for what she has done for the Italian people of Chicago and even of the whole country. It should not be forgotten that years ago when one of the first acts against immigration from Italy and Southern Europe was before the House of Representatives for consideration, it was thanks to the intervention of Miss Addams that "Uncle Joe" Cannon left the speaker's table to plead in favor of Italian immigration, thus causing the defeat of the act.

The Justinian Society of Advocates is an organization to which belong exclusively Italian lawyers. It was organized by its president, Mr. John De Grazia, in October, 1921. The name is that of Justinian, the Roman emperor, under whose reign the basic law of the civilized world (Justinian Code) was codified and promulgated. According to its president, the purpose of the society is to promote the social, intellectual and moral welfare of its members; to create that mutual understanding between them which brings about a true meeting of the mind; to elevate the prestige of the people of Italian birth and extraction residing in the United States of America; and to cooperate with the local and national governments in propagating the ideals of Americanism.

The organization has steadfastly adhered to its principles and purposes, as evidenced by the noteworthy achievements of many of its members, who have and are discharging their duties faithfully and honorably in offices of public trust and in private practice.

The Associazione Combattenti of Chicago is composed of veterans of Italian wars, but Americans of Italian descent who took part in actions in Europe are admitted. Its president is Mr. Michele Butera.

Of a social nature, rather than political, is the local section of the Fascisti League of North America, the Fascio Giorgio Moriani. The following statement made by Chev. Mario Lauro, the Fascista Interstate delegate, on November 11, 1927, before a group of Italians of Chicago, gives an idea of the aims of the Chicago Fascisti:

> Our aims as Fascisti in America as well as our systems are beyond reproach on the part of the Americans. As a matter of fact, the Americans ought to thank us for the propaganda against subversive ideas which we are spreading among our countrymen.
> We neither do nor try to place Italy before America. We want to be good Americans or good guests of the Americans, in order to deserve the respect which is due to good Italians or to Italy. That is all. If you like the expression: We love America as one could love his own wife; we love Italy as one loves his own mother.
> All members of the Fascio must take the following oath:
> "I do solemnly swear on my honor: To serve with loyalty and discipline the Fascist idea of a society based on religion, country and family and on respect for order, law, superiors and race traditions."
> In order to be admitted to the Fascisti League of North America a member must swear:
> "To love, serve, obey and extol the United States of America and to teach obedience to its Constitution and laws."

At the time of the tornado in South Illinois, March, 1925, a squad of local Fascisti left Chicago with the first train sent out by the William Heart papers and gave its aid to Murphysboro, Carbondale and West Frankfurt.

The local Fascio supports a popular university, described in Chapter IX, and is very active in the celebration of Italy's national events, with the cooperation of the leading Italian organizations in the city.

An important Italian organization in Chicago is the Italian Chamber of Commerce. It was organized in 1907 by Cav. Guido Sabetta, then Italian consul in Chicago. Its purpose and functions, according to the Italian Directory edited by the Chamber in 1927, are the following:

> The Italian Chamber of Commerce is an association constituted under the laws of the State of Illinois and is recognized and subsidied by the Italian Government.
> The purpose of the Italian Chamber of Commerce is to promote, facilitate, and protect the commercial relations between Italy and the United States, protect the interests of Italian

businessmen, encourage and guide the commercial and industrial aspirations of the Italians, protect and expand the national production.

The Italian Chamber of Commerce works for the betterment of the Italians in the commercial world, furnishes to Italian merchants and manufacturers the names of the leading concerns in America and Italy interested in the either country, and furnishes also the names of representatives capable of acting for them.

The Italian Chamber of Commerce certifies commercial signatures, releases certificates and declarations of a commercial character, settles commercial divergencies by nominating commissions of arbitrators or experts; suggests, at request, names of legal advisors; assumes financial informations, statistics on tariff duty, on freight, etc.; takes care of translations of commercial documents and correspondence; keeps the members, through a monthly bulletin, informed as to matters pertaining to Italo-American commerce.

Its first president from 1907 to 1911 was Chev. Frank Cuneo. Its president today is Chev. Italo Canini. NOTES TO CHAPTER 8

(1) In 1880 the Societa' di Unione e Fratellanza Italiana was so composed: President, R. A. Caproni; secretary, A. Valetra; treasurer, A. Valentine.

In 1890 the officers of the Bersaglieri di Savoia were: President, Luigi Spizzirri; treasurer, G. Spizzirri; secretary, E. G. Meli. The meetings were held at 228 Fourth Avenue.

The Societa' Cristoforo Colombo had as its officers: President, G. Ginocchio; vice president, Paul Basso; secretary, E. G. Meli; treasurer, Louis Spizzirri. Meetings were held at 208 La Salle Street.

Societa' Italiana di Unione e Fratellanza, 112 Randolph Street; president, A. Arata; secretary, G. Segale.

(2) Marie Leavitt, Report on the Sicilian Colony in Chicago, manuscript, quoted in R. E. Park and H. A. Miller, Old World Traits Transplanted, page 158.

(3) Provana del Sabbione, Condizioni della emigrazione nel R. Distretto Consolare in Chicago, Bollettino Emigrazione, 1913, No. 1.

Of the old Societa' di Mutuo Soccorso nobody knows exactly how many exist, who are their presidents and where they meet. At a recent installation of the supreme officers of the Italo-American National Union the following mutual benefit societies were represented:

Crocifisso di Ciminna	Societa' San Rocco
Societa' S. Raffaele Arcangelo	Societa' Fratelli Testa
Societa' Burgio	Societa' Sant' Anna
Societa' Rende S. File	Societa' Santa Lucia
Societa' M. S. S. Udienza	Societa' Alimena
Societa' Treste Conca	Societa' Maria Maddalena
Societa' Italian Loan	Societa' Santa Fortunata
Societa' Caltranese	Societa' M. S. S. Immacolata
Societa' Ventimiglia	Societa' S. Crocifisso
Societa' Madonna delle Grotte	Societa' Vefrano
Societa' Piemontese	Societa' S. Leo Luca
Societa' Imera	Societa' Santo Liberato
Societa' Mola di Bari	Societa' Unione Morale
Societa' Maria S. S. della Croce	

Other societies that are said to be still existing are:

M. S. S. Stella Mattutina	Italiano di Barogiano
Star of Italy	St. Anna di Cantalupo nel Sanno
Operaia Umberto	Corona d'Italia
M. S. S. Di Lugano	Alessandro La Marmora
Brindisi di Montagua	Madonna della Zotta
Cristoforo Colombo	Societa' San Giacomo
Fratellanza Italiana	Nuova Italia
Giovane Italia	San Giovanni di Poali
G. Marconi	Societa' Cialdini
Regina Elena	Societa' Pisana
San Cono e figli	Societa' Firenze
Santo Liberato di Pizzone	Societa' Torino
Santo Stefano di Castellone	Unione Morale Udulena (10 lodges)
Madonna di Roti Rochetta	Alleabza Italiana (18 lodges)
Figli di Calvello	Trinacria (14 lodges)
San Vito	Maria S. S. del Rozzo di Capurso

Some of the lodges that belong to the United Italian Benevolent Association are:

Societa' C. Colombo	Societa' G. Marconi Pleasure Club
Societa' Amerigo Vespucci	Societa' Lucca Athletic Club
Societa' Nuova Italia	Societa' Sorana
Societa' Firenze	Circolo Toscano
Societa' Torino	Societa' Arti e Professioni
Societa' Giovane Italia	Societa' Cialdini
Societa' Marconi	Societa' Fratellanza

CHARITABLE AND PATRIOTIC CONTRIBUTIONS OF THE ITALO-AMERICAN NATIONAL UNION

To victims of Calabrie earthquake...$2,000
To victims of Messina earthquake.. 2,500
To families of Tripoli war dead... 2,000
To families of the disaster of the Province of Catania........................ 500
To families in the earthquake zone of Toscana and Romagne..................... 1,500
For a gold medal to General Cadorna... 500
To Queen Elena for the orphans of the Great War............................... 2,000
To H. E. Avezzano for the war blind... 2,000
Contribution to the Chicago Bazaar of the Allies in World war................. 2,000
To the Italian invalids of the World war...................................... 2,000
For entertainment of the Italian Mission in America........................... 1,375
For entertainment of the Mission of Italian Newspapermen...................... 600
For entertainment of the Italian Military Mission............................. 1,000
For the California earthquake... 1,500
For the Ohio flood.. 2,000
Pro Fiume, through Progresso Italo-Americano.................................. 2,000
Pro sufferers from Aetan eruption, through Comm. Barsotti, of Progresso Italo-Americano... 6,000
Italian Loan 3,000
Pro Istituto Salesiano war orphans in Palermo................................. 750
Pro Istituto Industrie del Mezzogiorno, Abruzzi...............................,1,000
Pro Illinois flood victims.. 200
Crown and sword to King and Mussolini... 1,000
Airplane to De Pinedo... 1,495
Comm. Zopito Valentini, for an orphan asylum.................................. 1,500

The Italians have not contributed only to Italian causes. American appeals have always found the Italians ready to "chip in" their share. During the World war the Italians of Chicago presented an ambulance to the American Red Cross and otherwise helped to alleviate the sufferings of the "doughboys". At the time of the Florida tornado in 1927 local Italians, headed by Mr. Antonio Lombardo, collected over thirty-three hundred dollars which they presented to Mayor Dever.

CHAPTER IX

EDUCATIONAL ACTIVITIES

C HEV. ALESSANDRO MASTRO-VALERIO, the well known editor of the Chicago "Tribuna Transatlantica," will tell you that back in the nineties there was in Chicago no Compulsory Education law and that the children of the immigrants could be seen romping in the streets or loitering around saloons and cafes. Italian children, especially, were the ones to suffer most from the lack of such a law. They would get up at 2:30 in the morning, in time to get the first edition of the local newspapers, and then spend the rest of the day shining shoes, playing tricks in the streets or dozing in some hallway. In the late afternoon they were again out selling papers, coal and wood, staying out, at times under the rain, until all their wares were sold.

But as to schooling, none whatever.

Such state of conditions would have certainly spelled disgrace to the coming generation of Italians had not Mr. Mastrovalerio, with the help of Chas. Kozmvnski, a representative of an Italian Steamship line and a member of the Board of Directors of the Chicago Board of Education, started to work for the passing of a Compulsory Education Law in Illinois. The law was passed. Chev. Mastrovalerio was the first truant officer in the city. Oscar Durante, the editor of "L'Italia", was the second. Judge Francis Allegretti was another truant officer.

Another service that Chev. Mastrovalerio rendered the community was the opening of five evening schools for foreigners, thanks to the interest and support of Mr. George Howland, then Superintendent of Chicago Public Schools. Senator Chas. Deneen was one of the first teachers. Evening schools for foreigners, however, had been established in the city long before that time.

Mastrovalerio, Durante and Allegretti took a very active interest in the Italian children. Quite a few of the Italian professional people in the city today were taken away from the streets and guided, paternally, to schools. One of those boys now is a well known judge of the Municipal Court.

At times, however, the truant officer could not very well keep the children in the school because of their necessity to peddle newspapers. Late at night those children could be seen in the streets of the city, with a few papers in their hands, emaciated, ragged, hungry, sometimes soaking wet, importuning or begging passers-by to buy their papers. They would not go home until all their papers were sold.

In order to take those children away from the streets, the truant officer, according to Chev. Mastrovalerio, would buy the papers, coal and wood they had left and send them home. And the salary of the truant officer would dwindle away.

From those days to our own, the leading Italians of Chicago have never ceased advising and spurring Italian fathers to send their children to school. Of course, the compulsory law has helped a lot, and no doubt has been the biggest deterrent in the case of ignorant and greedy fathers. But without editorials in the Italian papers and speeches by Italian leaders, Italian children would not be making such fine records today.

Dr. Beck tells us in his study on "the Italians in Chicago" that "naturally, Italian parents, coming from a country in which there is an inadequate school system, do not value education for their children as much as do those from the countries in which popular education is of higher grade and more universal." (Page 20.) That statement is entirely misleading, or at the most could have been true, to a certain extent, twenty years ago. But today the contrary is the fact. The Italians in Chicago, even the poorest and the most ignorant, value education perhaps more than any banker on the gold coast. The poor Italian realizes that today education is more necessary than ever in the struggle for life and is anxious to give to his children what he was unable to get for himself. The statistics for high school and college attendance of Italian children proves it conclusively. But even twenty years ago conditions were not as bad as it was thought. The Immigration Commission reported the following figures for children 6 and under 16 years of age, at home, at school and at work, for native born of foreign father:

Father born in	No.	At home	School	Work	Father born in	No.	At home	School	Work
South Italy	188	3.7	92.0	4.3	Ireland	150	6.0	91.3	2.7
North Italy	44	6.8	86.4	6.8	Sweden	158	9.5	85.4	5.1
Germany	148	10.8	81.1	8.1					

The Italians, however, have not gone in for the higher grade of learning. When they enter college, it is with an utilitarian purpose in mind. They invariably choose a profession which they can make use of among their own people. So we find that most Italian boys in college study medicine, law, pharmacy and dentistry. There are very few Italian post-graduate students in our universities, with the exception of those in the fields of medicine and law. A sensible change, however, is bound to come in the next few years. With immigration closed, and all available opportunities for professional activities among the Italians filled, the college student of Italian origin either must choose a profession different from those mentioned above or struggle to secure a cosmopolitan clientele. As a matter of fact, there are today in Chicago quite a few Italian physicians and lawyers whose practice is almost exclusively American. Architects for example, do very little business with their own people.

In the fields of education at large the Italians have been represented for many years past. Dr. A. Lagorio, Joh. G. Garibaldi, Lawrence Cuneo, Michael Iarussi have been members of the Board of Directors of the Chicago Public Library, at one time or another, since 1906. Mr. Iarussi is now its vice president.

Dr. Antonio Lagorio, especially, has played an important part in the administration of the affairs of the Public Library. He was president of its Board of Directors twice, in 1913 and 1917. According to Mr. H. G. Wilson, secretary of the board, "Dr. Lagorio's administration was marked by his endeavors to extend the branch library system and to increase the effectiveness of the library service throughout the city and his desire to better the conditions of the employees both from the standpoint of living wages and conditions of employment."

At present one of the members of the Chicago Board of Education is Mr. Oscar Durante, the editor of the local Italian daily. Mr. Durante is chairman of the school administration committee. Another Italian in the employ of the Board of Education is Prof. Militello, Inspector of School Property.

In the field of public education in Chicago the Italians have been ever present even before Civil War days. Back in 1869 there was an Italian school, directed by Prof. John Franzoni, in the Meyer Block. The Italian language was taught at the University of St. Mary's on the Lake as early as 1846. Prof. De Salvo has been teaching at Northwestern University since 1904. Professor Altrocchi for many years was connected with the University of Chicago.

It is almost impossible to mention here all the schools of languages which Italians have directed or at which Italians have taught in the city. Most music colleges and conservatories have been teaching the Italian language for many years past. Probably all the teachers of the language have been Italian.

At present there are in Chicago several schools of languages in the loop which are directed by Italians. One of the best known is that of Prof. Gino Monaco, whose pupils have been to a large extent all members of some of the most aristocratic families in Chicago. Another well known Italian teacher in Chicago is Madame Consiglia Bartolomei, who has taught Italian at Lewis Institute, Bush Conservatory, and De Paul University. Professor Riggitano's studio in the Kimball Building is also well known. The various schools of music and singing directed by Italians are described in Chapters 11th and 12th.

An important part in the popular education of the Italians of the city, play the various philodramatic clubs and educational clubs. There are no less than ten in the city. The most important are: Circolo Giusti, with 110 members; Circolo Salvini, Circolo Galilei, Circolo Novelli, Eleonora Duse, Giovanni Grasso, etc. Some of those clubs maintain their own quarters, well furnished in all instances, with a small circulating library and a reference library. Every now and then they have public lecturers and in the winter they give out some Italian play. Each member pays a small monthly fee, from fifty cents to one dollar.

Apart from the dramatic clubs there are in Chicago two Italian dramatic companies, which occasionally go out of town. One is directed by Mr. Remo Conti and the other by Mr. Serafino Lami. They give mostly drama, although from time to time they produce comedies and farces. Mr. Lami's company is composed of 12 men and four women, Mr. Conti's of about the same number of persons. Usually a play is given at the request of local "mutual benefit societies" who pay the actors a lump sum and then sell their own tickets. But at times the two companies handle also the administrative side of the production. The plays are in most cases given at Turner Hall and Italian Hall on the near North Side. The admission price is 75 cents, although on a few sporadic occasions a dollar has been charged. The repertory of the companies is limited. Lami's company in the past has given Shakespeare's Otello and Hugo's Hernani, but their preference is modern dramas, especially Niccodemi's Scampolo, and

Quinera's Feudalismo. Bernini's "Il Beffardo" has also been produced by the Lami Company. Mrs. Esther Lami is its prima donna.

There is also in Chicago a small theatre devoted exclusively to Italian pictures and vaudeville. It is the "Dante Theatre", located on Taylor Street, near Halsted, in the heart of "Little Italy". Of the famous Italian artists who have played in Chicago Eleonora Duse is the outstanding. She was last here in 1924, on which occasion she played in Praga's La Porta Chiusa and Ibsen's Ghosts and Doll's House.

An Italian educational center in the city is the "Circolo Italiano" of Loyola University. It meets once a month. At each meeting, usually, a lecture is delivered on some phases of Italian life or culture. Dr. Italo Volini is its president and Dr. Vincent Carofiglio is secretary.

The University of Chicago and the University of Illinois also have a "Circolo Italiano" each. The "Circolo Italiano" of Hull House was the first one to be established in the city many years ago. Miss Ellen Gates Starr and Chev. Mastrovalerio were the founders. Mr. Hector Toniatti is in charge at present. The "Circolo" has been famous for many years past for its masked balls, which, it is said, have been considered by many Italians as the chief event of the season.

The Chicago Council for Civic Education has an Italian section, presided by Countess Lisi Cipriani. To said section belong representatives of the Italo-American National Union, Order Sons of Italy, Italian Chamber of Commerce, the Chicago Fascio, the Italian Arts Club and other similar organizations. Countess Cipriani is really indefatigable in arranging lectures and meetings at which problems that vitally interest the Italians are discussed.

Of late a new national fraternity original in some respects has been organized by Italian students in Chicago. The name of the fraternity is Sigma Phi Gamma, formerly the Juventas Club. It has 45 members. Its officers are the following: Consul, Ettore Ferrari; Pro-Consul, Remigio S. Cafaro; First Tribune, Maurice Militello; Second Tribune, August Sansone; Quaestor, Ray Meola; Legionnaire, D. Ambrosino. The Roman names given to the various officers, apart from the originality, suggest a new movement among the children of the Italian immigrants, a movement American in all respects, but nevertheless reminiscent of Rome's glory.

Of course Italian students are members of other national Greek Letter fraternities.

An interesting Italian institution in the city is the "Fascisti Popular University of Chicago", established in 1926 by the local Fascio Giorgio Moriani. Instruction is free. The lectures in 1926 were held at the office of the Fascio, but of late have been given at Loyola University. In 1926-1927 46 lectures were given, with a total presence of 940 students. An idea of the work of the Fascisti University may be had from one of the circulars describing the courses given. In 1927 lecturers and courses were: Mario Lauro, Doctor of Jurisprudence, University of Pisa, lecturing on Philosophy of Fascism, Fascist Legislation, Rights and Duties, Italian Literature; Alfredo Kniazzeh, Commercial Expert, Royal Institute of Technology (Naples) on Political Economy; Aurelio Pagano, M. D., University of Naples, on Hygiene and Prophilaxis; Giovanni De Grazia, Attorney at Law, on English Language; Ugo M. Galli, M. D., University of Rome, on

Natural Sciences, History, Cosmography, and Geography; Aurelia Nardi, graduate of Normal School, University of Bologna, on History; Tito L. Macarini, Titular Professor of the Royal Institute of Fine Arts (Rome), on Art in Italy; Armando Micheli, Titular Professor of the Royal Institute of Fine Arts (Rome), on History of Art; and Countess Lisi Cipriani, Ph. D., on "The Italian Factor in Anglo-American Civilization."

A "circolo d'inglese" "English circle" has been established recently among the Italians of Kensington, with the purpose of promoting the knowledge of the English language among the natives of Italy. Only English is allowed at the "circle". A branch of the Italy-America Society was established a few years ago in Chicago. The society aims to promote a better understanding between Italy and America. Mr. A. H. Price is the secretary and Mr. Giuseppe Garibaldi the treasurer. In all the society has about 160 members, of whom only about twenty-five or thirty are Italians.

A club of the same type was organized about 1907 by the then Italian Consul, Signor Guido Sabetta. The name given to it was "Lovers of Italy". Most of its members were American Society women.

Also educational in type is the Italian Arts Club mentioned in Chapter 8.

As a whole, if we consider the glorious traditions of Italy in literary pursuits and achievements the Italians of Chicago have not done well. Under the circumstances, no doubt, their accomplishments are worthy of notice, but they could do much better if some of the leading Italians in the city would just give the example. Today there are in Chicago probably ten Italian book stores, but only few of them keep books of real literary merits, with the exception of some old classics. Very few copies of modern Italian writers are to be found there. Even Brentano's does not seem to carry in Chicago any diversified stock of Italian books, although in its New York and Washington stores copies of the leading contemporary Italian authors are always on hand.

The reason probably may be due to the fact that the children of Italian immigrants cannot read Italian and those Italians who ought to keep up the knowledge that they acquired in Italy are so interested in making money that they neglect the finer things in life which form the heritage of Italy. Of course there are due exceptions. There are in Chicago Italians whose knowledge of world literature and affairs is profound, but, as said before, they are exceptions. The sad fact is that the Italians of Chicago, as a whole, have no Italian culture to amount to anything—what they may consider culture is simply rudimentary education.

Probably their lack of culture may be another of the various phases of the immigrant's life. The English themselves did not cultivate literature as soon as they landed. Sixteen years from the landing of the Pilgrim Fathers passed before Harvard was founded! And the Pilgrim Fathers were not illiterate immigrants!

The future is in the lap of the gods. Perhaps in a few years from now the Italians will wake up to the fact that higher education, just as well as money, is valued by the people of this country, and that being rated in "America's Who is Who" is just as important, if not more important than being quoted in "Dun" and "Bradstreet".

Graduating Group, Our Lady of Pompei School (1927 class). Rev. Chas. Fani in the center.

Church, School and Convent of Our Lady of Pompei, 1224 McAllister Place.

S. Maria Incoronata School

Assunta School on Erie Street

CHAPTER X

RELIGIOUS ACTIVITIES

APART from Monsignor Rosati (see Chapter II) and other high prelates who have displayed their activities in favor of the Catholic Church in Illinois, quite few have been the Italian missionaries who ever since the times of LaSalle have taught the principles of Christianity in the state. Very few, however, were the priests who came over to administer religious services to Italian immigrants.[1]

The result was that, thrown out in overcrowded slums or railroad camps, the Italians neglected the practices of their religion. The priests themselves, it is even claimed, did not seem to care. Back in the nineties there was only one Italian Church in the city, that of the Assunta, located on Illinois Street, near Wells, although some of the priests from that Church would celebrate every Sunday the Holy Mass in a hall on Forquer Street, not far from the present location of the Church of the Angel Custodian.

Probably one of the reasons why the Catholic Church seems to have neglected the Italians years ago was the practical impossibility to provide adequate Churches and priests in proportion to the rapidly increasing flood of Italian immigrants.

As a matter of fact, the first priests to minister to the Italians were to a large extent Irish. The founder of the Church of the Angel Custodian was an Irishman, Father Dunn, now a bishop of the Catholic Church.

It is said that Father Dunn was moved to establish a Church for the Italians on Forquer Street by the opening of Hull House by Jane Addams, although it is asserted by people who are in a position to know, that never did the leaders of Hull House try to do proselytism among the Italians.

At any rate, one of the chief incentives for an active interest in the Italians on the part of the Catholic Church was the fear that unless the Italians received more attention from Catholic leaders, the Protestant churches would have been the gainers.

Today there are in Chicago twelve Catholic Churches. They are:
Angelo Custode, 717 Forquer.
Addolorata, 909 W. Grand Ave.
Assunta, 313 W. Illinois.
Incoronata, 218 Alexander Street.
San Callisto, Polk and De Kalb Sts.
Madonna di Pompei, 1224 McAllister Place.
San Marcello, Rees and Vine Streets.
S. Filippo Benizi, Oak Street and Cambridge.
SS. Rosario, 612 N. Western Ave.
Sant' Antonio, 218 E. Kensington Ave.
Santa Maria di Monte Carmelo, 6722 S. Hermitage Ave.
San Michele Arcangelo, 2525 W. 24th Place.

St. Philip Benizi's Parochial School on Cambridge and Oak Streets

St. Anthony's Parochial School on Kensington Avenue

With the exception of the Church of San Michele Arcangelo, all the Italian Churches in the city maintain a parochial school, with the following attendance for 1927 (figures from Catholic Directory):

Assunta	321	San Callisto	100
Holy Guardian	349	Holy Rosary	426
Our Lady of Pompei	600	St. Anthony	246
St. Philip Benizi	680		
St. Mary Incoronata	401		3,323
St. Mary Mt. Carmel (estimate)	200		

Interior of an Italian Church (Guardian Angel's)

Figures for last year seem to be even higher. The Church of San Callisto, for example, in 1928 had an attendance of 85 boys and 105 girls, a total of 190, compared to 100 for 1927. Probably 4,000 more Italian children attend the parochial schools of Catholic Churches in their vicinity.

It is impossible to estimate the number of Italian families that really follow the practices of the Catholic Church. It may be safe to assert, however, that probably over ninety-five per cent of the Italians in Chicago go to Church at one time or another of their life, even if they profess to be atheists, agnostics, freethinkers and what not.

Two groups of Italian children of the "Guardian Angel Church" after their first communion.
Rev. M. Ciufoletti in center.

On the Protestant side there are the following Churches and missions ministering to the Italians:

Saint John Presbyterian Church, 1208 W. Taylor Street.

First Italian Methodist Ep. Church, Polk and Sholto Sts.

Second Italian Methodist Ep. Church, Princeton at 26th Street.

Waldesian Presbyterian Church, Superior Street.

Olivet Italian Church.

Moody Italian Church.

Campbell Park Presbyterian Church.

American Catholic Church.

Italian Reformed Church.

Three Evangelical Christian Churches, one on Erie Street, one on Grand Ave. and the other on the South Side. There is also an Italian branch of the International Bible Students Association which meets on Sundays at Hull House.

According to Rev. P. De Carlo, all the Protestant churches, including the missions, have probably four thousand members. Four thousand more adherents occasionally attend Protestant services. One of the first Italian Protestant Churches in the city was that organized by the Marquis Pietro Petacci, on Polk and Sholto Streets, back in the nineties. Marquis Petacci was the nephew of the Pope's physician but having married the daughter of the pastor of the English Protestant Church in Rome became a Protestant himself. Another old church was that of Rev. Grilli on W. Ohio Street.

The Protestant churches maintain two educational institutes for the Italians: The Garibaldi Institute, on West Taylor Street and the Samaritan Neighborhood House on Superior Street. Both do the same kind of work.

The following is the program of service of St. John Presbyterian Church and Garibaldi Institute:

Worship—St. John Presbyterian Church: Sunday Morning Service and Midweek Meeting.

Religious Education—Sunday School, Italian Bible Class, Sunday Evening Club, Friday and Saturday week-day classes.

For Little Children—Kindergarten every morning, Primary play room afternoons.

For Boys and Older Boys—Gymnasium classes, basketball, baseball; social, athletic and dramatic clubs; manual training, Wolf Cubs, Boy Scouts.

For Girls and Older Girls—Gymnasium classes, volley ball, folk dancing, dramatics, sewing, clubs, Camp Fire.

For Adults—Mothers' Club, Filodramatic Club, English and Citizenship classes under public school teachers, tutoring for Naturalization.

Music—Chorus; private lessons in piano, violin and voice.

Health—Nutrition class, lectures, publicity; medical and dental service in cooperation with dispensaries and hospitals.

Family Service—Friendly visiting; advice and assistance in solving family problems; temporary relief; helping to make contacts with specialized organizations; emergency service available day and night.

Summer Activities—Camping at Camp Gray, Saugatuck, Mich., and for Boy Scouts at Owasippe. Street play, trips and outings. Daily Vacation Bible School.

The Institute also maintains a free employment bureau for the benefit of any Italian who may want to avail himself of its services.

Garibaldi Institute

1208 Taylor Street

The Italian Protestant churches are organized along the lines of the American Churches. The following, for example, is the organization of the Saint John Presbyterian Church:

Mrs. Viola Baker, Clerk of the Church.

Nicola Gallo, Treasurer.

The Church Council (Consiglieri)
Nicola Gallo
Angelo Mancini
Nicola Panarese
D. M. Sorrentino
Riccardo Santilli
Giuseppe Ventrella
Anthony L. Porcelli
Gennarino Di Benedetto

The Visiting Committee (Comitato Visite)
Prof. Tommaso Gasbarra
Fortunato Papandrea
Nicola Gallo
Angelo Di Benedetto

Angelo Pennisi
Michele Burdi
Salvatore Bevilacqua
Giuseppe Siciliani
Angela Pennisi
Grazia Aronica
Amelia Cenite

The Social Committee (Comitato Sociale)
Walter C. Brousard
Luigi De Nardo
Angelico Di Iorio
Bernardo Chiodo
Michele Pennisi
Sam Aronica

Miss Rose D'Amico

Mrs. Adele Bucaletti

Mrs. Viola Baker

Mrs. Caterina Sperinteo

Mrs. Eleonora Eells

The Flowers Committee (Comitato
Fiori)

Mrs. Germana Gasbarra

Mrs. Concetta D'Amico

Mrs. Giovannina Cozzolino

Mrs. Giuseppina Carcerano

Mrs. Filomena Ferri

Mrs. Elisabetta Santilli

Mrs. Maria Ventrella

Mrs. Santa Capoccio

The number of freethinkers, atheists, agnostics, and anti-clericals among the Italians today is very negligible.

Back in the nineties an anti-clerical club, the Club Giordano Bruno, was organized by a group of educated Italians, but it had only a short life.

The president was Prof. Luigi Carnovale and its secretary Mr. Mastrovalerio. Some of its members were Mr. Alberto Gualano, Mr. John De Grazia, Mr. Stephen Malato, Mr. G. Bertelli and a few others. It lasted less than six months.

The origin of the club more than a sign of adversion to the Catholic Church was as a protest against the action of Rev. Dunn in preventing the School of West Polk Street being named in honor of Garibaldi, the Italian Liberator who took Rome from the Pope.

As a whole, the Italians have remained Catholic, at least nominally. That is, a large number of Italians may go to the Catholic Church only on special occasions, such as weddings, funerals, christenings and similar events. But relatively few of them follow all the practices of their Church, although they may not refuse to contribute to Church activities.

The new generation, on the other hand, brought up under the vigil eye of the priest, is growing as staunch Catholic as the most fervent Irishman. Not only are they generous with their money but they also seem to follow the teachings of Rome.

All the members of the various Catholic Churches are organized in sodalities which are named after a Saint or some religious affiliation. Some of them are the Holy Name, the Children of Mary, St. Anne's, the Sacred Heart, Madonna Incoronata, Young Ladies Sodality, St. Agnes and similar others.

* * *

(1) In the education of a Christian conscience in the Italians of Chicago, mention should be made of Mother Cabrini, Rev. Gambera, and Monsignor Giuseppe Tonello, Knight of St. George, who in April 1928 celebrated in Rome his fiftieth year of priesthood.

Rev. Tonello has founded two churches in America, one in Joliet and another in Los Angeles. He also founded the Corpus Christi Lyceum in Galesburg, Ill. For many years he was Enrico Caruso's almoner. He is well known as composer of religious music.

Rev. Gambera, of the Missionaries of San Carlo, formerly connected with the Italian Immigrant Society of New York, came to Chicago in the early nineties. For many years he was connected with the Mother Cabrini Hospital. He left for New York in April 1928.

Mother Francesca Saverio Cabrini was the founder and General Superior of the Missionaries of the Sacred Heart, an organization that has built many hospitals, orphan asylums and schools for the Italians throughout the world, especially in the United States and South America. Mother Cabrini first came to Chicago in May 1899, a guest of Dr. Antonio Lagorio. Here she was asked by Father Morecchini, pastor of the Church of the Assunta, to direct the first Italian Parochial school in the city, for which she secured the services of fourteen sisters of her organization. Mother Cabrini also founded in Chicago the Columbus Hospital and the Mother Cabrini Hospital. (For further particulars, see "La Madre Francesca Saverio Cabrini" Torino, Societa' Editrice Internazionale, 1928.)

CHAPTER XI

THE ITALIANS IN MUSIC

OF THE two races in the world with greatest musical traditions, the German and the Italian, the former was favored by circumstances in acquiring a position of leadership.

Already in large numbers in the city when the Italians first started to come over, the Germans have been able to exert a considerable influence on the musical taste of the people of Chicago. More nationalistic than the Germans at home, the Germans of Chicago have almost excluded the music of other nations so that while in Germany, for example, Italian music and musicians were holding sway and were even preferred to German composers, in Chicago Italian music was banned with very few exceptions from the musical programs offered by German teachers and musicians. Even Italian musicians have not received a warm reception in Chicago.

Only two Italians were connected with the Chicago Symphony Orchestra while Mr. Thomas was at the baton, neither one of them, however, being known as Italian. Louis Amato, a cellist, gave his nationality as French, but one day that he was surprised by Mr. Thomas while talking in Neapolitan to a friend of his, he did not hesitate to assert his real nationality. Enrico Tramonti, a well known harpist, used to call himself a Swiss, although he was a native of Sicily.

During Mr. Thomas's rule only on rare occasions was Italian music played. It is said, as a matter of fact, that the only Italian pieces in Mr. Thomas's library were "William Tell" and "Semiramis".

The adversion to Italian musicians was general throughout the city, and especially in labor quarters where the coming of the Italians was regarded as an intrusion to be checked at any cost. Not even some of the most famous Italian composers were spared.

When Mascagni was in Chicago years ago, bringing along one of the finest orchestras of Italy, he received such an indecorous and shameful reception that the better element of the city protested against it. The Chicago Daily News, on the occasion, published a cartoon deploring the incident.

Leoncavallo was not much more fortunate. He was even accused of having a poor orchestra, he, Leoncavallo!

Only in the last few years have Italian music and musicians received a fairer treatment. Since Mr. Frederick Stock has been at the direction of the Chicago Symphony Orchestra not only have well-known Italian composers and musicians been his guests (Respighi, Casella, Scionti, Consolo, Buzzi-Pecci, and others) but also Italian musicians have been regular members of the staff. Today the Chicago Symphony Orchestra has five players of Italian origin. R. Bolognini is one of the two violin principals, J. Vito is a famous harpist, W. Fantozzi and C. Morello are violinists, and F. Napolilli is the only player of English Horn in the orchestra.

Out of sixty-five members of the orchestra of the Chicago Civic Opera Company at present twenty-eight are of Italian origin. All of them are American citizens, that being a prerequisite for admission. Out of four conductors three are Italian, namely Giorgio Polacco, Roberto Moranzoni, Antonio Sabino, Mr. Polacco being the musical director of the company. Out of four assistant conductors two are Italian, namely, Dino Bigalli and Giacomo Spadoni. The orchestra manager is also Italian, Mr. Joseph Raffaelli, like Mr. Attico Bernabini, the chorus master, and Mr. F. Giaccone, the prompter. The players in the orchestra occupy the following positions:

Vittorio Parrini, second concert master.	S. Lavatelli, violencello.
G. Maffi, principal second violin section.	J. Tedeschi, bass.
M. Nicastro, first viola.	A. Bartolomazi, bass.
Amelia Conti, first harpist.	A. Montanaro, oboe.
Fortunato Covone, first flute.	L. Cancellieri, clarinet.
Paolo Renzi, first oboe.	L. Bucci, first bassoon.
Joseph Siniscalchi, first clarinet.	J. Turso, second bassoon.
Frank Crisafulli, first trombone.	A. Beghe, contra bassoon.
M. Perrone, tuba.	P. Di Lecce, third horn.
Bruno Beghe, first violinist.	T. D'Onofrio, first trumpet.
Antonio Colla, first violinist.	M. Manna, second trumpet.
Luigi Rossi, first violinist.	D. Palma, third trumpet.
A. B. Damiani, second violinist.	A. Russo, second trombone.
G. Lazzaretti, viola.	A. Bortolotti, base drum.

The various musical colleges and schools of the city have had Italian teachers for many years past. One of the first was Eliodoro De Campi, who in 1878 became the musical director of the Chicago Musical College. He was the author of the "Bells of Palermo". Before coming to Chicago he had been head of the vocal department of the National Conservatory at New York in 1861 and chief vocal instructor at the Beethoven Conservatory of St. Louis in 1872.

Sig. Pasquale Capone, also in the eighties, was for five years head of the violin department and director of the symphony orchestra and chamber music of the Chicago Conservatory.

Attilio Parelli was connected, just before the World war, with the Bush Conservatory as instructor of composition. Previous to that he had been conductor of the Chicago Civic Opera Company. Mr. Sacerdote and Mr. Scionti, the pianist, occupy today important positions in the teaching staff of the American Conservatory of Music.

Mr. Jan Joseph Chiapusso, a concert pianist, is the dean of the piano department of the Girvin Institute of Music and Allied Arts.

It is impossible to recall here the hundreds of Italian music teachers who have settled in Chicago in the last fifty years. Some of them have made a name for themselves, like Mr. Ernesto Libonati, father to the Libonati Brothers, attorneys, who was first violinist in the orchestra of the world's fair and one of the founders of the musicians' union; Mr. Giuseppe Vecchione, well known composer, formerly on teaching staff of the famous San Pietro A. Maiella conservatory of Naples and who, it was rumored at the time of Mr. Stock's absence during the world war, was scheduled to assume the direction of the Chicago Symphony Orchestra; Mr. N. O. Berardinelli, president of the Venetian Art Studio and head of the Berardinelli Music School; Mr. John Borino, with studio in the Fine Arts Building; and many others.

A new organization, the Classical Symphony Orchestra, appeared in May, 1928, at the Eighth Street Theatre under the direction of M. A. Panzella. According to the critic of the Chicago Daily News, the orchestra at its first appearance showed evidences of careful training.

Of the old teachers one of the best known was Mr. Giuseppe Valisi, who scored a great success with the composition of a waltz called after the "Ferris Wheel" at the time of the World's Fair. His brother, Tommaso Valisi, was considered one of the best mandolinists in the city, like Salvatore Tommaso, who was one of the first mandolin players and teachers to settle in the Middle West.

Italian players of musical instruments have come to Chicago in large numbers.

The United States Census of 1900 records 227 Italian musicians and teachers of music in the city. Today the Chicago Federation of Music, headed by an Italian, James C. Petrillo, has about seven hundred members of Italian birth or descent. Other musicians who are not affiliated with the union or who maintain independent studios of their own probably are over two hundred.

Italian solo players have taken part in Chicago concerts on too many occasions to be recounted here. A little Italian prodigy who came over in 1853 was Camilla Urso, a little violinist, ten years old, who came over with the Germana Society at the first symphony orchestra to be heard in Chicago.

Italian musicians maintain an Italian Musical Club, the "Circolo Musicale Italiano", established in 1924 and presided by Maestro Sirignano. Its offices are at 30 North Wells Street.

It is also difficult to estimate the number of private orchestras which are directed by Italians. Under the heading "Members taking business under names other than their own" the Chicago Federation of Musicians lists thirty-six orchestras and three bands which are directed by men of Italian origin. Of the thirty-six, seventeen are owned and directed by Russo-Fiorito. To those orchestras we should add probably fifty more orchestras, scattered throughout the city and especially in the Loop, which are also directed by Italians, such as the Bamboo Inn's directed by Joe Pacelli, the Rialto Garden's directed by Frank Nuzzo, and many others connected with cabarets and hotels in the city. One of the best known in the city is that of Guy Lombardo and his Royal Canadians. Joseph Gallicchio, well known violinist, is the director of the Daily News Concert Orchestra and Nicola Panico is the leader of Guyon's Paradise Orchestra. Louis Panico is the manager of two famous recording orchestras at the Navy Pier. His programs are broadcasted through station W. C. F. L.

The *Hull House Boys Band,* directed by Mr. James Sylvester (Silvestri), is composed to a large extent of Italians. Four of its members have been at various times members of the Chicago Symphony Orchestra. Some of the former members are now playing with the best known bands and orchestras of the country.

If the signs that school teachers seem to notice in their pupils of Italian descent are of any indication whatever, then it is not improbable that in the near future the Italian community of Chicago may produce a musical genius of its own who will add glory to the fair name of the city.

QUOD EST IN VOTIS.

* * *

The title of "Champion Amateur Junior Pianist of Greater Chicago" in the Children's Piano playing Tournament sponsored by the Chicago Herald and Examiner, for 1928, was won by an Italian girl, Johanna Siragusa, 15 years old, in competition with some 6,000 other aspirants at the Palmer House on June 18. The prize carried with it $1,000 in cash.

An idea of the type of concerts that Italians arrange and of how difficult it would be to give a list of the many Chicago Italians who frequently appear at public concerts in the city, may be had from the following program of a concert given by Madame Celeste Stasio Grieco at Kimball Hall, May 27, 1928:

Night Brings the Stars and You.....................By Clay Smith
Love's Enchantment............................By John Dowers
ROSE CANGELOSI
In quelle trine morbide (Manon Lescaut)........................By Puccini
ELEANOR DE NICOLO
Lieti Signor (Les Huguenots)........................By Meyerbeer
Dawn.........................By Pearl G. Curran
MABEL CRAFTON
O mio babbino caro (Gianni Schicchi)........................By Puccini
At Dawning........................By Cadman
La Folletta........................By Marchesi
LINA DI VENERE
Meditation (Thais)........................By Massenet
Serenade ....By Franz
ADAM ROMANO, Violinist
Beauteous Night, O Night of Love (duet)........................By Offenbach
MABEL CRAFTON   ANGELINA LO BUE
Villanella ....By Sibella
Lift Thine Eyes........................By F. Knight Logan
ELEANOR DE NICOLO
De' parlate d'amor (Faust)........................By Gounod
Cradle Song........................By Mac Fadyen
ANGELINA LO BUE
Il Bacio (The Kiss)........................By Arditi
The Star........................By James H. Rogers
MABEL CRAFTON
THERESA FORMUSA and GOODY HOLDEN at the piano

CHAPTER XII

ITALIANS IN GRAND OPERA AND SINGING

IT IS interesting to trace the origins of grand opera in Chicago.
The first opera to be given in Chicago was "La Sonnambula". The date,
July 29, 1850. The place, "The New Theatre", located on the second story
of a wooden frame building, measuring 80 feet in length by forty in width, and
situated on the South Side of Randolph Street, midway block between Clark and
Dearborn Sts. It was owned by J. B. Rice.

Admission tickets for that night and the following night were of fifty cents
for the boxes and 25 cents for the pit.

The artists were not world famed. They were Eliza Bienti, Mr. Vanvers and
Mr. Grubel.

Apparently the first opera in Chicago met with some favor, because the following night "La Sonnambula" was repeated, but unfortunately the season was
brought to an abrupt end as the theatre, during the performance of the second
act, burned down.

The owner, Mr. Rice, however, did not get discouraged.

He soon planned a new theatre, larger and more luxurious than the first. It
was to be the "Chicago Theatre". It was opened on October 24, 1853, and
started its life with grand opera.

The capacity of the theater was of 1,400 people. It was lighted with gas and
had all the conveniences that the times could afford.

The first company to perform there was the New York Italian Opera Company, managed by a Sig. Poliani. The prima donna was Signora R. De Vries,
the tenor Sig. Pozzolini, the baritone Sig. Toffanelli and the basso Sig. Colletti.
The first opera given in the new theatre was "Lucia di Lammermoor". The
following actors played the different parts:

Lucia	Signora De Vries	Lord Arthur	Signor Baratini
Edgardo	Signor Pozzolini	Raimondo	Signor Condi
Lord Ashton	Signor Toffanelli		

The admission to boxes and dress circles was two dollars, private boxes ten
dollars and thirteen dollars. Parquette one dollar and a half, gallery fifty cents.
The next performance was "Norma".

"The house was so full for the performance of 'Norma' and the public so
well pleased that the company decided to remain over until the following Monday to give 'La Sonnambula'.

"With the performance of 'La Sonnambula' the second season of opera in
Chicago ended, leaving an impress in the minds of the people which established
Italian opera and Italian singers as supreme in the world of opera. This original
bent given our forefathers has had a determining effect in our attitude toward
the art which still shapes our thoughts at the present moments, a stubborn fact

86

which is not to be denied." (K. Hackett, The Beginning of Grand Opera in Chicago, 1913.)

In 1864 Uranus H. Crosby erected the first real opera house, with a seating capacity of 3,000 and at a cost of $600,000. The new house was located on the north side of Washington Street, between State and Dearborn, and was called the Crosby Opera House. The opening night was postponed on account of Lincoln's death. The first opera given there was "Il Trovatore" under Grael. The performing company was from New York and included Zucchi, Morensi, Lotti, Susini and Brignoli.

From that year to date the tradition of Italian grand opera in Chicago has not been broken. Today Chicago boasts one of the greatest opera companies of the world and soon will have what undoubtedly will be the largest and most magnificent opera house in the country.

It is outside our purpose here to recount all the performances of grand opera that have been given in Chicago in the last seventy years or even to mention all the great Italian artists who have sung in Chicago theatres and halls.

From Adelina Patti to Bonci, to Tamagno, to Caruso, to Gigli, to Galli-Curci, to Martinelli, to mention only a few, the leading Italian singers of the world have all visited Chicago.

Adelina Patti first came to Chicago in 1853 when she was only ten years old, and sang in the dancing hall of the Tremont House. She was to visit Chicago many other times in her life. She was here in 1883 with the Abbey Opera Company, formed for the opening of the Metropolitan Opera House and on that occasion gave a two-week season at the Haverley's Theatre with Scalchi, Italo Campanini, Novano, etc.

When the "Chicago Opera Festival Association" was organized in 1884 "to provide grand opera for the people at popular prices and to raise the performance to a higher standard of excellence" many artists from Mapleson's Italian Opera Company joined it, including Adelina Patti, Mlle. Dotti, Madame Scalchi, Mlle. Seruggia, Mlle. Nevada and Signor Giannini, Sig. Rinaldini, Sig. Cardinali, Sig. Vicini, Sig. Bielletto, Sig. Nicolini, Sig. Cherubini, Sig. Caracciolo, Sig. Manni, Sig. De Vaschetti, Sig. Serboli, all tenors; Sig. De Anna, baritone; Madame Malvina Cavallazzi, premiere danseuse. The director was Luigi Arditi.

A new impetus was given to operatic fervor at the end of 1891 by the Grau & Abbey Opera Co. with the Ravogli Sisters, Madame Albani, Madame Scalchi, De Reszke Brothers, Polacchi and others.

Other Italian singers that had preceded them had been Paulina Lucca at McVickers in 1873, Madame Albani in 1875, Madame Rossini at Haverley's New Theatre in 1880, and Madame Cellini and Madame Parepa Rosa as early as 1868. With Madame Parepa at Crosby's Theatre in 1868 were Campanini, Tamagno and Trignoli. Another Italian singer of renown was Elena Varese, who came over in 1887 as assistant to the prima donna in the Gilmore Concerts. Elena Varese was the daughter of the great baritone Felice Varesi, for whom Verdi wrote the Rigoletto and the Traviata, and of Madame Boccabadati. One of the first Italians to sing at Chicago concerts was Madame Fabbri, a noted artist of the time, who sang at two concerts of the first season of the Philarmonic Society, in October 1860. Before her, Madame Theresa Parodi, assisted by

Madame Amelia Patti, had given two concerts in May 1856 under the direction of Maurice Strakosch. (Madame Parodi had been in Chicago before with the Patti family in 1851.) On June 27 of the same year, Adelina Patti, already surnamed the "young Malibran" (she was only sixteen years old at the time) sang at a concert with Signor Morino and others. It seems, however, that the first Italian singers in Chicago were Signor Marviotte and Signor Falocinni, who sang at public concerts in the year 1840.

Madame D'Angri gave a concert here in 1857.

Many Italian singers have appeared as soloists with the Chicago Symphony Orchestra. Antonio Galassi and Italo Campanini appeared at its first season.

Marescalchi was one of the famous tenors of the last century who visited Chicago in the nineties, later settling in the city where he opened a vocal studio.

Italian artists have been closely associated with the development of the Civic Opera Association, which until 1915 was known as the Chicago Grand Opera Company and then until 1922 as the Chicago Opera Association.

Instrumental in the organization of the Chicago Grand Opera Company, in 1910, was the former Italian Consul, Cav. Guido Sabetta, who is said to have convinced Mrs. McCormick to finance the great enterprise. The first musical director of the new opera company was Signor Cleofonte Campanini, who became its general director in 1915 when it reorganized under the name of Chicago Opera Association. Campanini retained that position until his death in 1919. He was succeeded by Gino Marinuzzi as conductor. Other Italian conductors of the opera association have been Pietro Cimini, Angelo Ferrari, Giorgio Polacco, Ettore Panizza, Roberto Moranzoni and Signor Parezzi. Giorgio Polacco is today the musical director of the association.

(The list of Italian artists who have sung at the various seasons of the association will be found in the appendix.)

The Italian community of Chicago has already given several promising young artists to grand opera. Gaetano Viviano, Giovanni Pane-Gasser, Enrico Clausi, Maria Fanelli are some of the young people of Italian descent who, according to musical critics of both Italy and America, are bound to add lustre to America's name in the field of grand opera.

Concert and radio singers of Italian origin there are aplenty in Chicago. From Don Sebastian to the Salerno Brothers, it is a long list of Italian tenors and baritones who daily bring joy to the hearts of thousands of people.

In the education of American vocal artists Italian teachers have played an important part, ever since the times of Marescalchi and Varesi. There are today in the city of Chicago not less than fifteen teachers of "bel canto", some of them world famous artists themselves. From Umberto Beduschi, until not very long ago famous throughout the world as a tenor, formerly with the Massimo of Palermo and Covent Garden of London, teacher of William Rogerson of the Chicago Civic Opera Association, to Francesco Daddi, formerly with the Manhattan Opera Company of New York and the Chicago Opera Association, to

Vittorio Trevisan, basse of the Civic Opera Association, to Angelina Di Giovanni Tilden, on the staff of the Hull House Music School, to Mario Carboni and Eusebio Concialdi, baritones, to Ettore Titta Ruffo, to Sacerdote, to Ciancarelli, to Servillo, it is all a well known list of artists whose services to the community have been and are bound to be of great value.

An Italian artist of renown who should be mentioned here is Vittorio Arimondi, who died in Chicago in April 1928. Signor Arimondi at the time of his death was teacher of "bel canto" at the Chicago College of Music. Previously he had sung as a basse at the Scala of Milan, the Costanzi of Rome, the Covent Garden of London, in Leningrad, in Paris, in Vienna, in Berlin, in South America, etc. He was considered as one of the leading teachers of singing in Chicago.

CHAPTER XIII

ITALIANS IN ART

I T IS a truism that if all the art galleries of the world were to return to Italy all the works of art created by Italians, not to say those created by foreign artists under Italian guidance or influence, the world would not have very much left.

The Art Institute of Chicago, for example, secured a high standing among the art museums of the world by the acquisition of the famous Demidoff Collection consisting of paintings of immense value, including original Rembrandts, Rubens, Van Dyck, Franz Hals, Holbein and others.

The reception of those paintings "marked an epoch in the artistic development of the city." (Wm. M. R. French, The Art Institute of Chicago, 1910, page 22.)

The Demidoff collection was started by Count Nicolai Demidoff, a learned and rich Russian nobleman, who settled in Italy towards the end of the eighteenth century. His son Anatoli was an Italian by birth and likewise was his grandson Paul, who in 1880 sold his famous palace of San Donato in Florence and moved to Pratolino.

The Art Institute of Chicago contains many Italian originals and a large number of reproductions of famous Italian works of art. Of great interest is the collection of 109 fac-similes of the most famous statues, busts, tripods, statuettes, lamps and other objects found at Hercolaneum and Pompeii.

Throughout the city, on the other hand, are scattered works of art created by Italians. Grant's statue in Lincoln Park, for example, was made by an Italian, Rebisso. Most of the decorations in the old Palmer House were made by another Italian, Mele. The Edgewater Beach Hotel, the City Hall, the Courthouse were decorated in part by Francesco Bartolomei. The postoffice, the new Palmer House, the Stevens Hotel have been decorated by Italian artists, the latter hotel by Bonanno, Micheli, and Benvenuto Pellini. To the leading theatres, hotels, and cabarets of the city Italians have contributed decorations and designs.

Catholic Churches, above all, have been made beautiful by the hand of Italian painters and sculptors. In the Church of St. Thomas the Apostle in Hyde Park are to be found some of the finest examples of Faggi's and Iannelli's sculpture. In the Church of St. Mathews are several mural paintings by Macarini. Religious statues by Italian sculptors can be admired in scores of churches in the city. The Da Prato Statuary Company turns out such admirable pieces of sculpture that has been appointed purveyor to the Holy See. Marcello Rebecchini is one of the well known sculptors connected with the Da Prato Company.

In the field of architecture the work of Rebori alone would be enough to give a first place to any one nationality. As chairman of the architects committee for the extension of Michigan Boulevard, in 1914, Mr. Rebori has certainly

The 13th Station of the Via Crucis, by Alfeo Faggi

In the Church of St. Thomas the Apostle
in Hyde Park.

contributed a good deal to make the city beautiful. Some of his other architectural conceptions are considered city landmarks. The Studebaker Theatre, the Four Cohans Theatre, the Racquet Clubs have been designed by him.

To be chairman of the architects committee selected by the Association of Commerce to supervise the construction of the new Civic Hall of Chicago, has been called another Italian, Mr. Joshua D'Esposito, formerly general manager and chief engineer of the Chicago Union Station Company, for the construction and a great deal of the designs of which he was responsible. Mr. D'Esposito is also consulting engineer for the new Daily News Building.

Louis Pirola, a young architect, is the winner of the twenty-eighth annual foreign traveling scholarship given by the Architectural Sketch Club, the Chicago Chapter of the American Institute of Architects and the Illinois Society of Architects. "A striking plan for the Chicago Building, designed to represent the principal structure at the 1933 World's Fair" won him the award (Chicago Tribune, May 13, 1928). In 1925 Mr. Pirola won a scholarship offered by the Massachusetts Institute of Technology.

Scipio Del Campo, another architect of Italian birth, was in full charge of the designing of Wacker Drive. He also designed the $2,000,000 Arlington Park Race Track at Arlington Heights, Ill. Mr. Capraro is the author of one of the most beautiful branch libraries in the city and of some imposing apartment houses in the exclusive residential districts of Chicago. Angelo Zucco, formerly with the Chicago Rapid Transit Company, also is considered a first class architect.

As a whole, architects of Italian blood are contributing perhaps more than their share in making Chicago beautiful. In painting and sculpture Italian artists are fast making a name for themselves.

Today Alfonso Iannelli is the head of the Department of Design at the Art Institute. Angelo Ziroli, a sculptor, was awarded the Shaffer prize for 1924 and the first prize in sculpture by the Society of Washington Artists in 1928. Leo A. Marzolo is considered one of the finest restorers of paintings in the Middle West. Tito Livio Macarini is well known for his mural decorations.

Adriano Benedetti is rapidly forging ahead as a sculptor of merit. Enrico Vannucci is the sculptor of the statute of Lindbergh in the Robert Burns School. But two Italian artists, above all, have left an indelible imprint in Chicago art. They are Angarola and Faggi.

Born in Chicago of Italian parents, Antonio Angarola spent eight years at the Art Institute, the first three years attending only in the evening. An idea of his standing may be had from the following awards he has received:

Business Men's Art Club prize of $200 in 1925.

Silver medal by Chicago Society of Artists, 1925.

Second prize, Chicago Galleries Association, 1926.

John Simon Guggenheim Memorial Foundation award of $2,500 for one year of creative work in Italy and France. This award is given to scientists, artists, musicians and writers and is considered one of the most important awards in the country.

Some of the early prizes that Mr. Angarola carried were the Frederick Magnus prize in color composition, Art Institute, Chicago, 1916; the William

The First Born, by Angelo Ziroli.

Awarded first prize for Sculpture Medal, Society of
Washington Artists, 1928.

A. Goodman painting prize, New York Art Students' League, 1917; the Clyde M. Carr landscape prize and the honorable mention at the American Artists' Exhibition, Chicago, both in 1921. His work is permanently represented at the John Vandepool Public School. Mr. Angarola at present is connected with the Kansas City Art Museum and has been on the faculties of the Art Institute, Chicago, the Layton School of Art, Milwaukee, and the Minneapolis School of Art.

Alfeo Faggi, a native of Italy, and at present residing in Woodstock, New York, has lived in Chicago for many years. To borrow an expression from the "Brooklyn Eagle" (Feb. 27, 1921), Alfeo Faggi is as great as any sculptor America has ever had. Ernest L. Heitkamp has said of him that he is "rapidly becoming, if he is not now, the most interesting, powerful and promising of sculptors working in the United States (Chicago Herald and Examiner, December 7, 1924). His work is at times "strongly reminiscent of that of the Serbian Mestrovic, especially in a figure of St. Francis of Assisi. He has made a number of other statues in which there is the same mystic quality, and his portraits point to considerable powers of characterization." (Richard Perry Bedford, in Encyclopædia Britannica, 13th edition.)

His exhibitions are invariably hailed as the most significant events of the art season. (New York Sun, March 4, 1921.)

"His art is founded upon that of the great primitives, but he merely uses the older art as a foundation on which to build a new palace of art. To avoid detail, while yet seeking to express motion, is the evident purpose in his work. The way in which he has succeeded in making his emotional aims comprehensible is a feat in modern sculpture." Some of Faggi's works are in Chicago. His "Head of Noguchi" is owned by the Art Institute. "Eve" is in the Arts Club, a replica of St. Francis is owned by Mrs. Frances Crane Lillie, and "Mother and Child" by Mrs. Martin Ryerson.

The Church of St. Thomas the Apostle has some beautiful examples of his work, including the famous "Pieta", reproduced elsewhere in this book.

In the field of commercial art, Rocco D. Navigato stands out as one of the foremost poster artists in the country.

While still a very young man Mr. Navigato was art director for the former Thos. Cusack Company, the largest outdoor advertising company in the world. In the last few years Mr. Navigato has maintained a studio of his own in the Wrigley Building, catering to such institutions as the Field Museum, for which he designed a series of fascinating posters, the Rapid Transit Lines, the Wrigley Company, the Stevens Hotel and other equally important firms. Some of his illustrations have been used in leading magazines, such as Printers' Ink. One of his most recent paintings is the reproduction of the Buckingham Memorial Fountain.

Rico Tomaso is another Italian of Chicago birth who has achieved national prominence as an illustrator. A former student at the Art Institute, Tomaso has also studied under Dean Cornwell and Harvey Dunn. A whole page was devoted to him in the "Red Book" for February, 1928. Armando Monaco also has "made good".

*Two
examples of work of
Chicago artists of Italian
origin*

-

Above: *The Cathedral of Lucca*, by T. L.
Macarini.

-

Below: *Ovis Poli*, one of a series of posters
drawn by Rocco N. Navigato for the Field
Museum.

-

*(Marco Polo was a Venetian traveler and author
who ventured as far as China in the 13th century.)*

Other Italian artists are C. Grieco, L. Amorosi, Miss Blanca Maggioli, P. A. Magnini, C. A. Nicolai, Bernard Mellerio.

In conclusion we may remain satisfied of the accomplishments of the Italians in the field of art. However, if we take into consideration the natural dispositions in the Italians towards art, they could and should have achieved much more had they been guided and directed properly. But apparently Chicago Italians are waking to the fact that they need to get together in order to pool energies and talents. One of the most promising signs is the Venetian Art Studio, organized by Prof. N. O. Berardinelli "to provide a meeting place for young Italian artists and art students eager to stimulate the intellect by discussion and mutual criticism.

The secretary of the studio is Mr. Angelo Mannarelli. The studio is located at 905 South Ashland Avenue, where young Italian artists convene to work and debate. Paintings are on view.

Already the studio has produced some results. One of the members, Mr. Joseph D. Salvo, received honorary mention at the 1927 exhibition of Chicago artists, for his painting "The Broken String". Paintings by other members of the "studio" have been accepted at the Illinois Exhibition (1926), South Side Exhibition (1926), and Exhibition of Chicago Artists (1927).

Those young men certainly deserve encouragement and support. Just as Ruotolo and Piccirilli have worked wonders in New York with their "Leonardo" school, so could the Italians in Chicago establish a popular school of art where the latent talent existing in our "Little Italies" could be cultivated and properly directed.

PRIZES WON BY ITALIANS

Norman Wait Harris Silver Medal, carrying a prize of $500 awarded in 1913 to Giovanni Battista Troccoli for Portrait: Mr. Ferry.

The Business Men's Art Club prize of $300 for a meritorious landscape in oil, awarded in 1925 to Anthony Angarola for Norwegian Village.

The Clyde M. Carr prize of $100 for a meritorious work in landscape, awarded in 1921 to Anthony Angarola for Backyard Paradise.

The Silver Medal of the Chicago Society of Artists, to the artist who presents the most artistic work, awarded in 1925 to Anthony Angarola for a group of paintings.

The Mrs. John C. Shaffer prize of $100 for an ideal conception in sculpture awarded in 1924 to Angelo Ziroli for The Dancing Girl.

Honorable mentions awarded to meritorious paintings and pieces of sculpture in the annual exhibition:

1919—Victor Salvatore, Dawn (marble).

1921—Anthony Angarola, Compassion.

1922—Cartaino Scarpitta, Prayer piece (sculpture).

1927—Gaetano Cecere, Francesca (sculpture); D. Salvo Joseph, The Broken String.

Prize in Architectural Department, Art Institute Scholarship, 1918, to Armando Monaco.

Annual Exhibition Art Students' League of Chicago, 1919: Fourth prize to Armando Monaco.

Logan prize of $100, 1921, between Celestino Celestini for etching "Monte Frumentario" and E. T. Hawly.

Twentieth Annual Exhibition of Applied Arts, 1921: Thomas J. Dee award to Mr. and Mrs. Peruzzi for jewelry collection.

Exhibition of Art Students' League, award for best poster in 1925 to Terquata Caselli.

Twenty-eighth annual foreign traveling scholarship given by Architectural Sketch Club, the Chicago Chapter of the American Institute and Illinois Society of Architects, (1928) to Louis Pirola, for a striking plan for the Chicago Building, designed to represent the principal structure at the 1933 World's Fair.

Honorary Mention for drawing and painting at the Children Exhibit of the Art Institute in the spring of 1928 was given to an Italian boy, fifteen years of age, Mike Gamboni, of Hull House.

* * *

Italian artists represented at the first and latest (1927) annual exhibitions of the Chicago Art Institute:

First Annual Exhibition, 1882:

Villa E., Going for a Drive.	De Nittis, A Cold Day.
Bruneri, F., Golden Wedding.	Chierici, Interior.
Luzzi, A., Ponte a Ema.	Rico, Martin, Grand Canal.
Gabrina, R., Market Scene in Rome.	Guardabassi, G., At the Toilet.
Pasini, Halt at the Well.	Michetti, The Day That Is Gone.
Glisenti, The Old Paper Vender.	Lessi, Two Old Cronies.

Thirty-first Annual Exhibition by artists of Chicago and vicinity at the Art Institute of Chicago, February 3 to March 8, 1927:

Anthony Angarola, "Boul. Mich." Docks; Kansas City Hills.
Joseph De Salvi, The Broken String.
Edward Gentile, The Spirit of Culver.
Romolo Roberti, Cass Street.
Gasper H. Ruffolo, My Pal.
Enrico Vannucci, My Son (marble); The Age of Iron (plaster).
Fortieth Annual Exhibition of American Paintings and Sculpture, the Art Institute of Chicago, October 27, December 14, 1927:
Paintings:
Anthony Angarola, Kansas City Workmen; Mushroom Cove, St. Paul.
Antonio P. Martino, The Canal.
Joseph Rollo, Louis.
Matteo Sandona, Julia.
Giovanni B. Troccoli, Mrs. William Saville.
Sculpture:

Gustavo Arcila, Hindu Youth.
Adriano Benedetti, Pouting Boy.
S. F. Bilotti, A Study in Rose Marble.
Olympio Brindesi, Beaver; Desolation.
Gaetano Cecere, Francesca.
Dominic D'Imperio, Fantasy.
Simon Moselsio, Circe; Daughter of Indra.
Richard H. Recchia, Down and Out.
Antonio Salemme, Charlotte.

CHAPTER XIV

THE ITALIANS IN BUSINESS

THE successes of the Italians in business have been the successes of the pioneers. Unschooled, poor, without any business training of any sort, discriminated against, handicapped at every turn, the Italian had to work his way up from the lowest rung in the business ladder.

Commercial traditions, of course, the Italians brought with them. From the Genoese world traders to the Sicilian fishermen, who would venture as far as the Levant to sell their coral or sponges, the Italian had been trading for centuries. Until the discovery of America the commerce of the then known world was practically in the hands of the Italians.

But the type of people who came to America from Italy was not that of the trader with sufficient capital to carry on his business on a large scale. As a matter of fact, the first Italian traders in the United States were former Genoese and Sicilian seamen. Only around the '90s did wealthy Sicilian lemon growers and Lombard silk merchants come to America for business purposes.

Perhaps no one of those men ever came to Chicago.

The first Italian *merchants* in the city were the Genoese. The first business ventures were the push-cart and the street organ. Saloons were next tackled and in short time developed into spaghetti houses.

As early as 1880 we find in Chicago twenty-two fruit stores and thirty restaurants and thirty-three saloons owned by Italians. Statuette makers in the city were first established apparently as early as 1860.

Other "lines of business" developed later with the increase of the local Italian population on whose patronage it was dependent.

In 1880, for example, there were only six Italian grocers, whereas today they amount to more than six hundred.

From those humble beginnings the Italians have acquired today leading positions in the commerce and industry of the city.

The list of the one hundred outstanding Italian firms in Chicago as given at the end of the present chapter will prove it beyond question.

Of course, there are many Italians in the city who occupy responsible positions with large Chicago firms but most of them are not known among the Italians as they have little to do with the Italian colony.

There is, for example, Mr. H. Fabbri, who from messenger boy rose to the presidency of the Northwestern Expanded Metal Company, a corporation doing several million dollars of business a year; there is Mr. John B. Zingrone, who from an immigrant elevator boy twenty-two years ago has become today the head of the X-ray department of the Mercy Hospital and one of the leading radiologists in the country; there is Mr. Joshua D'Esposito who in less than fifteen years rose from the position of draftsman to that of chief engineer of the Pennsylvania Railroad Company and later of general manager of the Chicago Union Station; there is Mr. Fred Salerno, who from an immigrant "greasy pans" boy has become vice president and general manager of the Sawyer Biscuit Co., one of the largest in the country; there is Mr. Joseph Soravia, who was just a clerk not many years ago and is today in charge of four important departments at Sears Roebuck & Company; there is Mr. J. Solari, secretary for the Peabody Coal Company, one of the largest coal operators in the world; there is Mr. Frank R. Florentine, general manager of the Congress Hotel; there is Mr. Melchiorre, chief designer for Hart, Schaeffner & Marx; there is Mr. A. Marimpietri, vice president of the Amalgamated Trust & Savings Bank; there is Mr. Speranza, manager of the clothing manufacturing department of Marshall Field; there is Mr. Joseph Malatesta, formerly vice president of the Consumers Coal Company; there is Mr. John Spala, general merchandising manager of the Hub; Mr. Fumagalli, maitre d'hotel at the Sherman House; Mr. Anton Negri, head chef of the Belden-Stratford, Parkway and Webster hotels; Mr. Michael Bondi, one of the leading designers of the city, with Marshall Field; Mr. Paonetti, head quality man for Hart, Schaeffner & Marx; Mr. Mule, assistant manager of the City News Bureau, an organization maintained by the various newspapers of Chicago to gather local news; Mr. Simon Moraco, secretary to the managing editor of the Chicago Daily News; Mr. Giuseppe Mastro-Valerio, engineer with the Western Electric Company; Mr. M. Butera, engineer with the Sanitary District; Mr. Andreuccetti, of the Northwestern Railroad Company; and many and many others whose names are not well known to the Italian community.

Italians who occupy minor office positions in the city, there are by the thousands. In the loop banks alone it is estimated, work over two hundred clerks of Italian blood.

Italian women, on the other hand, are almost absent from business positions, with the exception of those of "salesladies" in department stores and dressmakers and milliners at the most fashionable shops of the loop.

If we consider the rather short length of time in which the Italians have settled in the city, the Italians have done well; but they undoubtedly could have done more had they received some of the guidance, protection, encouragement and, one might as well say it, opportunities which have been offered to the children of older immigrant groups.

ITALIANS IN BUSINESS

(From Selected Directory of the Italians in Chicago, Compiled by Countess Lisi Cipriani, 1927-28)

Accountants, Public	3	Billiard halls	34
Advertising	2	Booksellers	3
Architects	9	Boxes, manufacturers	2
Artists	21	Cafes	30
Artists' materials	1	Canned foods	3
Art patterns and models	1	Carpenters and builders	7
Automobile accessories	4	Caterers	2
Automobile dealers and mfrs. agents	5	Cement	2
Automobile filling stations	7	Cheese, wholesale	8
Automobile garages	12	Chemicals	4
Bakers	60	Cigar manufacturers	8
Bakers' supplies	1	Cigars, wholesale	4
Banks	2	Cigarettes, manufacturers	1
Barbers	216	Cigars and tobacco	85
Barbers' supplies	3	Cleaners and dyers	4
Bedding	1	Coal, wholesale and retail	16
Beverages, manufacturers	6	Coffee shops	8
Beverages, retail	85	Commission merchants, produce	61

Confectioners (manufacturing)	10	Marble manufacturers and contractors	3
Confectioners, retail	240	Meat markets	172
Confectioners, wholesale	11	Medical institutes	1
Contractors	3	Merchandise brokers	3
Contractors, commissary	1	Monuments	7
Contractors, R. R.	4	Mosaic and tiles	2
Contractors and builders	5	Music publishers	2
Delicacies	48	Music (artists and teachers)	33
Dentists	32	Music and musical instruments	13
Dress, ornaments and rhinestone mfrs.	2	Newspapers and periodicals	6
Druggists, retail	55	Novelties	5
Drugs, importers	3	Nuts, edible	23
Dry goods, retail	11	Orchestras	11
Dry goods, commission	1	Painters	10
Engineers, consulting	1	Paints, oils and glass	4
Exporters	3	Paper boxes	1
Expressing and moving	26	Paper dealers	2
Feed stores	1	Pavements	1
First aid supplies	1	Photographers	16
Fish dealers	9	Physical culture	1
Florists	19	Physicians and surgeons	133
Forwarding agents	2	Plasterers	6
Fruits, wholesale	47	Plumbers	22
Fruits and vegetables	84	Presses, grape crushers and filters	2
Furnished rooms	55	Printers	13
Furniture manufacturers	18	Publishers	3
Furniture cleaners	1	Proprietary medicines	4
Furniture, retail	6	Radio apparatus and supplies	3
Furriers	2	Radio cabinet	1
General merchandise, retail	2	Railroad supplies and equipment	2
Granite	1	Real estate	115
Grape juice	1	Restaurants and lunch rooms	257
Grocers, retail	500	Riding clothes	1
Grocers, wholesale	33	Salad dressing	2
Gummed products	1	Sausages	12
Gunsmiths	2	Sausages, manufacturers	12
Hairdressers	22	Sewer builders	18
Halls	3	Shoe ornaments	2
Hardware and cutlery	27	Shoe shining	8
Hats and caps, manufacturers	1	Shoemakers and repairers	28
Hay, grain and feed	1	Shoes, retail	9
Horse-shoers	3	Soda fountain supplies	1
Hospitals	2	Statuary	9
Ice cream manufacturers	2	Steamship lines and agencies	20
Ice cream parlors	27	Stone cutters	2
Ice cream supplies	2	Studios	1
Importers	8	Sugar	2
Insurance agents	8	Tailors, manufacturers	21
Insurance brokers	2	Tailors, merchants	106
Jewelers	13	Teaming and motor trucking	13
Ladies' tailors	2	Terrazzo, mosaic and tiles	2
Ladies' waists	1	Theatres	10
Lamp shades and supplies	3	Tiles and tilings	4
Lamp manufacturers	1	Tin, copper, sheet metal work	4
Lamps and lanterns	6	Trunks, manufacturers	2
Lawyers	65	Undertakers	27
Macaroni dies and moulds	1	Upholsterers	2
Macaroni manufacturers	15	Watch and jewelry repairing	2
Machinery	3	Welding	2
Malt extracts and syrups	6	Wines, sacramental	3

The above list is not complete by any means. It registers only Italian firms as listed in the Chicago Classified Telephone Directory. Apart from the hundreds of Italian business firms not listed in the telephone book, there are quite a few concerns controlled by Italians but not bearing Italian names and therefore very hard to distinguish from the others. With the exception of a few lines of business not reported above, Countess Cipriani's directory is representative of the business activities of the Italians in Chicago and as a whole may be considered as an accurate index of the ramifications of the Italians in all fields of human endeavor.

CHAPTER XV

THE ITALIANS IN POLITICS

* * * If, for example, our city governments are corrupt, the most flagrant evidence of that corruption will usually be found in an immigrant community, because here administrative officers can defy decency without fear of the condemnation of American public opinion. But the corruption is in no sense confined to such neighborhoods; those who organize it or profit by it are not there. Eliminating the immigrant would not end it. To delude ourselves with the belief that except for his presence among us we would have been able to avoid these fundamental difficulties in our social and economic relationships, is only to delay the solution of these difficulties. Prejudice against the immigrant only confuses the issue.

—GRACE ABBOTT: "The Immigrant and the Community," page 295.

THE ITALIANS have been quick to take advantage of political opportunities offered to them in proportion to the strength of their vote.

When the Italians started to come over in the nineties, the Germans and the Irish were already well entrenched in the politics of the city. In 1888, according to L. P. Nelson (Statistics showing the original nationalities of Chicago), the following vote was cast in Chicago:

Italians	451	Norwegians	2,998
Germans	23,957	Bohemians	2,935
Irish	15,263	Poles	2,214
Swedes	4,401	Austrians	1,247

In 1892, according to the same source, the Italian vote had increased to 1,032 against 45,005 for the Germans, 23,578 for the Irish, 10,838 for the Swedes, 4,832 for the Norwegians, 2,333 for the Danes, 5,721 for the Bohemians, 4,861 for the Poles.

The Italians of those days were of the "migrant" type and as such did not have any desire to remain in the country or to take any interest in the political affairs of the community. Those who did vote, in the majority of cases did so in order to "return" the favors done to them by the politicians of their ward or because their votes were bought.

Viscount Bryce tells us of how illiterate immigrants, recently arrived from Europe, were given the franchise: "Droves of squalid men, who looked as if they had just emerged from an emigrant ship and had perhaps done so only a few weeks before, for the law prescribing a certain term of residence is frequently violated, were brought up to a magistrate by the ward agent of the party which had captured them, declared their allegiance to the United States, and were forthwith placed on the roll." (The American Commonwealth, vol. 2, page 99.) Further he says:

"It is even alleged that many of the immigrants (especially Italian) brought over to be employed on railroad making and other similar works come under what are virtually contracts to cast their votes in a particular way and do so cast them, possibly returning to Europe after some months or years, richer by the payment they have received for their votes as well as for their labor." (Loc. cit., Vol. II, page 103.)

Those men, however illiterate, exerted some influence on the politicians of their wards. Mastrovalerio tells us how in the early nineties Mr. Oscar Durante and other leading Italians, in order to stop the indecent practice of poor immigrants gathering rags in the streets, had an ordinance passed against it, which was soon ignored because of the pressure that rag-pickers brought to bear on the politicians in their ward.

Of course, the Italians of those days had some sort of Italian political leaders. John Ginocchio, for example, was republican leader. F. Cugno was a democratic "boss".

Some of the first Italians to occupy public offices were Stephen Malato and William Navigato, who were state representatives in the nineties. Frank Gazzolo was elected alderman in 1892, and Frank J. Brignadello was a member of the Illinois Legislature for three consecutive terms from 1894 to 1898. Rocco Navigato was deputy sheriff and special investigator in the city attorney's office as early as 1896. Anthony Trimarco was state representative in 1907. Stephen Revere was alderman twice in the late nineties. Paul Dasso was superintendent of the House of Correction at about the same time. Thomas Froley, an Italian with an Irish name, was state representative in 1918.

There have been many other Italians who have occupied minor political offices in the last twenty-five years. But it has been of rather recent date that they have started to climb the political ladder.

The first Italian to be elected to the Municipal Court was ex-Judge Bernard P. Barasa. Other Italian judges of the Municipal Court have been Mr. Alberto A. Gualano (1922), Mr. Francis Borrelli (. . . .), Mr. Francis B. Allegretti (1924), Mr. John J. Lupe (1923), Mr. John Sbarbaro (. . . .). The following Italians have filled the office of assistant state's attorney: Mr. Stephen Malato, Mr. Vito Cuttone, Mr. Thomas Landise, Mr. Michael Romano, Mr. John Sbarbaro, Mr. Michael Rosinia, Mr. Joseph H. Nicolai, Mr. Guy C. Crapple.

Mr. Crapple has also been assistant United States district attorney. Mr. Francis J. Cuneo has been assistant attorney general in Illinois from 1922 to 1927.

Other Italians who occupy political offices today are:

State Officials

James B. Leonardo, state senator.
Joseph Perina, state representative for Fifteenth District.
William V. Pacelli, state representative for Seventeenth District.
Charles Coia, state representative for Seventeenth District.
Michael R. Durso, state representative for Twentieth District.

Cook County Officials

Lawrence A. Cuneo, private secretary, state's attorney's office.
Dominic F. Volini, clerk, Bond Department, Cook County.
Peter Calo, investigator, state's attorney's office.
Alexander Conforti, investigator, state's attorney's office.
Nat. Biancalana, investigator, state's attorney's office.
Dan. Abbamonte, deputy coroner.

City Officials

Daniel A. Serritella, inspector of weights and measures, and republican committeeman for First Ward.

A. J. Prignano, alderman, Twentieth Ward.

Peter C. Granata, chief clerk, prosecuting attorney's office.

F. C. Martini, in charge Contracts Division, city engineer's office.

James Vignola, member Board of Local Improvements.

The leading Italian in politics in Chicago is former Judge Bernard P. Barasa. He has been candidate for mayor, for state's attorney and lately for member of the Board of Review. In the last election he ran ahead of his ticket, with over three hundred thousand votes. Although Mr. Barasa has been defeated in all three instances, he has rendered an invaluable service to the Italian community because he has paved the way for other Italians to get up the ladder of public life.

Today there are in the city of Chicago over 65,000 Italian votes, which are increasing at the rate of at least 5,000 a year.

The Italians as a whole are either Republican or Democrats. About 200 are are members of the Socialist Party; the latter have five sections, called after the ward in which they are located, such as the section of the Nineteenth Ward, the section of the Seventeenth Ward, the section of the Eleventh Ward and so on. The first Italian section of the Socialist Party was organized with 22 members in the old Nineteenth Ward by Mr. G. Bertelli, on September 15, 1907. In all, the Italian Socialists have about 800 members throughout the United States. They support a weekly of their own, "La Parola del Popolo", published in Chicago. The Italian Socialists of America profess to adhere to the platform of the United States Socialist Party, although they seem to be active in the organization of anti-fascist movements in this country.

The chief medium for the political education of the Italians is the Italian newspaper and the political club. Of the latter there are no less than twenty in the city, both republican and democratic.

These clubs are organized along the lines of pleasure clubs. Each man pays a small quota a month (between fifty cents and a dollar). They maintain in many instances luxurious quarters, such as those of the Italian-American Citizen Club at 1914 W. North Avenue, where they gather in the evening to listen to political speeches or to lectures on civic problems. These clubs are the best school for the Americanization of the Italians. In all of these clubs several men, invariably politicians, offer their services free of charge to assist the alien in the naturalization process.

As in other fields, so in politics is the evolution of the Italian very remarkable.

Brought up in a corrupt political environment, under the influence of Irish politicians, the Italian has not evolved yet a political conscience of his own. He is still following in the footsteps of the Irish. His methods, his ambitions, his ideals, his goals are the same as those of the Irish. The Italian has not fully absorbed, so far, the political beliefs of the better element in the country. When he votes, he does not look beyond the personality of the candidate. He has not learned to distinguish issues from men. In his opinions, one politician is just as corrupt as the other. Once a man gets into power, the average Italian reasons, he will become as bad as his predecessor. And the history of Chicago politics cannot give him the lie.

The clinic eye of any observer, however, will note that the Italians are fast abandoning the favor system of politics with their moving from their old districts. Twenty years ago they needed to go to their ward politician to get a license for a peddler's cart, to have their taxes reduced, or to get in good standing with the local police officer. Today the Italian is fast getting beyond that stage. He has learned the language, he has taken up American customs, he is independent of the politician. He is acquiring a political conscience of his own, like that of other races. Today he believes more than ever in team-work. Old jealousies are quickly forgotten. The immigration restriction has been a tremendous lesson for him. He has learned that unless he uses the same methods that the Irish, Germans and Scandinavians have used for the last fifty years, his children will never keep pace with the progress of other nationalities.

So we have today the Italian vote—strong, compact, increasing rapidly every year. A vote that will be reckoned with in the next few years. But here a question becomes imperative: "What will be the contribution of the Italians to American Government in the future? Will they continue to maintain their own identity as Italo-Americans or will they merge in the caldron of American politics, adhering strictly to American political traditions?

The answer is not very far. The Italians have already shown signs of breaking loose from ward politics. With their moving to American neighborhoods they are discarding old theories and acquiring the ways, manners and even beliefs of their neighbors. The Italian is just as much interested in politics as the average American. That is, he is chiefly interested in his family and his work. Politics do not allure him.

As it has already been stated in this volume, the Italian is instinctively democratic. All the leaders of modern Italy, with the exception of a few, have been the product of the middle class and in some cases even of the proletariat. Mussolini is the son of a blacksmith.

The principles that underlie the American Government are not new to the Italians. The Sicilians had a Constitution and a Parliament even before England. The love for freedom, on the other hand, has never been extinct in the Italians. The Italians have always been fighting for their freedom and for the freedom of other races.

The fear expressed by the Chicago Tribune in an editorial appearing in the issue of May 14, 1928, that the Italians might "cherish a divided allegiance and enjoy the powers and privileges of American citizenship as a means of advancing the interests of Italy" will seem ridiculous to any student of Italian immigration in the United States. This point is further illustrated in another chapter. Here it will suffice to state that no power in the world can keep the Italians from being interested exclusively in American affairs. Sentimental ties will exist, no doubt, just as they exist in the other nationalities, but they will never amount to anything more than that. As Mussolini himself has stated to the correspondent for the "New York Sun", Italy considers American citizens of Italian extraction as foreign citizens with no duties whatsoever towards their mother country. But even if Mussolini and all Italy entertained entirely different ideas than those expressed above, the Italians will ever remain faithful to the oath taken in becoming citizens.

On the other hand, any feeling of devotion to Italian traditions and culture which may exist in the Americans of Italian birth is almost entirely extinct in the first generation of Americans of Italian descent.

Mr. Fairchild's drastic desire that the traits of foreign nationality which the immigrant brings with him are not to be mixed or interwoven, but must *be abandoned* unfortunately has come true as it regards the Italians.

The children of Italian immigrants today are not interested in the least in Italian affairs or Italian beliefs or Italian political traditions. It is significant to note that the Socialist Party has not been able to gather any recruits among the children of the Italians, not even of Italian Socialists. And to say that the Socialist movement in Italy received a very strong support before the advent of Fascism.

Not even Fascism with all its attractiveness of efficiency and prestige has appealed to the Americans of Italian descent. As a matter of fact, although the masses of the Italians in the United States are indifferent to the political experiments of Fascism, quite a few Italians are against Mussolini because of their belief in the freedom of the press, freedom of speech and other democratic tenets.

It cannot be denied, however, that most Italians will vote for an Italian on the democratic or republican tickets. But even such tendency is fast disappearing. A young lady of Italian extraction remarked a few days before the primaries of April 1928, "I will vote for any good Italian, but I will never vote for a bad Italian." The spirit that prompted that remark is not peculiar of her alone.

With the recognition of the Italian vote, the descendants of the Italians will merge the interests of their race with the interests of the community at large, and will not vote for a man of their own race simply because he happens to be one of their own.

A recognition of Italian ability is necessary before the Italians will vote for issues and not for men. In the East the ability of the Italians is being recognized. Congressman La Guardia of New York, Congressman Palmisano of Maryland, Justice Cotillo of the Supreme Court of the State of New York, Francis A. Pallotti, secretary of state for Connecticut, Anthony Ruffo, mayor of Atlantic City, to mention only the outstanding, all men of undisputed high calibre and ability, could have never attained the high positions that they are filling now if the Italian vote in their own communities had not been recognized.

The day that the Italians will be given equal opportunities as other races to fill public offices, the Italians will forget the hyphen and will vote as Americans.

* * *

ITALIAN VOTE FOR 1898, BY WARDS

Ward	Votes	Ward	Votes	Ward	Votes	Ward	Votes	Ward	Votes	Ward	Votes
1	121	9	2	17	42	5	7	13	58	21	7
2	11	10	5	18	30	6	1	14	8	22	4
3	19	11	17	19	76	7	2	15	6	23	40
4	8	12	19	20	4	8	3	16	1	24	11

Total, 451.

CHAPTER XVI

THE ITALIAN PRESS

*The immigrant's language, like his memories, is part of his personality. These are not baggage that he can lose en route to his destination. Furthermore, it is not always desirable, even if it were possible, to extirpate or suppress these heritages. * * * The aim of Americanization is not the subjugation, but the assimilation, of the immigrant. Assimilation takes place more readily when there are no mental conflicts and new relationships breed new loyalties from the old heritages.*

—ROBERT E. PARK, The Immigrant Press and Its Control, page 468.

THE ITALIANS in the city support several publications. The Italian daily, "L'Italia", was established in 1886 by Chev. Oscar Durante, its present editor. "La Tribuna Transatlantica" was established in 1898. Chev. Mastrovalerio is its founder and editor. "Vita Nuova", a weekly, is edited by the Rev. P. De Carlo. "La Parola del Popolo", a weekly, is the official organ of the Italian Federation of the Socialist Party of America. "L'Idea", a weekly, was established by the late Cav. Uff. Antonio Ferrari eighteen years ago. "Germinal", a weekly, small size, is supposed to be published by a small anarchist group in the city. There is also the monthly "Bollettino delle Societa' Italiane", issued by Mr. Peter Nanni, and "Il Messaggero della Salute", a monthly devoted to hygiene, physio-psychic therapy and eclectic culture. Its editor and publisher is Mr. T. Lucidi. There are several other weekly and monthly organs of societies, lodges, churches and organizations of one kind or the other. Of late a new magazine has been established in Chicago: "Mens Italica", a monthly of about one hundred pages. To its first number, the only one out while this chapter is being written, leading Italian men of letters and university professors have contributed, from Fausto Maria Martini, the famous playwright, to Alfredo Petrucci, famous artist, from Prof. Biondolillo of the University of Palermo to Prof. Calligaris of the University of Rome. Among its contributors are Admiral Bravetta, Gen. Bertotti, E. Corradini, L. D'Ambra, E. Ferri and many other illustrious Italians. It is a magazine that is bound to have a great influence in the moulding of the culture of the Italians in America if it will be supported by the various communities in the country. Its editor and publisher is Mr. Vito Losacco.

With the exception of "Mens Italica" and "Il Messaggero della Salute" the Italian periodicals of Chicago are written in a language accessible to the average Italian with grammar school education. Mastrovalerio, especially, has made of his "Tribuna Transatlantica" one of the most picturesque and interesting newspapers in the country. Although he possesses a full command of the Italian language and a general culture to be equaled by very few Italians in the city, Mastrovalerio uses his literary Italian only on special occasions. His everyday prose is such that everybody can understand. It is full of idioms, provincialisms and English—or rather American—Italian neologisms. "Storo"

for "store", "Olzoppare" for "hold-up", "Mascina" for "machine, automobile", "gliarda" for "yard", "tostamasto" for "toastmaster", "grosseria" for
"grocery", "munsciainatori" for "moonshiners", "ghelle" for "girls", "bosso"
for "boss", "barra" for "bar", "ganga" for "gang" are some of the new words
that Mastrovalerio uses in his newspaper.

The Italian press of Chicago has played a very important part in the
progress of the local Italian community and in its increased prestige in the last
few years. Mr. Oscar Durante, the editor of "L'Italia", for example, was the
leader of a group of Italians who obtained from the Chicago South Park Commissioner that a new drive, from the extreme North Side to the extreme South
Side, be named Columbus Drive in honor of the great navigator. It was also
due to Mr. Durante's efforts that a Chicago public school was named in honor
of Giuseppe Verdi. Other public schools that have names of great Italians
are the Dante, the Columbus, the Tonti and the Volta.

To a certain extent the Italian newspapers of Chicago have had more
freedom and independence than most newspapers of the kind in the country,
and, in some cases, they have not hesitated to ridicule and expose men and conditions. Their chief source of revenue is from advertisements. Some periodicals, although widely read, seldom collect the yearly subscriptions. "L'Italia",
the local daily, is sold at public stands. It has a circulation of over 35,000.
Editorial policies they seldom have. They are all a one-man paper and as such
they are governed according to the principles that rule its publisher in his
private life. Editorials usually appear on the first page. The second and third
pages are devoted to local news and the rest to articles reproduced from other
newspapers. At election time the local papers usually sponsor one party or
the other, but they do not refuse paid advertisements from any other political
group.

The statement by Park & Miller[1] that "There is no doubt, for example, that
the nationalistic newspapers do not want their readers to become Americanized" is not true of the Italian publications of Chicago. As a matter of fact, the
Italian editors of Chicago have always been preaching Americanization to the
Italians. An Americanized group of Italians means more circulation for the
Italian papers and a greater source of revenue at all times, especially at election
times. It is a fact that the Americanized Italian will spend more than the
Italian who contemplates to return to Italy, and it is only a common sense matter
to expect business firms to advertise to spenders rather than to savers.

Equally erroneous is the other statement that the Italian press has been
carrying a propaganda of hate. The accusations moved by the Rev. Sartorio,
quoted by Park & Miller,[2] are true, no doubt, but the motives that actuate them
are misunderstood, if not misrepresented.

The Italian is quick to resent injustices and partialities.

It is not fair on the part of American newspapers to keep on harping on
Italian crimes and Italian bootleggers, when right here in this city more dastardly crimes are being committed every day by members of other nationalities,
mostly natives, than the Italians would ever think of. The campaign of hatred
in America is conducted not by the Italian press, but by the American press.
Recently in Chicago postal inspectors found the following weapons and explosives in the house of a Charles Cleaver:

2 machine guns.

7 shotguns.

137 full sticks of dynamite.

2 bombs, complete with caps.

1 bomb, uncapped.

Half bushel of assorted revolver bullets and rifle cartridges.

Drills (such as used in opening safes).

Hunting knife (ten inch blade).

Two jars containing dark fluid (believed to be an explosive).

Hundreds of detonating caps and several strands of wire used in the manufacture of bombs.

If Mr. Charles Cleaver had been an Italian, and especially a Sicilian, we may rest assured that the news would have received first page honors, but as Mr. Cleaver, unfortunately, did not happen to be a Southern European, the news was relegated by the "Chicago Tribune" on the twenty-second page, although a picture of the "arsenal" appeared on the last page (April 28, 1928). The other newspapers did not lay much stress on the matter.

It is therefore only natural that the Italian press should retort in its own way.

The condescension that some of the natives seem to show to the foreign born is poppy-cock. Of course, as a whole, the natives are superior to the immigrants in some respects, but, at the same time, there are many foreign-born in the city who are the superior of the average American.

By showing its readers the other side of the story, the Italian press has been and is doing an invaluable service to Americanization. Americanization implies some sort of superiority over other races, and by that standard the Italians will become real Americans only if they learn to look at their fellow citizens as they are, despoiled of all the pretentiousness with which some of them cloak themselves. No hatred has ever been preached by the Italian newspapers. They have done really constructive work and have helped the Italians to identify themselves with America. On the other hand, they have made the Italians maintain "their sense of social responsibility."

The Italian press of Chicago has always cooperated with local authorities, with Americanization bureaus, with social welfare agencies, in a word, with all public organizations, in any activity that could spell civic improvement.

In the future, unless a greater contingent of Italians will be admitted every year in the country, the Italian press is bound to die or to be written, at least in part, in English. Several newspapers in other sections of the country have already started along those lines.

NOTES TO CHAPTER 16

(1) R. E. Park & H. A. Miller, Old World Traits Transplanted, New York, 1921, page 290.
(2) Loc. cit. above, page 291.

CHAPTER XVII

INTELLIGENCE AND INTELLIGENCE TESTS

Huxley once described the Italian people as being some of the brightest on earth. Huxley, however, died too early to study the results of the Army Intelligence tests taken during the war. Had he had that wonderful opportunity, certainly he would have changed his opinion.

It is true that even Madison Grant, the famous exponent of the Nordic theory, admits the superiority of the Mediterranean race over the Nordic and Alpine races in intellectual attainments[1] but, reasons Prof. Bingham of Princeton, the attainments of the Mediterranean race date back to several centuries ago, whereas the army intelligence tests were taken in 1917-1918.[2]

It would be out of place to enter here into a discussion of the army intelligence tests, of the alleged superiority of the Nordics or even of the factors that go to make up intelligence.

"Definitions of intelligence are as varied as the minds that create them, but no matter which of the many formulas may be accepted, a foreigner never seems to possess the normal degree of the elusive quality. He is supernormal or subnormal: either dazzling the native born with the grasp and brilliancy of his intellect, or displeasing them with his mental backwardness and incapacity. He is either above the accepted standard or below—mostly below."

The real question here is:

"Are there in the foreigner any innate and unchangeable qualities of intellect, unaffected by environment, social status, education, experience in life, surroundings and emotion of the moment? Is there an intelligence that can be isolated, measured and classified as hopelessly inferior?"

"No matter how useful for some purposes may be the mental tests applied to immigrants and others, no yardstick has yet been devised to measure the values of human beings everywhere at all times. No matter how simple and easy the problems to solve and the questions to answer, there is no test that is not conditioned by the specific intelligence of the tester, by his environment, experience and education."[3]

Some teachers have tried to draw some conclusion (far-fetched, in most cases) from intelligence tests taken among the children of the foreign-born, but, points out Miss Mead of the American Museum of Natural History, "classification of foreign children in schools where they have to compete with American children, on the basis of group intelligence test findings alone, is not a just evaluation of the child's innate capacity." Having applied intelligence tests on 276 Italian children and 160 American children from the 6th to the 10th grade in the public schools of Hammonton, N. J., Miss Mead reaches the following conclusion: "The scores of the Italian children have been shown to be influenced by: the language factor as demonstrated by the classification according to language spoken at home, the social status factor and the length of time the father has been in this country, the last factor being somewhat interwoven with the language factor."[4]

In the absence, therefore, of definite scientific (not pseudo-scientific) formulas, we must abide by the points of view of people who can discuss the argument with authority and without prejudice.

A public school principal who for years has supervised a large Italian school makes the following observations, "Italian children are no readier to learn than are other children; on the other part, they are no less so." In most cases they improve the first opportunity to quit school. This is more the faults of the parents than of the pupils. The parents are content with their position and do little to inspire their children to be more than they are. But taking the illiteracy of Italy into consideration and the attitude of the parents it seems to me that the Italian group of school children is possibly doing better than are the children of any other foreign-speaking group of the city.[1]

Mr. Wm. J. Bogan, Superintendent of the Chicago School Board, who has had the opportunity to observe Italian children for several years past, recently stated that he "finds Italian children very intelligent, adaptable and quick to take up American customs and ideals."

Rev. William Murphy, Rector of the Church of St. Callisto, has found Italian children in his school "of splendid intelligence, of vivacity of intellect and very affectionate."

In answer to a questionnaire sent out by the Board of Education to principals of high schools in the city, the following answers were received:

Miss Nellie White, Acting Principal, Haines (Grammar) School: "My general opinion as to the qualities shown by Italian children in their studies is good." (717 Italian children.)

Miss Elvis L. Hicks, Principal, Andrew Jackson School (Grammar grades only, 1,423 Italian children in school): "In group intelligence tests, and standard reading and thought tests, there are on the average about twenty per cent who are at or above the standard norm, and eighty per cent who fall below the norm. This apparent deficiency is more than likely due to environmental difficulties; in particular to being required to use and hear a foreign language in the home. The group intelligence tests are, as you probably know, based to a large extent on reading ability. I should say that while the children rate below the average in scholarship ability (due perhaps to the facts mentioned above) they are above average in the general interest shown in their work and in responsiveness to the efforts of their teachers."

Miss Visa McLaughlin, Principal, J. A. Sexton School (grammar grades, 165 Italian children): "The Italian children are responsive and quick to grasp new ideas. Our chief trouble in this district is that the Italian language is used almost exclusively in the homes and therefore the children are backward in the use of English."

Mr. Aaron Kline, Principal, Pullman School (grammar): "Their teachers report their qualities in their studies thus: Excellent 30, good 133, average 146, poor 94."

F. J. Lane, Principal E. Jenner Public School (1,109 children of Italian parentage): "Noticeable qualities: Responsive, thrifty, affectionate, loyal, respectful, highly imitative. If attention is secured and interest is aroused good results follow. Not especially orderly but in no way opposed to good order. If interested, very eager to succeed."

Miss June H. MacConkey, Principal, Dante School (grammar, 581 children of Italian parentage): "Dr. Burton of the University of Chicago recently conducted an examination of sixth grade pupils of various nationalities. His statement was, I believe, that children of other nationalities, living in similar economic conditions, gave approximately the same results. This places the cause of the low scholastic attainment of the Italian children in the poverty of their environment and not in their nationality. Good qualities: Affectionate, eager to please, appreciative of music and art, responsive to kindness and attention. Qualities unfavorable for school work: Restlessness, lack of concentration, lack of persistence in the face of difficulties, lack of ambition regarding scholarship, slowness of comprehension, small power of retention, lack of reliability."

Mr. W. S. Schoch, Principal, Morgan Park High School (5 children of Italian origin): "One of the boys is characterized as affable and indolent, the other is good. The three girls are excellent students, capable and fine."

Miss Rose M. Kavana, Acting Principal, Medill High School (137 Italian students): "We find them capable but not studious or regular in attendance. They cooperate well and are pleasant to work with in school activities outside the classroom."

Mr. C. Pettersen, Assistant Principal, Carl Schurz High School (173 Italian pupils): "We find the average distribution as to abilities in their studies—some rank well and some not so good."

Mr. James T. Gaffney, Principal, Roosevelt Senior High School (15 Italian children) comments: "Capable students, quick-witted, inattentive, honor student, fair, excellent, above average, enthusiastic, cooperative, loyal, not particularly industrious or accurate."

Englewood High School, Mr. Davis M. Davidson, Principal (60 Italian children): "The teachers' opinion is expressed as follows: Four teachers find these pupils excellent. Ten teachers regard them as good; sixteen teachers find them fair; two teachers vote these pupils as poor."

Mr. Wm. J. Bartholf, Principal, Crane Technical High School (407 Italian children): "Number of students above the average, 319; below the average, 88."

Mr. H. D. Smith, Assistant Principal, Parker Senior High School. Five students. All very good students.

Mr. John Jacobson, Acting Principal, Tuley High School (34 Italian children): "We notice no difference in the qualities of Italian children when compared with children of other nationalities."

Mr. John E. Addams, Principal, Waller High School (180 Italian children): "We endeavor to meet each pupil as an individual without reference to race or parentage, and we find among the Italian pupils, as we do in other nationalities, all varieties both as to intelligence, character and industry. Some are excellent, others medium and some poor."

Mr. Grant Beebe, Principal, Lane Technical High School (221 Italian pupils): "We have some 15 or 20 nationalities represented at Lane and the Italian boys are making a very good showing in comparison with those of other nationalities. We find them particularly successful in our architectural and freehand drawing departments and in our musical organizations."

Mr. Chas. H. Perrine, Principal, Lake View High School (40 Italian pupils): Scholarship standing, 1.60 plus. Scholarship median of school, 1.71.

Mr. C. Melody, Principal, Calumet High School: "Of pupils of Italian origin, eight are classified as excellent, eight as good, seven as fair, two as poor and one as very poor."

Miss Dora Bells, Principal, Flower Technical High School (42 pupils): "Answers based partly upon knowledge of these students and partly upon previous experience. Studious: 36 report no, 6 report usually. Lazy: majority report no, 7 report usually or yes. Brilliant: 37 report no, or uncertain or lively, 2 report yes. Dull: majority report no, 1 reports yes. Average: 39 report yes or usually. Well disposed: majority reports yes, 9 report yes or usually. Troublesome: majority reports no, 9 report yes or usually."

Miss Caroline L. Reilly, Principal, McKinley High School (968 Italian children): "General mental ability of pupils as shown by intelligence tests and regular class-room work to be similar to that of other groups found in our cosmopolitan high schools. Outstanding in their accomplishments in the languages, Latin, French and Spanish. Number of pupils electing science courses is limited but the superior pupils are outstanding in their accomplishments. Keen interest in music and drawing, but lack of sustained effort is noticeable. Interest in athletics is keen and outstanding, in city contests standing is excellent."

Mr. W. J. Harrower, Principal, Harper Junior High School (171 Italian children): "We find that they range from the best to the poorest * * * and that where Italian parents attempt to become Americanized and do not hold to the old country customs the children are on a par with those of other nationalities."

Miss Mary E. Tobin, Principal, Cregier Junior High School (440 Italian pupils): "As to my opinions of the qualities of these children, I can only speak of them in praise. They are earnest and industrious; excellent in music, art, English and social studies; good in all studies. I see no difference between this group and all other pupils of whatever origin—all fine young Americans."

From letter by Assistant Superintendent Bogan to Mr. J. Gonnelly, about Cregier Junior High School, dated March 11, 1927: "Most of the children are of Italian descent. A more interesting and lovable group I have never met. The discipline is beautiful. The self-control shown by the pupils in the corridors is remarkable. I was thrilled time and again by the accomplishments of this school under serious handicaps."

Miss W. R. Hatfield, Principal, Parker Junior High School: "We find that one is superior, eight above average, eleven average, and two below average."

Mr. Wilbur H. Wright, Principal, Austin High School (206 Italian children): "In general the children of Italian origin do satisfactory work. Many of them are superior students and are on our honor roll. A survey of the work of this group shows their accomplishment to be on a par with that of other nationality groups in our school."

Mr. Geo. White, Principal, Lindblom High School (134 Italian children): "Out of these, 106 have good qualities and 28 have bad qualities. We also wish to add the following: Leonard Fragassi, one of our Lindblom students, gave his life in defense of his father. The student body of Lindblom has erected an expensive memorial in his honor."

Miss Dorothy M. Sass, Assistant Principal, Tilden Technical High School (107 Italian children): "Eleven of them failed in each subject, six in two subjects, three in three subjects, one in four and one in five. The regular program per pupil is five subjects. The general feeling of the teachers seems to be that they are quick to learn, loyal to those they like, but quick-tempered, quick to resent, and some of course are lazy."

Miss Sophie A. Theilgaard, Principal, Curtis Junior High School (250 Italian children): The following comments by teachers are representative: "A wide spread of intelligence. Where home life is clean and industrious the children reflect the same traits. I find many children who have to be taught the most elementary principles of citizenship; but I also find a large number of excellent students." "The majority of Italian children are satisfactory. Those that come from good homes are excellent in all respects; those that come from poor homes reflect their environment." "Fourteen out of 47 are of Italian parentage. The majority of these rank in the upper third of the class. Good qualities: loyalty to school, punctuality, good scholarship, most desirable school citizens, personal appearance excellent. Bad qualities: tendency toward "gang spirit" among several of these boys, lack of home training in some instances. The only bad qualities noted are among those ranking lowest in their groups." "About twenty per cent of the children in my class are of Italian descent. Fifty per cent of this group are class leaders in scholarship and citizenship. All of the others, but two, are of average ability. The special two are slow. One is a problem case as far as running away from a very poorly organized home is concerned, and the other is the naturally slow type with very little ambition." "I find my Italian pupils on a par with the other nationalities, both in mind and body. Most of them are exceptionally quick to learn." "I find the Italian pupils intelligent and ambitious. As a rule they have fine ideals of citizenship. Often the language is a serious handicap." "The Italians of my group come from homes of the better class and seem highly intelligent." "As compared with other nationalities about same proportion of studious and non-studious."

Mr. Chas. J. Lunak, Principal, Hirsch Junior High School (95 Italian children): "Nine children fair, 10 children fair, four children fair, five children average, eight children a great variety of abilities and attitudes shown. On the whole my eight are slow but industrious. One is decidedly lazy and one inclined to dishonesty." "Six children in the class —widest range of abilities." "Six children in the class, emotional, excitable, industrious." "One child in the class, good." "One child in the class, good." "Two children in the class—these are good." "Two children in the class, good."

Miss Mary Boughan, Sabin Junior High School (14 children of Italian origin): Scholarship, 4, 90 to 95; 6, 80 to 90; 4, 70 to 80. No failure. Conduct: 1, 95 or above; 7, 90 to 95; 6, 80 to 90; 2, 70 to 80.

Harrison High School (78 Italian children): 40 good, 5 very good, 8 excellent, 22 fair and 3 poor.

Mr. Frank W. Stahl, Principal, Bowen High School (44 Italian students): Ten poor students, 15 fair, 16 good, 3 excellent. The opinion of these teachers seems to be that these fair and poor students have the ability but will not apply themselves.

Mr. C. E. Lang, Principal, Kelvyn Park Junior High School (48 Italian students, 21 girls and 27 boys). Girls: Scholarship—superior 1, excellent 3, good 10, fair 7; deportment—superior 4, excellent 11, good 4, fair 2; attendance—superior 2, excellent 10, fair 1, good 7, poor 1. Boys: Scholarship—excellent 3, good 11, fair 10, poor 3; deportment—superior 7, excellent 8, good 6, fair 5, poor 1; attendance—superior 4, excellent 12, good 8, fair 3.

Miss Helen Corcoran, Assistant Principal, Sullivan Junior High School: "Twenty-five Italian children are registered in our files, their work averaging good, though several are above that average."

ITALIAN CHILDREN IN THE HIGH SCHOOLS OF CHICAGO
Senior High Schools

(n. r.) indicates "not reported".

Austin	206	Marshall	n. r.
Bowen	44	McKinley	968
Calumet	26	Medill	137
Crane Technical	407	Morgan Park	5
Englewood	60	Parker	5
Fenger	n. r.	Philipps	n. r.
Flower Technical	42	Roosevelt-Albany Park	15
Harrison Technical	78	Schurz	173
Hyde Park	n. r.	Senn	n. r.
Lake View	40	Tilden	107
Lane Technical	221	Tuley	34
Lindblom	134	Waller	180

Junior High Schools

Cregier	440	Kelvyn Park	48
Curtis	250	Parker	22
Farragut	n. r.	Phillips	n. r.
Harper	171	Sabin	16
Herzl	n. r.	Stockton	25
Hibbard	n. r.	Sullivan	n. r.
Hirsch	95	Westcott	n. r.

Total reported, 3,949.
Schools that did report, 27.
Schools that did not report, 9.

NOTES ON CHAPTER 17

(1) "The mental characteristics of the Mediterranean race are well known, and this race, while inferior in bodily stamina to both the Nordic and the Alpine, is probably the superior of both, certainly of the Alpines, in intellectual attainments. In the field of art its superiority to both the other European races is unquestioned, although in literature and in scientific research and discovery the Nordics far excel it." (Madison Grant: The Passing of the Great Race, page 229, quoted by Brigham.)

(2) Carl C. Brigham, Ph. D., Assistant Professor of psychology in Princeton University: A Study of American Intelligence, page 184.

(3) The Interpreter, March 1928, pages 3-5. The article continues as follows:

If there is such a thing as an inborn intelligence and if it can be defined and measured, let us hope that some day science will find a more precise method of measuring it and grading mental values.

Until it is done it may be better not to codify what is hardly more than a point of view. It may be still better to see what can be done to bring the intelligence of the foreigner—both the subnormal and the supernormal—somehow nearer to what would be normal and common.

If the native born—here or elsewhere—could free themselves from the habit of considering their intelligence as the standard of the world and of estimating anything that is different in terms of superiority and inferiority—perhaps some foreigners would not appear to be such mental giants and the mass would not seem quite so unintelligent. When the immigrant has gone through the American experience, has become accustomed to the American environment, and is given the equalizing opportunity of American schools, it may be that his "inferiority" will disappear altogether.

(4) Margaret Mead: Group Intelligence Tests and linguistic disability among Italian children: School and Society, April 16, 1927.

(5) F. O. Beck, the Italians in Chicago, loc. cit. page 21. As to accuracy of above statement confront figures for high school attendance by Italian children.

(6) The questionaire, mailed thanks to the interest and courtesy of Assistant Superintendent of Education Wm. Bogan and Mr. Oscar Durante, member of the Chicago Board of Education, asked for "a general opinion as to qualities good or bad shown by Italian children in their studies."

CHAPTER XVIII

THE ITALIANS IN THE LABOR UNIONS

D URING the garment workers' strike of 1910, a shabby dressed woman appealed for aid to Mr. A. Marimpietri, one of the leaders of the strike. "All I want is enough to buy a pair of shoes for my child," she mumbled. "He can't go barefooted, his shoes are worn out." Mr. Marimpietri looked at her: a wan, frail looking, emaciated young Italian woman. Instinctively he looked also at her shoes: they too, like her child's, were worn out. "But how about yourself?" Mr. Marimpietri asked her. "Well, do not bother about me, take care of my child—there are other children that need help too. We must win this strike."

The strike had been going for about fifteen weeks when that Italian girl asked for help. Fifteen weeks of sacrifices, of self-denials, of suffering. That strike was by far more trying than any other strike of our days. Today the Amalgamated has a large unemployment insurance fund. (In the last few years over four million dollars have been paid out.) But back in 1910 no such fund ever existed. The Amalgamated had not even been organized. The only help that strikers received was out of their own private savings and whatever public charity could afford. That girl well expressed the spirit that animated the Italian strikers.

In the Amalgamated strike of 1910 the Italians played a very important part. The strikers were mostly from Southern Italy and Tuscany, a determined nucleus of workers who fought valiantly to victory. Their efforts have been rewarded. Today the Italians of Chicago are well represented at the direction of the Amalgamated affairs. Mr. Marimpietri is member of the National Executive Board, is in charge of the unemployment insurance fund and has been made vice president of the Amalgamated Trust and Savings Bank. He is also director of the employment department, president of the local 39 (Coat Makers) and head of the pricing department. Mr. Grandinetti is one of the general organizers. Five other Italians are business agents. Several others occupy equally important positions. Out of 30,000 members of the Amalgamated, over 25 per cent are of Italian birth or origin.

Italians are also predominant in the *Hod Carriers' Building and Common Laborers Executive Council of Chicago and Vicinity.* Its executive officers are Samuel P. Luzzo, president; J. V. Moreschi, vice president; C. F. Balzano, secretary-treasurer; S. D. Giovanni, sergeant at arms; D. Paulella, M. Dineen, Chas. Powers, trustees. The Union contains fourteen locals, with over 14,500 members. Most of the presidents of those locals are Italians. Mr. Luzzo is also vice president of the Chicago Building Trades. The former president of the Hod Carriers' Union, Mr. J. V. Moreschi, is now its international president, with offices in Quincy, Mass. Italian is the president of the Chicago Federation of Musicians, over seven thousand strong, as is also one of the three members of the examination board.

115

It has been impossible to secure the list of the Italian presidents of the various union locals. The Official Labor Union Directory for 1928, however, gives the following Italian secretaries:

C. F. Balzano, Secretary Hod Carriers' Executive Council.

Frank Rango, Secretary Local 548, Journeymen Barbers Int'l Union.

Felix A. Valle, Secretary Park Employees Union.

William C. Marti, Secretary Scientific Laboratory Workers.

Steve Conforti, Secretary Street Repair and Section and Dump Foremen's Union.

Antonio Presi, Secretary Local 35, Granite Cutters Int'l Union.

Sam Lo Bue, Secretary Local No. 1, Hod Carriers B. & C. L. Union.

C. Damiani, Secretary Local No. 25, Hod Carriers Union.

Vito Miroballi, Secretary Local No. 76a, Hod Carriers Union.

M. J. Ballestro, Secretary Local 134, Machinists Union.

Alfred Rota, Secretary Local 24 (Wholesale) Upholsterers' International Union of North America.

N. Enrico Guidetto, Secretary Local 270, Amalgamated Clothing Workers of America.

Rose Carnovale, Secretary Local 275, Amalgamated Clothing Workers.

Chas. J. Lino, Secretary Local 937, Clerks, Brotherhood of Railway (Rock Island, Freight Handlers).

The Italians are now strong pillars of the American Federation of Labor. In some locals they are the predominant element. Probably there are in Chicago today not less than 50,000 Italians who are members of unions affiliated with the A. F. of L.

In answer to my inquiry regarding whether the Italians were good union men, Miss Elizabeth Christman, Secretary-Treasurer of the International Glove Workers Union of America, answered: "My experience in working with these groups is that they were loyal and sincere, and from the standpoint of comparison I can readily say they were good union men and women." Mr. Charles H. Sand, Secretary-Treasurer of the District Council of the United Brotherhood Carpenters and Joiners of America, Cook County, Ill., answered: "We find them to compare favorably with other nationalities and with respect to obedience to our laws and rules their rating is very good." The Secretary of the Journeymen Barbers International Union, Local 548, Mr. L. Rango, answered: "They are very good union men."

The answer of Mr. John Fitzpatrick, President of the Chicago Federation of Labor, does not need any comments. My letter to him read: "In view of the old charges that the Italians are not good union men, that they have been in many instances strike-breakers, and that they have done very little toward the development of labor unionism, I would like to have from you an opinion based on your personal experiences with the Italians of this country, and especially with those of Chicago." Mr. Fitzpatrick's answer was:

"In reply, I am compelled to say that this is the first instance in my forty years connection with organizations of labor that I heard that charge. My experience with the various nationalities is that those of any particular race may hold together a little closer than a group composed of different nationalities but when it comes to their economic interests where all workers have a common interest and a common cause the racial and nationalistic interests are forgotten. In the obligation of the American Federation of Labor we find these words: 'Race, creed or color shall not be a barrier to membership.'

"As a result of this we find the Italian workers in every occupation standing alongside of their fellow workers in every effort and every struggle, for the mutual benefit, protection and advancement of the workers generally.

"Therefore, we subscribe to the loyalty and unselfishness of the Italian members of our organization."

(See also Chapter VII on "occupations".)

* * * loyalty is not a self-pleasing virtue.

I am not bound to be loyal to the United States to please myself. I am bound to be loyal to the United States because I live under its laws and am its citizen, and whether it hurts me or whether it benefits me, I am obliged to be loyal.

Loyalty means nothing unless it has at its heart the absolute principle of self-sacrifice. Loyalty means that you ought to be ready to sacrifice every interest that you have, and your life itself, if your country calls upon you to do so, and that is the sort of loyalty which ought to be inculcated into these newcomers. That they are not to be loyal so long as they are pleased, but that, having once entered into this sacred relationship, they are bound to be loyal whether they are pleased or not; and that loyalty which is merely self-pleasing is only self-indulgence and selfishness.

—From an address by Woodrow Wilson before the Citizenship Convention held at Washington, D. C., July 13, 1916.

CHAPTER XIX

HEART ALLEGIANCE

One may be at heart an Italian, a German, a Pole, a Russian, but love of one's native land, of its language or art or culture, does not involve divided allegiance. Italians in the United States are expected to continue to seek citizenship, to become good Americans and so to emphasize their Americanism, not their Italianity, on all proper occasions. Still it is proper, of course, for them to maintain spiritual contacts with their native land, read its literature and, if they choose, favor it with gifts and endowments out of their legitimate earnings.

—Editorial in "The Chicago Daily News," May 23, 1928.

*While it is expected that you shall pledge undivided allegiance to America, America does not expect you to forego your love for the land of your birth. * * * Be proud of the country you come from.*

I will refuse citizenship to anyone who is not proud of the country of his birth. Anyone who does not love his own country is not apt to love the country of his adoption.

—From an address by Justive Salvatore Cotillo of the Supreme Court of the State of New York to applicants for citizenship at Bronx County Court. (United America, Jan. 7, 1928.)

BENITO MUSSOLINI, in his speech to the Italian Senate on June 5th, 1928, reiterated his previous statements on the relation of naturalized Italians in the United States to their mother country:

Immigration restrictions and Italy's quota—though we are sorry for the reasons which prompted this legislation—leave us quite indifferent. The Fascist government follows a policy of voluntary restrictions of emigration. Whether the Americans maintain or modify their immigration bill is an affair which concerns them alone.

As for naturalized Americans of Italian origin, they are American citizens and therefore foreigners as far as we are concerned. We limit ourselves to hoping they will continue to be proud of their Italian origin. (Chicago Tribune, June 6, 1928.)

But even if Mussolini's declarations had been of an entirely different nature, no power in the world could retard the assimilation of the Italians in the United States.

As Foerster points out, "Of patriotism as a Frenchman, for example, knows it, a proud devotion to the traditions and ideals of his nation, he (the Italian) has little. *La Terza Italia* is of recent birth. What is magnificent in an earlier age is unknown to the lower classes, remote, or thought of as not representative; or it is simply blended in the much acuter memories of secular, even millenary, alien conquest and oppression. Below Rome especially, there is a history of governments, but not a political history of the people. * * * Abroad the Italian's sentiment of patriotism, such as it is, may be reanimated. Thrown among men of other nationalities, put upon the defensive, the critic may find in himself a pride like that which other men show, and he may regard his own countrymen in a new light." (Loc. cited page 426.)

Especially in the last few years, since the advent to power of Mussolini, the "patriotism" of the Italians has been fanned to an extent probably never reached before. Italians who ten years ago would keep away from colonial activities or celebrations, today are always on hand to show their devotion to Italy—devotion so to say, because in the case of some of the prominent Italians of Chicago personal interests and ambitions more than devotion are the real motive.

The real essence of the admiration of the local Italians for Mussolini, however, is not of a political nature. The Italians of Chicago are not interested in the governmental experiments of Fascismo. They do not care whether Italy has a parliamentary form of government or not. They see in Mussolini only the savior of Italy, and they admire him because of what he has been doing for the good of Italy.

They look at Mussolini just as our business men do. But, possibly, their admiration may be due to the fact that the ever increasing prestige of Italy reflects to some extent on their increasing prestige in this country, and that whereas twenty years ago they had to be almost ashamed to declare their nationality today they can be proud to call themselves Italians.

On the other hand, there is a large number of Italians in the city who admire Mussolini for what he has done for the welfare and prestige of Italy, but who, at the same time, having been imbued with American democratic ideas, cannot reconcile political principles with economic attainments.

But real devotion or allegiance to Mussolini, as some people have stated, is totally absent among the Italians of Chicago. Today the Italian is interested in America. If he goes back to Italy it is only on a brief visit. His home is here. Here are his children, his interests, his future, the future of his children. The ties that exist today between the Italians in Chicago and their mother country are purely sentimental ties. There is no force in the world that can obliterate those sentiments. They exist in the Italians just as they exist among the Germans, the Scandinavians, the Irish and any other immigrant group in the United States.

Naturalization figures prove how rapidly the Italians are taking an active part in the life of the city. The following data were furnished by Mr. Schlotfeldt, Chicago District Director of Naturalization:

Aliens Naturalized	1922	1923	1924	Aliens Naturalized	1922	1923	1924
Russia	1,458	1,350	1,356	Sweden	555	484	407
British	908	917	....	Norway	191	170	159
Italy	1,292	1,235	1,290	Czecho-Slovak	975	1,148	945
Germany	1,621	780	588	Poland	1,657	5,153	3,084
Austria	1,367	363	215	Greece	166	232	458
Hungary	943	341	190				

(1922 and 1923 figures are for Cook County, whereas those for 1924 apply only to Chicago.)

The Italians do not become Americanized because of political or economic opportunism. Just as until not many years ago they were very reluctant to apply for their citizenship papers because they were contemplating a return to Italy and felt that Americanization under those circumstances would have been sheer hypocrisy, so today the Italians are eager to become Americans because they have made up their mind to remain permanently in the United States.

The tremendous decrease in remittances to Italy and the remarkable increase in real estate purchases among the Italians of the city prove that beyond any reasonable doubt.

The loyalty of the Americans of Italian descent is as unwavering as that of the descendants of the Pilgrim Fathers. Their devotion to America cannot be surpassed by any other immigrant group.

Even the editor of the most nationalistic Italian review in the United States has repeatedly stated that naturalized Italians should give to America unflinching loyalty and fidelity. "The naturalized American citizen must consider himself absolutely disassociated from his citizenship of birth and bound, instead, without legal or mental reservations, to the new citizenship. This for the Italian is a *duty* on account of the many problems of political, moral and economic character that are connected with the allegiance sworn to the American Constitution." (Agostino de Biasi, Cittadinanza Italiana e Cittadinanza Americana, Il Carroccio, February, 1928.)

If at times the Italian may seem to be attached more to Italy than to the United States, if to the average American he appears to be unduly clannish, it is because of the attacks of newspapers and writers on the Italian race as a whole. The Italians get together not because they cannot assimilate with the natives but simply because of self-protection. Otherwise they are as much interested in Italy as any educated native American.

The process of Americanization of the Italians can be hastened by the American press more than by any other agency of naturalization. The day that American newspapers will have stopped harping on Italian evils and instead of magnifying them will handle them as it handles the wrong-doings of the natives, then the Italian will forget that he came from across the Atlantic and will take as active an interest in community affairs as the most zealous member of our civic leagues.

CHAPTER XX

INDIGENCE

The fear that immigration increases poverty and pauperism found more general expression seventy years ago than it has at the present time. The declaration that the United States is being used as "the dumping ground for the known criminals and the paupers of Europe" was not only more frequently made from colonial times down to 1882, but the charge had in it more of truth then than since that time.

—GRACE ABBOTT: "The Immigrant and the Community," page 166.

E R. LEWIS in his book "America: Nation or Confusion" (New York, 1928) "cites Dr. Laughlin's testimony[1] before the Congressional Committee in 1922 to the effect that the aliens who were then 14.5 per cent of our population, contributed 31 per cent of our feeble-minded, 29.8 per cent of our morons, 225.76 per cent of their quota of our insane, 193.67 per cent of their quota of our maniacs, 229.12 per cent of their share of our senile psychosis, 138.58 per cent of their share of epileptics, 133.29 per cent of their share of tuberculars, and 137.78 per cent of their share of public dependents."[2]

Let us examine then to what extent the Italians of Chicago contribute to the above infirmities.

According to the latest report (1926) of the Illinois Department of Public Welfare, there were 646 feeble-minded white persons admitted to state institutions for the year ending June 30, 1926. Of these, only 19 were foreign born. Of the native born only 165 were of foreign parentage—275 being of native parentage, 47 of mixed parentage, 100 of parentage unknown, 33 of one parent native and the other unknown, 7 one parent foreign and the other unknown. Statistics by nationality are not given.

According to the same report the first admissions and readmissions to State Hospitals for the Insane, year ending June 30, 1926, were 4,387 and 1,755 respectively. By nationality (table 138) they are Germany 285 (16.08%), Poland 237 (13.37%), Sweden 146 (8.23%), Italy 145 (8.18%), Austria 128 (7.22%), Russia 124 (6.99%).

Here it should be added that out of 6,142 admissions and re-admissions only 1,772 or 28.9% of the total were foreign born. The Italian percentage of the total, therefore, was only 2.19%.

When we consider, however, the nationality of the parents of the patients we find the following figures: Germany 545, Poland 259, Sweden 185, Ireland 246, Italy 153 and Austria 141.

Over a five-year period (1922-1926) the Germans contributed 1,057, the Poles 919, the Swedes 555, the Irish 537, the Italians 513 and the Austrians 507.[3]

Over the same period, by race, out of 22,661 admissions the following quotas apply: Germany 2,665, Slavonic 2,291, African 1,631, Irish 1,614, English 1,431, Scandinavian 1,141, Italian 621. Still 5,252 cases were reported as mixed, and 4,129 unascertained. The same observation applies here that we made in regard to the nationality of criminals, namely that very seldom the nationality of an Italian is not ascertained and therefore if the mixed and unascertained cases were properly allotted among the different races, the Italian proportion to other races would be still lower than what it appears to be.

For senile psychosis the following statistics are reported in table 43 of the Illinois Department of Public Welfare, 1926 (page 322):

Race	Total	Senile	Race	Total	Senile
Mixed	32.3	36.5	Slavonic	10.4	4.2
German	12.1	18.3	Scandinavian	4.8	3.5
Unascertained	12.9	10.9	All others	3.7	2.9
Irish	5.7	10.6	Hebrew	2.2	1.0
African	7.8	5.4	Scotch	0.7	0.7
English	2.9	5.4	Italian	3.1	0.6

The above percentages are based over the five-year period 1922-1926.

In Cerebral Arteriosclerosis the Italian percentage is 2.2 against 17.7 for the Germans, 6.8 for the Irish, 5.2 for the Scandinavians, 5.0 for the English, etc.

In general paralysis the Italian percentage is 3.0 against 10.2 for the Germans, 7.7 for the Slavs, 4.6 for the Scandinavians, 3.9 for the Irish.

In alcoholism the Italians, excluding the mixed and unascertained, are the seventh with 2.7% against 22.1 for the Slavonic, 11.1 for the Irish, 8.0 for the Scandinavians, 6.7 for the Germans.

In Maniac Depression the Italian percentage is 6.1, against 15.7 for the Germans, 40.0 for the mixed and 11.7 for unascertained.

In Dementia Praecox the Italians occupy the eighth place (the tenth if mixed and unascertained are included) with the Germans on top (10.2) followed by the Africans (8.8), the Scandinavians (6.8), the Irish (5.2), the Hebrew (4.8).

If we consider on the other hand the nationality of people admitted to the Psychopatic Hospitals the following figures are found for the year Dec. 1, 1925, to Dec. 1, 1926. (Charity Service Reports, Cook County, 1926, page 41.)

Total 5,175. Negroes 442, Poles 400, Germans 266, Irish 188, Russians 179, Italians 173, Swedes 132.

By psychosis the Italians have 16 for senility, 4 for epileptic, 11 for mental deficiency (against 403 for Americans), 28 for alcoholism (Americans 469, Scandinavians 31, Irish 59), Mania depressive 3, general paresis 17, Dementia praecox 74 (Americans 979, Germans 73, Polish 134, Swedish 41, etc.).

Out of 40,592 patients admitted to the Cook County Hospital (1925-1926) (Charity Service Reports, page 87) only 496 were Italians, 34,028 were Americans, 608 Germans, 601 Poles, 524 Irish, 415 Austrians, 305 Czechs, 578 Russians, 356 English, etc.

At the Oak Forest Institutions (loc. cit. page 246) out of 4,254 patients only 86 were Italians. Germany had 308, Ireland 248, Poland 289, Sweden 154, Czechoslovakia 111, Austria 117, Russia 172.

It cannot be denied, however, that the Italians have over ten per cent of the persons who received parents pension fund for the year 1925-1926. (161 Italians out of 1,538; of the Italians 137 were widows.)

A little lower proportion maintains for the department of poor relief, 938 Italians out of a total of 9,571, over 50% (5,165) being Americans. The same proportion applies in the proportion of nationalities granted pensions during

New Columbus Hospital

Mother Cabrini Hospital

Both institutions are owned and administered by the "Missionaries of the Sacred Heart," an Italian organization which maintains several hospitals, schools, and asylums throughout the world.

(See notes to Chapter X.)

fiscal year Dec. 1, 1925, to and including Nov. 30, 1926. (Charity Service Reports, page 425.) Italians 35; total 363.

On the other hand when we consider the nationality of people who have stayed at the Chicago Lodging House we find the following statistics:

Sweden	794	Austria	237
Ireland	744	Canada	208
Poland	470	Lithuania	202
Germany	434	Scotland	186
Mexico	366	Russia	180
Norway	273	Italy	170

The above figures are reported in the Annual Report of the Department of Public Welfare, City of Chicago, 1925, and are for the year 1924. The unit in the statistical count is a night's lodging. The complete figures are: Total foreign born 5,008, native born 12,617.

NOTES ON CHAPTER 19

(1) The Laughlin report, or "Expert Analysis of the Metal and Dross in America's Melting Pot" as it was named by the Chairman of the Committee, Albert Johnson of Washington, was found shot through with grossest fallacies. A number of authorities made and published careful studies of it, notably Professor H. S. Jennings, noted naturalist of Johns Hopkins University, in "The American Journal of Sociology" of August, 1924, and the booklet "Social inadequacy of Foreign Nationals in the United States" published as special report 28 of the National Industrial "The Survey" of Dec. 15, 1923; Prof. Joseph M. Gillman, of the University of Pittsburgh, in Conference Board. These studies showed that the Laughlin investigation had failed to make a representative territorial selection of data, that the data had been misrepresented by means of an arbitrarily determined "quota". They showed also that Dr. Laughlin's own conclusions were at great variance with his findings, that he had not made the corrections necessary as to age and sex distributions, that he had assumed what is far from proven (the inheritability of certain defects or states) and that he had failed to take into consideration other well established facts having a direct bearing upon the investigation." C. Panunzio, Ph. D., Professor of Social Economics, Whittier College, in Immigration Crossroads, New York, The MacMillan Co., 1927, page 115-116.

Southernland (Criminology, page 99) says of this study that it is quite misleading in its conclusions.

(2) Quoted by John Carter, in "Looking into the Melting Pot," New York Times Book Review, April 15, 1928.

(3) Foreign population in Illinois in 1920 (U. S. Census): Germans 205,491, Poles 162,405, Italians 94,407, Swedes 105,577, Austrians 46,457, Irish 74,274.

CHAPTER XXI

SOME OBSERVATIONS ON CRIME IN CHICAGO
In Relation to the Local Italian Community

(Statements made in this chapter are corroborated in the following)

EXAMINATION of crime statistics for the city of Chicago, a study of the local crime situation, and a comparison between the number and types of crimes committed by Italians in Chicago and Italians in other cities of the country lead to the following conclusions:

1. That the Italians commit more crimes than any other racial group in the city is a myth which cannot be substantiated by facts.

2. The crimes committed by the Italians in Chicago in the last few years have few of the Italian characteristics. With due exceptions they are the product of environment rather than nationality. In hundreds of other cities the Italians are almost totally absent in all types of crimes.

3. In crimes of violence, such as murders and bombings, the Italian percentage is only a very small fraction of the total.[1] (See statistics at the end of the volume and notes in the following chapter.) The Italians, compared to other nationalities, have been pikers at the game.

4. The major portion of crimes of violence among the Italians would not take place were it not for the relative immunity guaranteed by lax local conditions and by the evident collusion between politicians and criminals.

5. The major portion of the crimes of violence among the Italians apparently is perpetrated by a small organized gang. To blame the whole Italian community, therefore, or only the Sicilians of Chicago, is unjust and idiotic.

6. Minor crimes among the Italians are due to little acquaintance with our customs and laws. The longer they stay in the country the fewer crimes they commit.

7. The so-called Black-Hand exists in the imagination of reporters in search of sensationalism and of police officials incapable or unwilling to solve a crime. As a matter of fact, it is much easier to charge a crime to the Black-Hand and forget about it than to go through the trouble of solving a murder. The term "Black-Hand", according to Chev. Mastrovalerio, was coined by Carlo Barsotti, editor of "Il Progresso Italo-Americano" of New York, in order to avoid using the word "Mafia". (See note 7 in following chapter.)

8. The "Mafia" as it is understood today in the United States is also a product of the imagination. Of course, Italian criminals of Chicago are acquainted and maintain contact with criminals in other cities in the country and even in Italy, but they are not, in any way, shape or form, organized or affiliated to each other. All criminal groups in the United States maintain contact with criminal groups in other cities. (See note 8 in following chapter.)

9. The charge that the Italians refuse to testify for the state in murder cases, however true to a large extent, applies just as well to any other nationality, even the native American. Irrespectively of nationality, a man will talk provided his life is not in danger, and provided his person and property are efficiently protected by the law. Of the total number of persons arrested in 1926, 19,410 had criminal records and 2,626 had major criminal records, but only 164 went to the penitentiary. (Editorial in the Chicago Tribune, Nov. 1, 1927, based on report of H. G. Clabaugh, chairman of the parole and pardon board, quoted by U. S. District Attorney George E. Q. Johnson before the Chicago Association of Credit Men.) Out of 704 murders for 1923-1926 only 14 were sentenced to hang and only 95 were sent to the penitentiary. (Reports of the Police Department for the City of Chicago.)

10. The Italian people abhor crime just as much as any nationality in the world. Mussolini started his campaign against the Mafia in Sicily because he knew that the Sicilian people would have helped him in his task. Without the help of the Sicilian people Mussolini (or rather Prefect Mori, for that matter) would have not gone very far. But the Italian people in Chicago are intelligent enough not to be made the scapegoat of corrupt politicians.

11. A notable change is taking place in the nature of the Italians. With the improvement of their economic conditions they are fast moving out of their old residences and moving in American neighborhoods where they are taking up American customs and manners. The spirit of vendetta is fast disappearing among the old immigrants and has totally disappeared among their children. Knives are out of fashion. Personal divergencies will be settled by fist fights. But sawed-off shotguns and machine guns will continue to be produced as long as immunity from punishment is within the range of probability and as long as these remain the prevailing weapons of violence among all national groups.

SEPARATE THESE SIAMESE TWINS

"Courtesy of Chicago Daily News. Cartoon by Shoemaker"

CHAPTER XXII

NOTES ON THE PRECEDING CHAPTER

The problem of citizenship is not a problem created by the immigrant and his presence makes it more difficult of solution only because we have not provided him with safe leaders and have not ourselves been very good examples. Indeed the primary corrupting influence in every city in which I am acquainted is either of native stock or belongs to the first or second generation of those immigrants whose coming does not disturb us and whose presence we regard as blessing. These are either German or Irish, and largely of the latter nationality.

—E. A. STEINER: "The Immigrant Tide," page 201.

(1) Detailed statistics are found in the following chapter.

(2) Before the Italians came to Chicago, the city was well known for its Paddy the Bear Ryan, Walter Stephens, Con Shea and some of the worst criminal types in the world. (See Chicago Commission on Race Relation.)

Judge Marcus Kavanagh of the Superior Court of Cook County, in a review of a book on "The Gangs of New York" by Herbert Asbury, appearing in the Chicago Tribune for April 14, 1928, informs us that before 1880, when the population of New York was made up of Anglo-Saxons and Scandinavians and Germans and Irish, "the conditions which existed" then "would not now be tolerated in any city of the civilized world." He quotes Asbury:

Conditions such as these soon prevailed throughout the Fourth Ward, and by 1845 the whole area had become a hotbed of crime; streets over whose cobblestones had rolled the carriages of the aristocrats were filled with dives which sheltered the members of celebrated river gangs. No human life was safe, and a well dressed man venturing into the district was commonly set upon and murdered or robbed, or both, before he had gone a block. If the gangsters could not lure a prospective victim into a dive, they followed him until he passed beneath an appointed window, from which a woman dumped a bucket of ashes upon his head. As he gasped and choked, the thugs rushed him into a cellar, where they killed him and stripped the clothing from his back, afterward casting his naked body upon the sidewalk. The police would not march against the denizens of the Fourth Ward except in parties of half a dozen or more, and when their quarry sought refuge in a dive they frequently besieged the place for a week or longer until the thug was driven forth by restlessness or hunger. The principal resorts were always well garrisoned and fully supplied with muskets, knives and pistols.

There existed many boarding houses where sailors were robbed and murdered and from which they were shanghaied. During the late sixties an investigating committee estimated that 15,000 sailors were annually robbed of more than $2,000,000 in these places.

According to Grace Abbott (The Immigrant and the Community), the nationality of those debarred and deported as criminals for the year ending June 30, 1914, shows "that so far as the records of the immigration service are concerned a larger per cent of criminals are found among the immigrants from Western Europe than among those from Southern and Eastern Europe, but that the numbers excluded are relatively very small for all nationalities." (Page 108.)

I do not need to recall the type of people who went after gold in California. "Feverish, boisterous, half-savage population," Hough describes them. In those days "western steamers reeked with gambling, swindling, duelling, and every variety of vice. Public law was almost suspended in some regions, and organized associations of counterfeiters and horse thieves terrorized whole sections of the country." E. Hough, "The Passing of the Frontier."

Comparisons are odious, still they are necessary for some people who think that their race has never been associated with the worst types of outlawry.

When the Italians first came to Chicago, they also committed their share of crimes, at times dastardly ones. But all races, no matter whether Nordic or Alpine or Mediterranean or what not, have lived in an illegal state of conditions until they acclimated. Probably even the Mennonites in Paraguay will have a higher percentage of crimes in the next few years than they will in the next few decades. And the Mennonites are the most peaceable people on earth.

Ignorance of the law at first was the cause of many crimes among the Italians (see note 6). Some of the murders were committed because many Italians tired of being called "Dago" and "Wop" and "Guinea" found that they could get some justice only through the use of a knife.

Other murders were committed because some people having been blackmailed found it easier to answer with bullets than with gold. Today there are very few blackmailing cases among the Italians and invariably they are reported to the police, as demonstrated by the reports of the police department. Still other crimes were the product of temperament, jealousy, a wrong conception of honor, animosities which could easily be avoided, and quite a few old feuds which had originated in Italy. Today very few crimes of that type take place among the Italians. Today in nine cases out of ten an Italian kills because of double-crossing in "booze" or "politics".

That such are the causes is easily verified by the total lack of murders in hundreds of Italian communities in small American cities. Unfortunately the same situation of Chicago is true of other large cities, such as St. Louis, Detroit, Cleveland, Buffalo and many others. The motives are the same: big profits and protection.

(3) Detailed statistics for murders, by nationality, are found in the following chapter. There are no statistics for bombings. However, in the list that the Chicago Tribune published on March 28, 1928, out of 68 bombings from October 11, 1927, to March 26, 1928, only 8 Italian names appear, including that of Judge Sbarbaro and of Lawrence Cuneo, brother-in-law and secretary to State's Attorney Crowe. Bombings in Chicago started with the gamblers' wars of 1907. No Italian was involved. (See "Organized Crime," Chapter III, a survey prepared for the Illinois Association of Criminal Justice by Prof. John Landesco of the American Institute of Criminal Law and Criminology.

(4) Lax conditions in Chicago and collusion between politicians and criminals are known throughout the world. As Judge Kavanagh states in his review of the Asbury book cited above, "Today the organized gang is in partnership with politics, and thus makes bold and great offense not only possible but safe. There has not been a city administration in Chicago during forty years when, to some extent, gambling and often other vice privileges were not extended in exchange for political favors—if not by the mayor himself, then by some one in power under him. There has not been a mayor in Chicago who by calling in his chief of police and saying to him, 'Clean up this town within thirty days or hand me your resignation,' could not have to a large extent cleaned up the town of vice and crime."

Present conditions, however, are not of recent date. Investigations have been made, causes of crime have been determined, but little improvement has taken place. In 1912 the Civil Service Commission of the City of Chicago conducted a police investigation. It arrived at the following conclusions:

That there is and for years has been a connection between the Police Department and the various criminal classes in the City of Chicago.

That a bi-partisan political combination or ring exists, by and through which the connection between the Police Department and the criminal classes above referred to is fostered and maintained.

Similar conclusions were arrived at in the Report of the City Council Committee on Crime, 1915, page 184 and 189:

There can be no doubt that one of the chief causes of crime in Chicago is that members of the police force, and particularly of the plain clothes staff, are hand in gloves with criminals. Instead of punishing the criminal they protect him. Instead of using the power of the law for the protection of society, they use it for their own personal profit. They form a working agreement with pickpockets, prowlers, confidence men, gamblers and other classes of offenders. The basis of this agreement is a division of the profits between the law-breaker and the public official. The exact extent of this system it is impossible to determine, but there is no doubt that its ramifications are so wide as to cripple the machinery for the enforcement of the law. * * *

That such collusion between police officials and criminals is a widespread practice there can be no doubt. The testimony of all the investigators converges upon this central point and coming from so wide a variety or sources, confirmed by the Civil Service Commission and the state's attorney in so many specific instances, leaves the way open to no other conclusion than the existence of an appalling system of partnership in crime between public officials on the one hand and habitual criminals on the other.

An idea of the crime situation existing in Chicago today may be had from the following charges hurled against the Thompson-Crowe regime in editorials and speeches just before and after the primaries of April 10, 1928.

Crowe should be defeated "because under his administration of the office of state's attorney of Cook County crimes of violence, particularly murders by gunmen and bombings by blackmailing gangs, have become unprecedently common. In a vast majority of cases the guilty have escaped punishment, so that fear of punishment is reduced to a minimum among the city's organized criminals, many of whom are affiliated politically and otherwise with men who sit in Crowe's political counsels." (Editorial, Chicago Daily News, April 9, 1928.)

"That there are hundreds of gambling resorts in Chicago, most of them well known to the police and the state's attorney's office is a matter of common knowledge. Ordinarily they are open and free to do an intensive business because they are protected by politicians and city officials. It is notorious that these resorts breed crime, particularly crimes of violence. * * * Chicago is wide open to protected gambling, beer running and other profitable forms of law-breaking because the city administration tolerates them, if it does not actually protect them." (Editorial, Chicago Daily News, March 26, 1928.)

"One savage murder * * * together with kidnapings, beatings and threatenings accompanied by displays of pistols, sufficiently prove that terrorism was an important factor in obtaining votes for candidates approved by the crime syndicate. Police protection for some reasons was ineffective where it was most needed. * * * Gunmen at the polls, assassins charging through the streets firing at and killing a fleeing candidate while their death car displayed the campaign banner of a high public official, kidnaped election workers herded in hidden places by armed hoodlums, repeaters openly voted in gangs while watchers' protests were stilled by the menacing muzzles of pistols, ballots forcibly removed by robbers from polling places, election officials wearing out erasers by changing the marks on ballots to suit their wishes—these are some of the incidents of the day which go to show how little the agents of the crime syndicate fear the police when those agents are working for the crime syndicate's political allies." (Editorial, Chicago Daily News, April 17, 1928.)

Headline, first page, Chicago Daily News, March 26, 1928:
POLICE STATION'S BOOZE STORE RAIDED.—Storeroom is discovered next door to Shakespeare Station. The alcohol salesman "has been meeting all alcohol customers at the Shakespeare Avenue Station and filling their alcohol wants as they loitered about."

"I told my audience that Robert E. Crowe, the state's attorney, is and has been all along the key to the whole crime situation in Chicago, including the bombings. I told them that if Crowe really wanted to clean these things he could without a question do it and that he is the man responsible." (Judge Daniel P. Trude, Chicago Tribune, March 27, 1928.)

"Investigators for the Tribune found and listed more than 200 gambling places last week. * * * Vice and politics have a ready affinity. One produces profits. The other furnishes protection. No city can have open vice without political protection. If the police cannot find and suppress what the normal citizen will find without difficulty it is because the police either have been pulled off the job by the political control or because they have declared themselves in on the game. The latter is the less likely because when the big profits are to be taken the politicians do not permit the police to get much of the take. Whenever Chicago or any other city becomes a wide open town it is because political management is taking a percentage from the operation of vice. * * * Politics never is in doubt as to conditions in any given area. Its success depends on precise knowledge and it has just that. Chicago politics has a sort of frontier crudeness in its taking of profits." (Editorial, Chicago Tribune, March 27, 1928.)

During the elections of April 10, in one precinct "Johnny put a revolver against Mason's head, but a policeman pushed away the gun just as Johnny fired. But the cop didn't arrest him." (Testimony before coroner's jury, Chicago Daily News, April 16, 1928.)

"I saw Granady's car (Granady was a colored lawyer running for committeeman. He was killed on primary day.) with a Swanson banner on the rear, and a man in a brown suit who was standing in the middle of the street pulled a gun and shot at the car. I rushed up to the sergeant and said, 'Arrest that guy before he kills some one.' The sergeant didn't do anything." (Testimony before coroner's jury, Chicago Tribune, April 18, 1928.)

"Bad government Chicago has known in the past, as has almost every large city. Graft there has been, protected vice there has been; unholy alliances between government and sinister business interests there have been. But never before has the control of the city been held by a gang that did not hesitate to bomb and kill those with the temerity to oppose them. * * * the office of the state's attorney of Cook County * * * has become in the hands of the present occupant * * * the key position in the operations of the most sordid, most rapacious political gang in the history of the state. Chicago is cursed with gang politics, protected vice, illegal voting and a general debauchery in its public life because of the power that has been concentrated in the office of state's attorney and of the way in which that power has been used and abused." (Editorial in "Christian Century" quoted by Chicago Daily News, March 30, 1928.)

(5) An idea of the protection and immunity that gangsters enjoy, as well as of lax conditions existing in Chicago, may be had from the fact that out of 20,186 arrests for felonies only 647 went to the penitentiary or reformatory. (Clabaugh statistics cited before.) For detailed statistics on convictions for major crimes see Appendix. The Employers' Association of Chicago, just before the primaries of April 10, 1928, stated that there were in the city forty-six different rackets still active when the statement was made, although twenty-nine racketering organizations had been destroyed. According to the "Chicago Tribune" for April 28, 1928, figures released for publication by the Illinois Association for Criminal Justice show that only 3.13 per cent of all persons charged with felonies during 1923 were punished for the crimes they were charged with committing.

(6) The kind and number of crimes committed by any members of any social group are largely determined by their economic status and the degree to which they are adjusted to their surroundings. The recent immigrant, as a rule, lives under less favorable economic and social conditions than the foreign born of longer residence, who have, for the most part, been able to win for themselves larger incomes and have become better adjusted to the laws, customs, and institutions of the country than when they first arrived. Accordingly, a relatively high percentage of crime might be expected from the newly arrived immigrant; and criminality in so far as it results from poverty and social maladjustment is likely to be less in proportion as the time in the United States is longer. Furthermore, the recent immigrant who commits a crime, owing to the handicap of poverty and ignorance of our laws and customs, is more likely than the offender of longer residence to be detected and sentenced. (Crime Conditions in the United States: Prisoners 1923, page 101.)

Also "care must be taken to consider the greater proportion of adults among the foreign born. Even then the amount of criminality may be due to the strange environment in which these foreigners find themselves, rather than to any influence of nationality." Prof. Mayo-Smith of Columbia University, in Statistics and Sociology, page 273, quoted by Edith Abbott in "Report of the City

Council Committee on Crime." 1915.

(7) There is the same scandalous situation with regard to the so-called "Black-Hand" outrages. One of the Chicago papers reported forty-five murders in seven months which the police charged to the "Black-Hand". The police method of preventing crime of this sort is as unintelligent as it is unjust. On one occasion following several "outrages" the police arrested quite at random fifty Italians in one neighborhood. The men were all fined one dollar and costs for disorderly conduct, and the inspector thought that this would frighten the colony into behavior. Instead, the arrest and conviction of men known to be innocent was teaching disregard rather than respect for law.

Prominent Italians and the leading Italian newspapers have tried to interest themselves in this situation. Most of these believe that, although there is probably a "Black-Hand" organization, very little of the murder, bomb-throwing, blackmailing and kidnaping charged to such a society are really committed by its members; and hold to the theory that a band of criminals are operating under police protection and that the police are covering up their failure to arrest the offenders to the satisfaction of the American public by attributing them to Italian "Black-Hand" organizations. These Italians refuse to believe that the police cannot discover the Italian perpetrators of the small per cent of these crimes which they hold the "Black-Hand" really commits. This seems a reasonable theory, because such a woeful police incompetence as the situation would otherwise argue seems impossible.

The Italian Consulate employed a man for a time to investigate every "Black-Hand" case reported in the newspapers. Out of the first thirty investigated, there was only one that could not be explained on some theory other than that it was committed by the "Black-Hand". The result of all this is that the Italian suffers at every turn. He is not protected against the criminal inside or outside of his own ranks; and the general public grows increasingly indignant, not at the police but at all the Italians. (Grace Abbott, The Immigrant and the Community, page 118-119.)

If we examine the police reports for 1923-1926 we find that out of 89 murders ascribed to the "Black-Hand" two were pending and 87 were marked "no arrest". I have mentioned already that out of 704 murders for the same period only 109 were convicted.

The "Black-Hand" is simply a sign that cowards and idiots use to scare people. Just as Hickman out in California signed his blackmailing notes "The Fox", so other criminals have signed theirs "Black-Hand". But no such thing really exists. In May 1928 a man by name Acci was found dead in a remote section of a Chicago suburb. His body was full of buckshots. The police found in his pockets six "Black-Hand" letters, the writing of which matched with that of twenty-six more letters that had been brought over to the attention of the police.

CHAPTER XXIII

CRIMINAL STATISTICS AND THEIR INTERPRETATION

INTERPRETATION

E. H. SUTHERLAND in his book on "Criminology" tells us that the statistics of crime are known as the most unreliable and the most difficult of all statistics. Still, one may arrive at a more or less correct conclusion by properly weighing the following factors:

1. "Some English-speaking immigrants, whose foreign birth was not easily indicated by their speech would probably be called 'American'; but on the other hand, quite as many American-born citizens who had loyally kept their foreign names or spoke with a foreign accent would undoubtedly be called Italian, Polish or Russian." (Edith Abbott: "Report of the City Council Committee on Crime," page 51.)

2. In accepting the statistics of the Illinois Department of Public Welfare care should be taken to properly compare the total number of crimes for each race in relation to environment. According to the U. S. Census for 1920 there were in the City of Chicago and in the State of Illinois the following number of foreign-born:

	Illinois	Chicago		Illinois	Chicago
England	54,247	26,420	Austria	46,457	30,491
Ireland	74,274	56,786	Russia	117,899	102,095
Norway	27,785	20,481	Italy	94,407	59,215
Sweden	105,577	58,563	Germany	205,491	112,288
Czecho-Slavia	66,709	50,392	Poland	162,405	137,611

In 1920 (U. S. Census) the proportion of urban to rural population for Illinois was of 67.9 against 32.1.

The ratio of commitments was from 67.95 in 1922 to 76.76 in 1926 for urban against 32.05 in 1922 to 23.24 in 1926 for rural.

In 1926 the Italian commitments were distributed as follows: Joliet 32, women's prisons 1, Menard 4, Pontiac 17, State Farm 9, boys 34, girls none; total 97 (96 men and one woman).

Still the environment of commitments, by institution, was as follows:

	Urban	Rural		Urban	Rural
Joliet Institution	671	31	Illinois State Farm	269	425
Women's prisons	23	13	St. Chas. School for Boys	447	60
Menard	489	93	State School for Girls	202	43
Pontiac	462	111			

In other words, over 85 per cent of Italian commitments were in institutions in which over 95%, 75% and 87% of the commitments, respectively, were of urban origin.

3. The proportion of the adult population among the foreign-born to their total population and to that of the whole state also should be considered. It is a well established fact that the number of adults among the Italians is higher than among many other nationalities, having the same length of residence in the United States.

131

4. Arrest statistics are not an index of crime.

> That is, an increase in arrests may be due to increased efficiency or, at any rate, to increased activity on the part of the police and not to an increase in crime; and a decrease in arrests may be due to an increased laxity or diminished activity due to the fact that the police are suspending the excessive use of the "drag-net" system and are no longer making wholesale arrests without adequate evidence of guilt. (Edith Abbott in Survey of Cook County Jail, 1922.)

5. Statistics of charges are not an index of crime either. Usually when a murder takes place in "Little Italy" the drag-net system is used and consequently many Italians not only are charged with crimes they never committed, but even charged with more than one offense. In 1926, for example, 211,317 persons were arrested. For the same year the total number of charges was of 243,600, or 32,283 more charges than arrests.

6. Statistics of the board of health, regarding deaths by homicide, are not an index to the nationality of the perpetrator—moreover, in order to arrive at a fair conclusion, the nationality of the mother of the deceased should be taken into account.

7. Hold-ups are potential murders. Unfortunately no statistics by nationality are kept. Statistics on burglary and robbery, however, clearly show what race commits most of these crimes. The Italian is almost absent.

8. In figuring the per cent of murders committed by each nationality, in relation to its total population in the state, the basis followed by the Illinois Department of Public Welfare is misleading. In the first place, the total number of murderers is too small to be allotted to each nationality on the percentage basis. On the other hand, if the total number of mixed or unascertained nationalities would be taken in consideration, the per cent for the older immigrant groups would be considerably higher than it appears. Urban and rural population for each nationality should also be taken into account. There are very few Italians in urban centers in Illinois. There are very few Italians of mixed parentage or whose nationality is not very easily ascertained.

9. The statistics for murder and manslaughter given by the Police Department conflict with those of the Department of Health, even on the basis of the nationality of the victims. For example, for 1923 to 1925 the Department of Health reports 419, 509, and 563 cases of homicide, respectively, against 233, 307, and 321 for murder and manslaughter by the Police Department. The nationality of the victims does not correspond either. For 1924, according to the reports of the Police Department, the victims of murders and manslaughter were: Total 307, Polish 12, Italian 36, German 5, Irish 2, American white 99, Austrian 1. For the same year the Department of Health gives the following figures for homicide victims (by nationality of mother of deceased): Irish 29, German 41, Austrian 11, Polish 30. No nationality for Italian victim's mother is given, but the total number of Italian victims of homicide does not differ much from that of the Police Department (38 according to the Department of Health and 36 according to the police).

STATISTICS ON CRIME

1. (Table 5) In 1926 the prisoners in State Institutions in Illinois were 93.0 native born and 6.5 per cent foreign born. The fathers of the prisoners were 2,310 native born (68.5%) and 785 (23.3%) foreign born.

2. (Table 6) By race of commitments the Italians occupy the fourth place, coming after the Irish, the Slavonic and the Germans. But out of a total of 12,849 commitments for 1922-1926, 6,145 or about 48 per cent were of mixed or unascertained nationality (see note 8 in this chapter).

3. (Table 7) Figures speak for themselves. The same consideration to be made as in preceding chapter.

4. (Table 8) Id.

5. (Table 9) Whenever there is a murder in Chicago, almost invariably the police makes heroic raids in the Italian wards. They arrest at random just to discharge the prisoners as soon as they arrive at police headquarters. In many cases they book them on hypothetical charges. By so doing, the police believe to justify themselves before the public. The number of crimes unsolved, however, proves how efficient is the Chicago Police Department. Still, the Italian per cent of arrests is of less than 2.5% against an Italian population of about 3% of the total. (Also see notes 1 and 4 in this chapter.)

6. (Table 10) The percentage of crimes committed by Italians is only a drop in the bucket. Figures do not need comment.

7. (Table 11) Italian women are almost absent from crimes.

8. (Table 12) See note 5 in this chapter.

9. (Table 13) See following note.

10. (Table 14) The Italians have, by charges, about 10 per cent of the total murders, 5 per cent of total manslaughter, and 5 per cent of total rape. It is well known in Chicago that when a murder takes place in the city, the Italians are the first to be booked on a murder charge, to be released soon after, and for each murder that takes place in "Little Italy" at times over ten Italians are booked on murder charges. Convictions, however, tell quite a different story.

11. (Table 15) In convictions for felonies the Italian per cent is of only 2.50, and in misdemeanors of 2.15.

12. (Table 16) The Italians are almost absent from crimes of arson, bigamy, burglary, confidence game, embezzlement, forgery, robbery, bastardy, extorsion by threats, being inmate of gaming houses, or keeping gambling houses and houses of ill fame, in vagrancy, etc.

13. (Table 17) Italian women are almost totally absent in prostitution.

14. (Table 18) Out of a total of 704 murders for the four-year period, 1923-1926, 332 murders, or 47% of the total were reported as not solved. Of those supposed to have been solved, 85 were pending, 29 were stricken off, 81 were killed, 68 were acquitted and only 107 (15% of the total) were sentenced. Figures for murder and manslaughter as reported by the Police Department are only a fraction of the deaths that the Department of Health reports as caused by homicide, even excluding those killed by automobiles or other accidents.

15. (Table 19) The per cent of the Italians admitted to probation during the three-year period 1921-1924 is of only 2.11 of the total.

16. (Table 20) The Italians who were prisoners at the Cook County Jail from Dec. 1922 to Nov. 1923 were 219 out of 10,400, or about 2% of the total. Almost the same proportion applies for the inmates of the House of Correction.

One hundred leading firms in the city owned or controlled by Americans
of Italian descent

1. Cuneo Press, reputed the largest printing establishment in the world. Printers of some of the leading magazines in America, at one time of the Chicago edition of the Saturday Evening Post. They are well known as some of the finest book printers in the country. The Harvard Classics, the annuals of the Encyclopædia Americana have been printed by them. Mr. John F. Cuneo, its founder and president, is the grandson of an Italian immigrant.

2. The Chicago Macaroni Company, one of the largest manufacturing establishments in the world. Established years ago by a group of Sicilian immigrants, it has today a daily capacity of 125,000 pounds a day, with sales of over two million dollars a year. Connected with it are the former firms of Morici and Matalone, importers and wholesale grocers, who do an annual business running into the millions.

3. The Da Prato Statuary Company, the largest of the kind in America. Established in Chicago in 1860 on an humble scale, it employs today from between two hundred fifty and three hundred men, of whom ninety-five per cent are Italian. It maintains offices in New York, Montreal, Canada and Pietrasanta, Italy. It specializes in ecclesiastical furnishings made in marble, bronze, mosaic and composition. Many cathedrals in the country, such as Denver's, Nashville's, Indianapolis's, and others, have been furnished entirely by the Da Prato Company. Years ago it was appointed by the Pope as purveyors to the Holy See. Mr. John Rigali has been its president since the incorporation of the company in 1893. A very interesting feature of the Da Prato Company is the Americanization class that it conducts at its own expense once a week and to which workingmen in the plant take part. It also maintains a good sized reference library specializing in religious art.

4. The United Fig and Date Company, importers of all kinds of nuts from all parts of the world. Also manufacturers of food products. The business of the firm, including the production of a New York branch, runs into several millions of dollars a year. Its president, and one of the two original founders is Mr. Pietro Costa. The company occupies one of the most valuable corners in Chicago, namely the northwest corner of La Salle and the Chicago River. Mr. Costa is also the founder of the West Indies Fruit Importing Company, which has a practical monopoly on the pineapple production of the Island of Cuba. It imports on the average from 850,000 to 1,000,000 cases a year of pineapples, and does a business of between three and four million dollars a year.

5. Peanut Specialty Company, the second largest firm in the United States dealing in peanuts. (The largest—Planters—is also Italian.) The Chicago firm does an annual business of over five million dollars a year. Mr. Joseph Galli is president and Mr. John F. Lavezzorio is secretary of the corporation.

6. The Chicago branch of the Grasselli Chemical Company, one of the largest in the world.

7. The Chicago branch of F. A. D. A. (F. A. D'Andrea), well known to radio fans.

8. The Isotta Motors of Illinois, affiliated with the Isotta Motors, Inc., of New York, and the Isotta Fraschini Corporation of Italy. The "Isotta" is the second largest automobile factory of Italy and specializes in marine and airplane motors. The "Santa Maria", De Pinedo's famous seaplane in which he made his *Four Continent* flight, was equipped with "ace" type of Isotta Motors. The Isotta is the originator of the four wheel brakes (1910) and the straight eight motors (1916). Mr. Ugo D'Annunzio, the son of the famous poet, is the president of both the Illinois and New York corporations. Mr. Mario De Tullio and Mr. P. F. Bronckhurst are, respectively, treasurer and secretary of the local concern.

9. The Chicago branch of the Di Giorgio Fruit Corporation, one of the leading in the United States.

10. Antonio Lombardo & Company, importers and wholesalers of Italian products. Although the firm is very young, it has had a very remarkable development. Today it does a business of about one hundred fifty thousand dollars a month and enjoys one of the most liberal credits in the city.

11. J. B. Canepa & Company, macaroni manufacturers ever since 1860. Well known throughout the city for their Red Cross brand, advertised all over.

12. Andrea Russo & Company, importers and wholesalers of Italian products. Established in Chicago in 1883. Its annual business averages about three million dollars.

13. Garibaldi & Cuneo, leading fruit merchants.

14. Cuneo Brothers, leading fruit merchants.

15. Ginocchio & Costa, leading fruit merchants.

16. Gazzolo Drug & Chemical Company, one of the largest jobbers and wholesalers of chemical products in the city.

17. The Munago Company, one of the largest furniture manufacturers in the city.

18. Sibilano Furniture Company, manufacturers and dealers. The Sibilano Company is considered one of the finest producers of upholstered furniture, especially of the antique type.

19. The Kedzie Theatre, *the home of the spoken drama,* the first theatre in the city to offer well known plays at motion picture prices. Mr. Frank Gazzolo is the originator. Mr. Gazzolo formerly was manager of the Studebaker Theatre and other well known playhouses in the city.

20. The Triangle Restaurants, one of which is considered to be the largest in the world. Mr. Dario Toffenetti is the proprietor.

21. Ralph L. Moni & Co., one of the leading dressmakers in the country. Patronized especially by artists.

22. Bayardi Brothers, large manufacturers of jewelry.

23. Lawrence P. Romano & Co., owners and developers of Marquette Road Terrace, *"the largest real estate development in Chicago"* (as stated in the firm's advertisements).

24. Lake Towns Improvement Company, subdividers; M. F. Schiavone, president.
25. Guarno Real Estate Improvement Corporation (capital and surplus over two hundred fifty thousand dollars).
26. D. Calamari & Company, one of the largest dealers in shelled nuts in the city.
27. North Shore Petroleum Corporation; A. Nannini, president.
28. Modern Wire Company; Guy D'Incognito, president.
29. Ricci & Company, dealers in edible nuts.
30. J. Barsotti & Company, dealers in shelled nuts.
31. John B. Chiappe Co., cigar manufacturers. Established in 1873, it being the eleventh in the state by year of foundation.
32. Colaianni and Di Re, railroad contractors.
33. Western Mosaic & Terrazzo Company, one of the largest in the Middle West, doing an average business of over two hundred thousand dollars a year. Some of the work it has done so far includes the mosaics for the dormitories of Northwestern University, for Woodlawn Hospital, State Hospital, Metropole Building, Midwest Athletic Club, Stop and Shop, Steuben Club, Morgan Park Soldiers' Academy, and others. Mr. A. Stella is its president.
34. The Ramaccitti Company, excavators. Does a business of over three hundred thousand dollars a year. It has undertaken some of the largest excavation "jobs" in the city, such as the widening of Halsted Street from Harrison to Twenty-second, of Clinton Street from Harrison to Twelfth, and others. It also undertook the excavation for 265 buildings of the Argo Corn Products Company, in Argo, spending a full year in that work.
35. The Mosaic Shade Company, Inc., manufacturers of onyx and marble lamp stands. Established in Chicago in 1908 by its actual president, Mr. Lawrence Vivirito. It does an annual business of over three hundred thousand dollars a year.
36. The Milani Company, manufacturers of the Milani's French Salad Dressing, recognized as the leading in America. The Milani plant has recently been taken over by the Kraft Cheese Company, who has opened additional salad plants in New York and San Francisco.
37. Dominic Marubio, teaming and motor service. Established in 1885 and considered one of the largest in the city.
38. Broccolo Paper Box Company, manufacturers.
39. Benedetto Allegretti Company, one of the oldest candy manufacturers in the city.
40. The Casazza Company, distributors of automobile tires and accessories. Although it has been established only a few years, it does an annual business of about two hundred thousand dollars.
41. Silvestri Statuary Company, one of the largest in the city.
42. Grego Railroad Construction Company, manufacturers of railroad supplies.
43. Venetian Wrought Iron Works Co.
44. C. A. Mosso Laboratories.
45. A. Pacini Laboratories.

46. Cavanna Drapery & Curtain Works, Inc.
47. Illinois Cut Glass Company; Mr. George Palumbo, president.
48. General Marble Company, manufacturers of onyx and marble for all purposes.
49. Lo Presti Brothers, importers and wholesalers of Italian products, doing an average volume of business of about four hundred thousand dollars a year.
50. Garofalo Bros., leading importers and wholesalers of Italian food products.
51. Liberty Lamps Manufacturing Company.
52. Sisco Brothers Candy Company, large manufacturing confectioners.
53. Olive Can Company, manufacturers of olive oil cans.
54. Pan-Ferrara Company, candy manufacturers.
55. V. Formusa & Company, leading importer and wholesaler of Italian food products.
56. Ferretti Health Institute (for physical culture).
57. American Designing and Cutting Academy; S. Sabucci, director.
58. Louis Sala Co., manufacturers and dealers in toys and novelties.
59. Thomas A. Garibaldi & Co., realtors and builders.
60. John Caretti Company, mosaic contractors.
61. Torino Bakery, one of the largest in the city.
62. Gonnella Baking Company, also one of the largest.
63. American Noodle & Macaroni Co.
64. Italian Importing & Manufacturing Co., one of the largest macaroni manufacturers in the city and importers of Italian products.
65. De Luxe Candy Company, wholesalers and jobbers.
66. Milano Furniture Company, manufacturers of high grade carved furniture.
67. Peter Maggiore & Brothers, importers and wholesalers of Italian food products.
68. American Art Furniture Manufacturing Co.
69. Angela & Company, caterers to the most exclusive families on the Gold Coast.
70. Otto Annoreno & Company, large receivers and distributors of fruits and vegetables.
71. Bert Packing Company.
72. Giannini & Hilgart, stained and ornamental glass manufacturers.
73. Giovannini Biscuit Company.
74. N. Rigoni, dress manufacturer.
75. Marganella Fur Shop.
76. J. Roncillo & Co., manufacturers of gummed products.
77. Imperial Malt Company, packers of some of the best known brands in the city.
78. Anderson & Christiano, tailors of riding clothes.
79. Venetian Upholstery Cleaning Company.
80. Geo. F. Sivore, leading real estate agents.
81. J. Ginocchio, soda fountain supplies.
82. Curto, V. J., & Co., leading uptown realtors
83. Albertelli, Paul, paper box manufacturer.

84. Venetian Art Lamp Company.
85. Agnini & Singers, manufacturers of novelties.
86. G. Viviano & Brother Co., wholesalers of Italian food products.
87. Orlando Upholstering Co.
88. Lemoneena Manufacturing Company, manufacturers of effervescent citrate of magnesia.
89. Orlandi Statuary Company.
90. Braschi Export Company.
91. Venezia Garden Ornament Co.
92. North American Accordion Company.
93. L. Bartolacci, manufacturing jeweler.
94. Ziroli Monumental Company.
95. Livorno Hat Manufacturing Co.
96. Forti Brothers, manufacturers of trunks.
97. Rome Bedding Company, manufacturers of mattresses.
98. Salerno Machinery Company.
99. Abruzzi Company, pants makers.
100. Modern Life & Accident Insurance Company; Ralph Manno, president.

United Fig and Date Building, N. W. corner La Salle Street and the Chicago River
(A concern doing several million dollars of business a year. P. Costa, President.)

Lists And Tables

Table I

ITALIAN EMIGRATION TO THE UNITED STATES

Year		Year		Year	
1820	30	1856	1,365	1892	61,631
1821	62	1857	329	1893	72,145
1822	35	1858	1,414	1894	42,977
1823	33	1859	1,051	1895	35,427
1824	45	1860	920	1896	68,060
1825	75	1861	954	1897	59,431
1826	57	1862	621	1898	58,613
1827	35	1863	514	1899	77,419
1828	34	1864	694	1900	100,131
1829	23	1865	594	1901	135,996
1830	9	1866	1,318	1902	178,375
1831	28	1867	1,585	1903	230,622
1832	3	1868	1,549	1904	193,296
1833	169	1869	1,489	1905	221,479
1834	104	1870	2,893	1906	273,120
1835	61	1871	2,816	1907	285,731
1836	115	1872	4,190	1908	128,503
1837	36	1873	8,757	1909	183,218
1838	86	1874	7,667	1910	215,537
1839	84	1875	3,631	1911	182,882
1840	37	1876	3,017	1912	157,134
1841	179	1877	3,195	1913	265,542
1842	100	1878	4,344	1914	283,738
1843	117	1879	5,791	1915	49,688
1844	141	1880	12,354	1916	33,665
1845	137	1881	15,401	1917	34,596
1846	151	1882	32,160	1918	5,250
1847	164	1883	31,792	1919	1,884
1848	241	1884	16,510	1920	95,145
1849	209	1885	13,642	1921	
1850	431	1886	21,315	1922	
1851	447	1887	47,622	1923	
1852	351	1888	51,558	1924	
1853	555	1889	25,307	1925	
1854	1,263	1890	52,003	1926	
1855	1,052	1891	76,055	1927	

Table II

ITALIANS ADMITTED TO THE UNITED STATES WITH DESTINATION ILLINOIS AND ITALIANS DEPARTED FROM ILLINOIS

| | Admitted | | | | Departed | |
	North	South	Total	North	South (Aliens)	Total
1898	.....	.....	1,289	.....	.....	.....
1899	956	2,100	3,056	.....	.....	....
1900	1,260	2,403	3,663	.....	.....	.....
1901	1,430	3,386	4,816	.....	.....	.....
1902	2,290	4,918	7,208	....	.....	.....
1903	.....	.....	.....	.....	.....	.....
1904	2,799	5,184	7,983	.....	.....	.....
1905	3,663	6,685	10,348	.....	.....	.....
1906	4,293	9,809	14,102	.....	.....	.....
1907	5,139	10,183	15,322	.....	.....	.....
1908	2,230	4,490	6,720	1,496	6,756	8,252
1909	2,755	10,240	12,995	1,487	3,166	4,653
1910	3,547	11,629	15,126	1,315	1,911	3,226
1911	3,055	7,889	10,944	1,301	3,671	4,972
1912	2,222	6,179	8,401	1,193	7,179	8,372
1913	4,773	12,764	17,537	1,178	4,131	5,309
1914	4,156	14,546	18,702	1,229	3,735	4,964
1915	929	2,234	3,163	765	4,373	5,138
1916	308	1,238	1,546	234	3,420	3,654
1917	177	1,362	1,539	160	381	541
1918	88	226	314	58	381	439
1919	64	103	167	79	1,344	1,423
1920	899	4,536	5,435	667	4,632	5,299
1921	2,451	9,976	12,427	914	1,906	2,820
1922	562	1,930	2,492	799	2,338	3,137
1923	747	2,321	3,068	205	1,054	1,259
1924	1,126	2,412	3,538	237	960	1,197
1925	146	323	469	218	1,077	1,295
1926	129	459	588	236	888	1,124
1927	230	796	1,026	190	832	1,022

Table III

(U. S. Census Figures)

	Italians in Illinois	Italians in Chicago	Italian stock in Chicago
1850	43	.....	......
1860	219	100	......
1870	761	552	......
1880	1,764	1,357	....
1890	7,876	5,591	8,219
1900	23,523	16,008	26,046
1910	72,163	45,169	74,943
1920	94,407	59,215	124,184
1928	.....	80,000 (estimated)	200,000 (estimated)

FOREIGN GROUPS IN CHICAGO

Natives of	1870	1900	1920	For Illinois, 1920
Germany	52,316	170,738	112,288	205,491
Ireland (figures for 1860)	19,889	73,912	56,786	74,274
Norway	6,373	22,011	20,481	27,785
Sweden	6,154	48,836	58,563	105,577
Denmark	1,243	10,166	11,268	17,098
Bohemia	6,277	36,362	50,392	66,709
Poland	1,205	57,713	137,611	162,405

Table IV

ITALIAN POPULATION OF CHICAGO, BY WARDS

Ward	Born in Italy	1910 Both parents born in Italy	1920 Born in Italy	Ward	Born in Italy	1910 Both parents born in Italy	1920 Born in Italy
1	3,045	1,853	3,913	19	14,649	8,757	15,199
2	346	231	428	20	519	335	1,207
3	189	170	216	21	461	202	2,064
4	1,892	1,242	1,766	22	8,216	4,564	6,183
5	136	52	287	23	113	79	522
6	1,119	79	140	24	219	116	488
7	146	97	253	25	172	113	250
8	660	272	1,059	26	100	115	261
9	314	245	3,100	27	323	281	886
10	41	44	447	28	154	156	337
11	94	56	1,311	29	200	30	1,499
12	813	348	140	30	448	400	420
13	287	273	1,548	31	638	637	175
14	1,652	1,402	3,540	32	224	187	507
15	158	123	658	33	2,963	1,091	1,301
16	131	83	275	34	119	96	119
17	4,910	3,593	5,199	35	209	173	908
18	509	242	2,611				
Totals					45,169	27,737	59,215

PRISONERS IN STATE INSTITUTIONS: ILLINOIS

Table V

(Reports of Illinois Department of Public Welfare)
161—Native born, foreign born and citizenship of commitments and fathers of commitments—
criminal and delinquent group, year ending June 30, 1926—all state institutions as per page...

Commitments	Number	Percent
Native Born	3,136	93.0
Foreign Born	220	6.5
Unascertained	17	0.5
Fathers of Commitments		
Native Born	2,310	68.5
Foreign Born	785	23.3
Unascertained	278	8.2

Table VI

160—Race of commitments—criminal and delinquent group, year ending June 30—all state
institutions listed on page....

Race	Total	1922	1923	1924	1925	1926
Irish	975	224	132	137	242	240
Slavonic	900	167	147	163	212	209
German	782	157	130	153	155	187
Italian	398	88	37	73	103	97
English	381	106	62	49	82	82
Mixed	4,225	578	519	575	1,173	1,380
Unascertained	1,920	354	396	449	347	374
Total	12,849	2,303	1,907	2,169	3,097	3,373

160—Race of commitments, year ending June 30, 1926

	Boys	Girls		Boys	Girls
Slavonic	91	4	Lithuanian	14	9
African	86	47	Mixed	1	189
Italian	34	none	Unascertained	225	2
German	20	3			
Irish	14	none	Total	507	254

Table VII

Race Distribution of Crimes of Commitments, year ending June 30, 1926

	Total	Murder and Manslaughter	Burglary	Larceny	Robbery	Confidence Game, etc.	Crimes Against Chastity	All Others
English	2.55	1.45	3.83	2.20	2.64	3.93	2.35	2.17
German	5.34	5.80	6.38	5.13	6.47	8.85	7.65	3.00
Irish	7.36	7.25	8.94	7.48	9.83	9.18	9.41	4.44
Italian	2.68	6.76	2.34	2.20	5.28	...	4.71	1.96
Scandinavian	1.17	0.97	0.43	1.06	1.20	0.98	...	1.96
Slavonic	6.03	4.35	5.74	7.57	11.27	2.30	6.47	3.41
Mixed	42.03	19.80	42.76	42.31	22.30	47.54	35.29	54.03
Unascertained	10.75	10.14	9.79	10.09	8.39	10.49	9.41	13.54

Table VIII

Race Distribution of Commitments and Crimes, year ending June 30, 1926

			Per Cent	
	Commitments	Crimes	Commitments	Crimes
African	608	668	18.03	17.74
Irish	240	277	7.12	7.36
German	187	201	5.54	5.34
Slavonic	209	227	6.20	6.03
Italian	97	101	2.87	2.68
English	82	96	2.43	2.55
Mixed	1,380	1,583	40.91	42.03
Unascertained	374	405	11.09	10.75
Total	3,373	3,766	100.00	100.00

Table IX

ITALIANS ARRESTED

(From Annual Reports of the Chicago Police Department)

Year	Total	Italian	Year	Total	Italian
1896	96,847	1,540	1912	83,853	2,632
1897	83,680	1,206	1913	107,257	3,347
1898	77,441	1,025	1914	111,461	3,357
1899	71,349	808	1915	114,625	2,981
1900	70,438	685	1916	104,531	2,532
1901	69,442	949	1917	129,270	3,194
1902	70,314	1,116	1918	105,632	3,198
1903	77,763	1,714	1919	91,457	2,828
1904	66,344	1,488	1920	87,197	2,479
1905	68,622	1,551	1921	132,190	3,363
1906	78,342	1,715	1922	132,290	3,576
1907	58,002	1,416	1923	181,980	4,837
1908	63,385	1,761	1924	242,602	6,781
1909	66,695	1,831	1925	264,494	5,810
1910	77,218	2,805	1926	211,317	4,954
1911	80,649	2,768			

Table X

NATIVITIES OF PERSONS ARRESTED

(Annual Reports of the Police Department)

	1885	1886	1887	1888	1889	1890	1891	1892	1893
Germany	4,735	5,249	5,664	5,910	5,557	6,889	7,210	8,928	8,926
Ireland	4,775	4,577	4,882	6,187	5,260	6,426	6,790	7,666	6,436
Sweden	763	764	895	1,060	1,073	1,575	1,530	1,888	1,729
Am. Whites	23,059	25,586	26,095	26,945	26,201	33,955	39,033	49,285	56,488
Italian	325	386	434	587	611	.....	.....	1,122	1,450

FOREIGN WHITE STOCK IN CHICAGO IN 1895

(Both foreign born and natives of United States)

(From Chicago Daily News Almanac, 1895)

Italian	14,194		Irish	111,037
German	216,324		Swedes	58,763

Table XI

ITALIANS ARRESTED, BY SEX

	Male		Female	
Year	Total	Italian	Total	Italian
1923	169,614	4,632	12,366	205
1924	225,523	6,528	17,079	253
1925	246,719	5,565	17,775	245
1926	194,290	4,748	17,027	206

Table XII

STATISTICS OF CHARGES PREFERRED IN THE MUNICIPAL AND CRIMINAL COURTS
OF CHICAGO BY OFFENSE AND NATIVITY

(From Annual Reports, Police Department)

Felonies—

	1923	1924	1925	1926	4-Year Period
Total Male	13,166	14,850	16,126	18,195	62,337
Total Female	1,222	1,666	1,793	1,991	6,672
	14,388	16,516	17,919	20,186	69,009
Italian Male	399	591	583	632	2,205
Female	40	50	37	36	153
	439	641	620	668	2,358

Italian per cent total, 3.40%.
Per cent Female, 2.31%.

Misdemeanors—

	1923	1924	1925	1926	4-Year Period
Total	177,890	239,829	264,341	207,385	
Italian	4,758	6,827	5,815	4,864	
Female:					
All Nationalities	11,489	16,134	16,819	16,029	
Italian	171	225	231	193	

Table XIII

STATISTICS OF CHARGES PREFERRED IN THE MUNICIPAL AND CRIMINAL
COURTS FOR 1926

	Total	Italian		Total	Italian
Burglary	1,762	43	Robbery	3,169	78
Confidence game	1,644	14	Disorderly conduct	95,078	2,100
Embezzlement	254	1	Inmates of disorderly house.	20,827	407
Larceny, etc.	6,375	125	Inmates of gaming house..	3,440	95
Manslaughter	301	7	Keepers of gaming house..	859	24
Murder	284	23	Keepers of house of ill fame	147	2
Rape	334	13	Soliciting for prostitution..	115	1

Table XIV

STATISTICS OF CHARGES PREFERRED IN THE MUNICIPAL AND CRIMINAL COURTS
BY OFFENSE AND NATIVITY

(From Annual Reports, Police Department)

Murders

	1923	1924	1925	1926	4-Year Period
Total	207	291	318	284	1,100
Italian	21	22	56	23	122
Murder, Accessory to					
Total	33	72	65	94	264
Italian	3	10	4	5	22
Murder, Assault to commit					
Total	347	421	470	527	1,765
Italian	38	34	43	45	160
Manslaughter					
Total	218	272	237	301	1,028
Italian	10	15	19	7	51
Rape					
Total	255	288	339	334	1,216
Italian	20	23	13	13	69
Rape, Assault to commit					
Total	80	78	78	81	317
Italian	3	3	2	4	12

Table XV

CONVICTIONS IN MUNICIPAL AND CRIMINAL COURTS

	1923	1924	1925	1926	4-Year Period
Felonies					
Total	4,014	4,856	5,000	3,052	16,922
Italian	107	114	122	82	425
				Italian per cent, 2.50	
Misdemeanors					
Total	63,470	68,347	79,118	52,922	263,857
Italian	1,637	1,605	1,483	1,046	5,771
				Italian per cent, 2.15	

Table XVI

CONVICTIONS IN MUNICIPAL AND CRIMINAL COURTS

Crime	1923 Total	1923 Italian	1924 Total	1924 Italian	1925 Total	1925 Italian	1926 Total	1926 Italian	4-Year Period Total	4-Year Period Italian
Arson	7	none	2	none	3	none	....	....	12	none
Bigamy	8	none	13	1	4	none	....	....	25	1
Burglary	351	8	518	14	493	15	....	....	1,362	37
Confidence game	201	none	236	none	214	2	....	....	651	2
Crime against children	23	4	35	1	57	3	....	....	115	8
Crime against nature	9	1	18	1	9	none	....	....	36	2
Embezzlement	39	none	38	none	44	none	22	none	143	none
Forgery	25	none	34	none	3	none	....	....	62	none
Robbery	259	5	473	13	594	14	....	....	1,326	32
Adultery	125	2	87	2	100	2	95	2	407	8
Bastardy	51	1	44	none	47	1	....	....	106	2
Extortion by threats	9	none	11	1	7	none	6	none	33	1
Carrying fire arms and concealed weapons	604	40	722	55	744	57	693	35	2,763	187
Inmates of gaming house	1,014	50	1,182	17	989	16	336	22	3,521	105
Keepers of gaming house	99	5	238	4	285	3	120	5	742	17
Keepers of houses of ill fame	227	4	258	6	33	none	40	none	558	10
Vagrancy	110	1	268	4	529	1	493	2	1,400	8
Compulsory education	138	22	148	18	40	5	47	5	373	50

Table XVII

FEMALE OFFENDERS—CONVICTIONS

	1923 Total	1923 Italian	1924 Total	1924 Italian	1925 Total	1925 Italian	1926 Total	1926 Italian	Grand Total Total	Grand Total Italian
Inmates of houses of ill fame	321	none	436	1	56	none	89	none	902	1
Keepers of houses of ill fame	118	none	126	none	22	none	35	none	301	none
Soliciting for prostitutions	171	none	208	none	28	none	none	none	407	none
Kate Addams Law	281	2	637	1	946	none	926	1	2,790	4

Table XVIII

NATIVITY OF WOMEN IN COOK COUNTY JAIL, 1914, 1916, 1920, 1921

(From Survey of Cook County Jail, 1922, page 223)

Total	2,692	
Poland	131	(includes Austria, Germany and Russian Poland)
Germany	87	
Ireland	81	
Lithuania	28	
Italy	25	
Canada	24	
Sweden	22	

Table XIX
DISPOSITION OF MURDER CASES
(From Annual Reports of the Police Department)

	1923	1924	1925	1926	Total
To hang	1	3	7	3	14
To Joliet, life	4	9	11	8	32
To Joliet, other sentences	11	20	14	12	57
Pontiac	1	1	...	...	2
Insane asylums	1	1	1	1	4
Acquitted	12	22	18	16	68
Not billed, stricken off, nolle prossed	4	6	8	11	29
Murderer suicide	12	20	20	13	65
Murderer killed	5	2	4	5	16
Unsolved	59	86	98	89	332
Pending in criminal court	26	10	18	31	85
Total	136	180	199	189	704
"Black-Hand" cases	20	24	28	17	89
No arrests	19	23	28	17	87

Table XX
NATIONALITY OF PERSONS ADMITTED TO PROBATION
(From Annual Reports of the Municipal Court of Chicago—for the years Dec. 4, 1921, to Nov. 30, 1924)

	1921-1922		1922-1923		1923-1924		Grand Total	
	M.	F.	M.	F.	M.	F.	M.	F.
Total	3,249	721	3,095	786	4,286	854	10,630	2,361
Italian	127	none	92	14	120	20	339	50

Italian per cent, 2.11

Table XXI
STATISTICS OF PRISONERS AT THE COUNTY JAIL FROM DEC. 1922 TO NOV. 1923
(From Annual Message from President of Board of Commissioners, Cook County)

Austria	113	Native	7,290
Germany	112	Poland	522
Ireland	211	Russia	164
Italy	219	Sweden	108
Lithuania	158		
Mexico	107	Grand total	10,400

Table XXII
NATIVITY OF INMATES AT THE HOUSE OF CORRECTION, 1921

		Nativity of inmates' parents
Total	8,566	8,566
Foreign	2,967	3,699
Austria	366	433
England	72	116
Scotland	38	74
Germany	179	545
Ireland	316	1,055
Italy	142	225
Poland	557	748
Russia	397	493
Lithuania	101	109
Norway	68	104
Sweden	191	252
Mexico	116	121
Greece	61	65
Bohemia	43	104

ITALIAN MEMBERS OF THE ART INSTITUTE OF CHICAGO

Life Members

Thos. W. Algeo
Wm. D. Algeo
Ed. F. Brizzolara
Mrs. Giovanni B. Bruno
Miss Bertha M. Carra
John F. Cuneo
Mrs. Hallie Damiani
Edward N. D'Ancona
Salvatore Ferrara

Mrs. George Abelio
Wm. J. Accola
Gaston L. Alciatore
Mrs. Bernard P. Barasa
Dr. Alfredo Bellizzi
Mrs. Christye Brizzolara
Vincent Carofiglio
Mrs. Eugene L. Cavanna
Mrs. J. A. Cecce
Barto Chiappe
John A. Chiaro
Mrs. Michele Chiodo
Dr. Eleuterio Ciotola
Mrs. Victor J. Curto
G. L. Manta
Roy Massena
Mrs. F. E. Matti
Mrs. Rose Mercurio
Louis Milani
Mrs. Wm. J. Miskella

Giuseppe Garibaldi
Leonard Anthony Gliatto
Dr. J. R. Lavieri
Leo. A. Marzolo
Mrs. James Minotto
Dr. Ralph Pagano
Dr. Morris Penchina
Mrs. Barbara Prato
Wm. C. Presto

Annual Members

Dr. Donat F. Monaco
Mrs. L. N. Nave
Joseph J. Nevotti
L. A. Pereira
H. E. Poronto
Mrs. A. Frank Cuneo
Frank Cuneo
Francesco Daddi
Alfred D'Ancona
Mrs. P. R. De Carlo
Mrs. J. D. De Feo
Sister De Pazzi
Mrs. J. D'Esposito
Peter Dolese
Albert H. Fabbri
Mrs. James P. Ginna
Mrs. John Ginocchio
J. C. Granata
Alberto N. Gualano
Alfonso Iannelli

A. Ramaccitti
John E. Rigali
Philip S. Rinaldo
Lawrence P. Romano
Miss Adele Schillo
Mrs. Joseph Soravia
Frank J. Stodola
David M. Zolla

Mrs. F. A. Lagorio
John La Veccha
Mrs. Gennaro D. Lavieri
Mrs. Franklin A. Luce
Mrs. Homer J. Luce
Egisto Orlando
Miss Marie Paldi
Peter E. Paoli
Robert L. Pioso
Mrs. D. A. Raggio
Mrs. Lawrence A. Rigali
Mrs. Michael A. Romano.
Mrs. Mamie Salamo
Mrs. M. J. Schiavoni
Mrs. Salvatore Sisco
Mrs. D. L. Toffenetti
Vittorio Trevisan
Mrs. M. F. Ventresca
Miss Caroline Vitellaro

CHICAGO SCHOOL TEACHERS HAVING ITALIAN NAMES

Algeo, Mary S.
Angeletti, Leila
Arado, Amelia
Arado, Grace
Arado, Stella
Arata, Albina
Arvia, Emily
Avondino, Josephine
Carciotto, Louise
Casella, Rose
Caverno, Cora
Cella, Nora
Canepa, Vincent
Cuneo, Veronica
Damato, Mildred
Dando, Anna
De Celle, Celeste Marie Louise
De Florio, Angelina
Del Banco, Bessie

Del Campo, Marie
Del Manzo, Hilda
Doria, Lillian
Durso, Margaret
Ferrero, Emma
Fortino, Michael
Francia, Lena
Gandia, Jane
Garroti, Christine
Giachini, Ida
Gliatto, Giulia
Guanella, Ethel
Guarino, Frances
Giuliano, Giusto
Lagorio, Patricia
Lagorio, Veronica
Lino, Frank
Lombardo, Janne
Maraviglia, Louise

Marini, Edna
Michaelis, Ruth
Miranda, Helen
Motto, Anna
Nardi, Teresa
Narmonta, Aldona
Navigato, Louise
Nicolai, Minnie
Pattullo, Milton
Paula, Mildred
Paves, Charlotte
Pesta, Rose
Rosa, Edith
Sbarbaro, Augustine
Sillani, Mabel
Tramatei, Gertrude
Varraveto, Marie
Ventresca, Francesco
Zarlenga, Lillian

Some of the teachers included above may not be of Italian origin, although they have an Italian name; on the other hand, it has been impossible to include the names of teachers of Italian descent who have Anglicized their names.

The above list does not include the large number of teachers of Italian descent who are not at present on the teaching staffs of Chicago schools.

CHICAGO STUDENTS HAVING ITALIAN NAMES
AT UNIVERSITY OF ILLINOIS, URBANA, ILL.
For the year ending 1926-1927
Undergraduate and Professional Colleges

Algeo, Thos. Wm.
Anselmo, Frank Michael
Bernero, Louis John
Boitano, Alfred
Cappetta, J. Virginia
Carbone, F. J. (Melrose Park)

Cella, Lawrence G.
Collora, N. A.
D'Ambrosio, Arthur
Gioacchini, Peter
Granata, Wm. Josephine
Lino, Frank Domenick

Metthei, Emm. A.
Piosa, E. B.
Prato, Ph. E.
Spira, Leonard
Tamburino, A. J.

Graduate
La Piana, Angeline

College of Medicine

Barone, A. Martin
Berardi, J. B.
Carelli, Paul V.
De Trana, G. E.
Franco, J. R.
Francona, Nicholas
Lavezzorio, L. M.

Lavieri, Frank J.
Limarzi, L. R.
LoBraico, Adeline
Mastri, Aquil
Oliviero, Vinc.
Pava, Chas.
Russo, Carmen F.

Salerno, Marie
Schiavone, J. M.
Scuderi, Carlo
Sodaro, N. E.
Varzino, L. S.

Dentistry
Bazola, Fred N.   Zaccaria, A. L.

Pharmacy

Barone, A. J.
Barone, Dante Rosario
Belli, Julius
Bisconti, Ed.
Cambio, Orlando
Colucci, Vito
De Gilio, Edith
De Gilio, Frank Nick
Esposito, Domenick
Gardella, Libero
Garramone, Pasquale

Gentile, Joseph
Gerbori, Wm.
Giurato, James
La Manna, Joseph
La Rocca, Frank
La Rocca, Salvatore
Martorano, Lawrence
Minarsini, J. Martin
Muzio, J. A.
Panzica, Nicholas
Perdenza, Joseph

Pesato, H. B.
Pinna, P. B.
Pinta, E. F.
Riccio, D. J.
Sallemi, Ernest
Sodaro, Anthony
Taglia, Amedeo
Triscinzzi, Victor
Vincenti, Fred (Melrose Park)

STUDENTS OF ITALIAN NAMES AT NORTHWESTERN UNIVERSITY
Evanston

Albi, E. L.
Alicata, J. E.
Belarmino, Eliseo D.
Bianucci, Henry
Biondi, Reno J.
Biondi, Rita M.
Cannizzo, Gregorio
Cassaretto, Frank P.
D'Esposito, Louise M.
Di Giovanni, Edith M.

Fedrizzi, Jos. A.
Giza, Stella
Garzonetti, Rose M.
Lazaretti, Raymond F.
Lettola, Matti G.
Lombardo, Ignace F.
Magatti, Francis W.
Malato, Emelie
Mancinelli, Ralph D.
Manello, Carl L.

Marrandino, Ralph A.
Masciola, Evelina
Masessa, Rocco A.
Minto, Virginia L.
Penza, Rudolph
Radosta, Sylvia V.
Raida, Theresa
Terrando, Dolores

Chicago

Colombatto, Domick Eowin
De Larco, Joseph E.
Galanti, Chas. Rascol
Madda, Vincent Albert

Maina, Edward G.
Sabbia, Donald Palmer
Eerritella, Della Mamie
Sippola, George W.

Galgano, John Henry
Ravelo, Fiorentino

THE ITALIANS IN CHICAGO

151

LOYOLA UNIVERSITY

Italo Volini, Professor of Medicine
Lisi Cipriani, Ph. D., Lecturer on Comparative Literature, Graduate School
John Anthony Suldane, Associate in Pediatrics
Anthony Sodaro, Assistant in Medicine
Anthony Partipilo, Assistant in Anatomy

School of Medicine—Loyla University

Carofiglio, Louis Ed.
Cella, Louis Ed.
Conforti, James H.
Drago, Rosario Chas.
Fusco, Patrick Henry
Geraci, Angelo Sam.
Geraci, Samuel Anthony
Barberio, Angelo Albert
Bellini, Albert Carl
Borruso, Camilla
Caliendo, Joseph Edward
Casciato, John James
Cirrincione, Francis A.
Di Leo, Joseph Anthony

Laurenzana, Frank Marion
Marzano, Joseph
Marzano, Mary Georgiana
Mennella, James Vincent
Metro, Michael Leo
Petrone, Marco Salvatore
Saletta, Frank John
Castro, Cosimo
Catania, Anthony Michael
Minardi, Joseph Anthony
Nigro, Salvatore Joseph
Pecoraro, Amedeo Michael
Samonte, Antonio
Valenta, Ella Helen

Cava, Jasper Francis
Firneno, J. R.
Lo Presto, Frank
Macaluso, Leonard A.
Muzzicato, Chas.
Pace, Anthony J.
Saladino, Anthony J.
Abramo, Dominick J.
Guerra, John Dante
Gullo, Chas.
Luna, Francesca R.
Serio, Thos. J.

School of Law—Loyola University

Santucci, J. B.

Marino, Lawrence N.
Gennaro, Albachiara

Furno, William M.

School of Commerce—Loyola University

Chianelli, Joseph
Curielli, Armida
Dasso, Stephen

Falore, Chas.
Ferrari, Marco E.
Mariano, Louis L.

Presentin, Marie L.
Quinturiano, Gervasio

College of Arts and Sciences—Loyola University

Addeo, Louis
Allegretti, Anthony James
Balsamo, Nicholas Joseph
Bartolucci, Raymond John
Casciato, Nicholas Anthony
Citro, John Alfred
Colangelo, Anthony
Copia, Paul Joseph
Corsiglia, Benedict I.
Cutrera, Hugo T.
D'Esposito, Joshua Paul

Fazio, Peter
Fazio, John Rocco
Freda, Vincent Chas.
Freda, Anthony William
Gualano, Carl Albert
Maggini, Renzo Grimaldi
Marzano, Joseph Adam
Monachino, Thos. Alfred
Montambo, Ray Jay
Novelli, Michael
Parenti, Michael Joseph

Pontecorvo Edmond Luca
Rocco, Paul Carl
Santucci, Joseph Bernard
Spiteri, W. Blase
Tambornino, Paul Joseph
Tomaso, Alphonse Rocco
Vincenti, Anton Peter
Volini, Camillo Eugene
Zvetina, Richard George

Graduate School—Loyola University

Rosatti, Sister Mary Lorettina, *Education*   Rossi, Madame Marie Aimee, *Education*

Chicago College of Dental Surgery—Loyola University

Baldassare, Lino A.
Lapata, Frank
Porto, Joseph F.
Contraffatto, Sam A.
Cozzi, William

Mascari, Frank J.
Rollo, James S.
Romano, Alfred
Tufo, Rocco P.
Canonica, Eugene P.

Lendino, Angelo
Rago, Michael F.
Reveno, Maurice
Salvino, James T.

There are many Italians studying at the University of Chicago and at the Art Institute, but as said institutions do not publish a directory of students, it has been impossible to give here the names of the Italian students, although, thanks to the intervention of Prof. E. Burgess, the files of the University of Chicago were open to the writer.

Many Italian students are to be found also at Chicago Kent College of Law, De Paul Law School, Armour Institute, Lewis Institute and the various educational institutions in the city.

ITALIAN OPERAS PRODUCED FOR THE FIRST TIME IN CHICAGO

1910-11—Puccini, The Girl of the Golden West.
1911-12—Wolf-Ferrari, Il Segreto di Susanna.
           I Gioielli della Madonna.
1912-13—Zandonai, Conchita.
1913-14—Franchetti, Cristoforo Colombo.
           Leoncavallo, Zingari.
1915-16—Leoncavallo, Zaza.
1916-17—Zandonai, Francesca da Rimini.

1917-18—Mascagni, Isabeau.
           Lazzari, Le sauteriot.
1918-19—Catalani, Lorelei.
1919-20—Montemezzi, La Nave.
1920-21—Marinuzzi, Jacquerie.
           Leoncavallo, Edipo Re.
1925-26—Franchetti, Namiko-San.
           Alfano, Resurrection.

1926-27—Giordano, La Cena delle Beffe.

ITALIAN SINGERS WHO HAVE BEEN CONNECTED WITH THE CHICAGO GRAND OPERA COMPANY, CHICAGO OPERA ASSOCIATION, CIVIC OPERA ASSOCIATION OF CHICAGO

1910-11
Enrico Caruso
Amedeo Bassi
Mario Sammarco
Antonio Scotti
1911-12
Luisa Tetrazzini
Alice Zeppilli
Mario Sammarco
Rosina Galli
Amedeo Bassi
1912-13
Luisa Tetrazzini
Titta Ruffo
Alice Zeppilli
Mario Sammarco
1913-14
Lina Cavalieri
Titta Ruffo
1916-17
A. Galli-Curci
Francesco Daddi
1917-18
A. Galli-Curci
Carolina Lazzari

Francesca Peralta
Giulio Crimi
Giacomo Rimini
1918-19
A. Galli-Curci
Guido Cicolini
Riccardo Stracciari
Alessandro Dolci
1919-20
Amelita Galli-Curci
Nina Morgana
Titta Ruffo
Carlo Galeffi
1920-21
Alessandro Bonci
Amelita Galli-Curci
Rosa Storchio
Titta Ruffo
1921-22
Amelita Galli-Curci
Anna Correnti
Lodovico Oliviero
Giacomo Rimini
Virgilio Lazzari
1922-23

Claudia Muzio
Tito Schipa
Giulio Crimi
Giacomo Rimini
Cesare Formichi
Virgilio Lazzari
1923-24
Amelita Galli-Curci
Doria Fernando
Tito Schipa
Virgilio Lazzari
1924-25
Toti Dal Monte
Olga Forrai
Flora Perini
Tito Schipa
1925-26
Claudia Muzio
Olga Forrai
Tito Schipa
Giacomo Rimini
1926-27
Claudia Muzio
Tito Schipa
G. Rimini

Virgilio Lazzari
Cesare Formichi
1927-28
Toti Dal Monte
Claudia Muzio
Tito Schipa
Lodovico Oliviero
Cesare Formichi
Luigi Montesanto
Giacomo Rimini
Virgilio Lazzari
Vittorio Trevisan
Conductors
Giorgio Polacco
Roberto Moranzoni
Antonio Sabino
Assistant Conductors
Dino Bigalli
Giacomo Spadoni
Chorus Master
Attico Bernabini
Orchestra Manager
Joseph Raffaelli
Prompter
Fernado Giaccone

DECORATIONS AWARDED TO ITALIAN SOLDIERS FROM CHICAGO

Beato, Corp. John, 2209 No. Karlow Ave., D. S. C.
Bruno, Tony, 528 W. 28th St., I. W. C.
Cassaga, Serg. Sam., 1023 Thompson, D. S. C.
Cecilia, Louis, 554 Taylor, D. S. C., Croix de Guerre.
Francisco, Serg. John, 3157 Division, D. S. C.

Gatanio, Cor. I., 1208 Washburn, D. S. C.
Reati, Corp. Mike, 1028 W. Polk, I. W. C.
Zappa, Steve, D. S. C.
Michaelis, Chas., D. S. C., British Military Medal.
De Bonis, S. T., M. M. Britain, Croix de Guerre, Belgium.

ITALIAN SOLDIERS FROM CHICAGO KILLED DURING THE WORLD WAR
(From Daily News Almanac, 1919)

Basone, Sam., 919 Cambridge.
Carravatta, Pasquale, 836 Garibaldi Place.
Catalano, James, 116 So. Sangamon.
Cuia, Corp. Andrew, 1755 Ashland Ave.
Corsiglia, Chas., 2742 No. Sacramento.
Cuza, Nick, 248 Alexander St.
D'Avolio, Guerrini, 1110 So. Morgan.
Damiani, Chas., 1008 Cambridge Ave.
Fillici, Fiori, 9370 Anthony Ave., So. Chicago

Fontana, F., 734 E. 104th.
Panozza, Dominik, Kankakee.
Pierucce, Joseph, 1367 Fulton.
Potampa, Frank, 2712 So. Kildare.
Saffore, Thos., 3723 So. State.
Scalzitti, John C., 2426 N. Tripp Ave.
Sinadi, Xavier, 1735 Wabausia Ave.
Strippi, Steve, 502 Eveylin Place.
Zucchero, N., 611 Sholto.

Zullo, Antonio, 1142 W. Taylor.

ITALIAN SOLDIERS FROM CHICAGO, KILLED DURING THE WAR, WHOSE BODIES WERE BROUGHT BACK FROM FRANCE

(From Roll of Honor, E. R. Lewis, compiler, published by Board of Commissioners of Cook County, 1922)

(*) indicates repetition of names listed above.

*Guerini Avolio
Carmen M. Broccolo
Thos. C. Carlino
Michael L. Luisi
Anthony Pinocci
Joseph T. Padula
*Joseph Pierucce
Stanley Sofolo

*Costantino Scalzitti
Macario Taglieri
Vito S. Scalise
L. N. Tortorelli
Julius Penno
Wm. R. Lamberti
Louis Grazia
Nick J. Benedetti

Frank Cielo
Frank Calabrese
Joseph Greco
Michael Libonati
William Palmisano
Frank Saetina
Martin Avignone
Mike Blasco

DECEASED SOLDIERS

Peter Malato
Pasquale Puzza

Victor De Blase
Carlo Morando

Alessio Remicco
Jos. Navarra

ITALIANS IN CHICAGO IN 1860

Badardio, Joseph, 276 So. Clark, home same, confectioner.
Lagorio, A., saloon, 179 S. Canal, home same.
Lagorio, F., saloon, 39 Chicago Ave.
Raggio, J., confectioner, 101 N. Clark, home same.
Raggio, A., confectioner, 172 Randolph, home 205 W. Van Buren.
Raggio, J., confectioner, 110 N. Clark, home same.
Raggio, J., confectioner, 183 So. Wells, home same.
Pentony, T., carpenter, 45 N. Dearborn.
Perigo, Anthony, machinist, Chicago House.
Garibaldi, F., 180½ So. Clark, home same.
Baggio, Lawrence, 206 Van Buren, home same.
Bozzola, Louis, engraver, 251 Illinois.
Castello, Conrad, teamster, Union Park House.
Pelo, Joseph, ship carpenter, 153 So. Clinton.
Milazzi, J., barber, 133½ So. Clark.
Milazzi, Gaetano, So. Wells, between Monroe & Adams.
Berna, Eugene, machinist, Butterfield near Commerce.
Berna, Peter, stone cutter.
Gazzado, Lewis, ice cream saloon, 45 W. Kinzie.
Gazzado, Peter, saloon, 31 W. Kinzie, home same.
Cavanna, Philip, hatter, 51 Buffalo.
Cavanna, Eugene, upholster.
Cella, Antonio, fruit dealer, 172 Randolph.
Cella, Louis, confectioner, 215 So. Clark, home same.
Casci, D. and Pierre L., moulding and figure work, 168 So. Clark, home same.
Pieri, Joseph, plaster work, home 48 Carroll.
Pierra, L., home N. Clark near Indiana.
Regonni, Dominick, pawnbroker, 79 So. Wells, home same.
Regneri, Lampert, cooper, Goethe St., between Clark and LaSalle.
Santa, Joseph, cooper, 36 Wesson.
Stemma, John, laborer, home North Ave.
Stegenza, J., carpenter, 334 So. Desplaines.
Pirro, Jacob, carpenter, Larrabee, N. Center.
Pirone, Conrad, teamster, Hickory near Green Bay.
Nicolai, Aug., tailor, 444 So. Clark.
Nicolai, Ed., plasterer, Indiana Ave., near Harding Place.
Nicolai, Fred, shoemaker, Quincy, between Wells and Franklin.
Nicolai, John L., teacher French, N. Wells, between Illinois and Michigan.
Nicolai, Wm., barber, Granger, between Wells and Sedgwick.
Passino, Joseph, machinist, Canal, between Wright and Meagher.
Pazzo, Marcus, clothing store, home 8 Buffalo Lake, cor. Franklin.
Piombo, J., rear Monroe between Wells and Clark.
Frazza, Giovanni, home 138 Madison.
Ribolla, Alex., home 136 Madison.
Lui, Michael, laborer, Butterfield and Commerce.

ITALIANS IN CHICAGO IN 1880

Artists

Borgella, F., 125 Dearborn.
Ernesti, R., 46 W. Madison.

Gregori, Luigi, 170 State.
Torrey, Eugene, 97 Clark.

Baker

A. Spera, 130 Brown.

Barbers

Carciotto, L. D., 83 Madison.
Cardella, John, 91½ Van Buren.
De Simone, A., 12 So. Water.
Geraci, A., 1800 State.
Liverno, F., 602½ W. Lake.

Milazzo, S., 157 Van Buren.
Nicolai, G., 105 W. Polk.
Nicolai, W., 141 N. Clark.
Paonessa, N., 127 Dearborn.
Paonessa, M., 60 Adams.

Boots and Shoes

Arnoldi, P., 430 Ogden Ave.
Arnoldi, A., 624 N. Paulina.

Schiavoni, L., 66 Polk.
Seneca & Ring, 195 Dearborn.

Bottler

Torchiani, H., 189 Washington.

Commission Merchant

Mattei, Angelo, 149 So. Water.

Confectionery and Fruits

Angelo, Chas., 278 Clark.
Anterelli, Louis, 276½ Clark.
Bacigalupi, D., 3744 Cottage Grove Ave.
 199 W. Lake.
Barboro, D. S., 18 No. Wells.
Bernaro, John, 431 No. Clark.
Biggio, L., 221 So. Halsted.
Brizzolara & Pfeiffer, 138 22nd St.
Caproni, Louis, 251 So. Halsted.
Catelani, A., 714 Milwaukee.
Cella, A., 124 Van Buren.

Chicoine, Valerio, Mrs., 888 W. Madison.
Ghiselli, Lodovico, 123 Blue Island.
Gozzelo, Anthony, 370 W. Madison.
Granelli, A., 19 W. Kinzie.
Longinotti, A., 31 W. Kinzie.
Loverzario, N., 173 Dearborn.
Malatesta, Mary, 365 W. 12th.
Millarina, Joseph, 221 Blue Island.
Manfredi, David, 221 W. Chicago.
Polsi, G., 220 W. Randolph.
Ratto, Gasper, 319 W. Indiana.

Grocers

Cuneo, G. B., 66 N. Franklin.
De Stefeno, Millie, 527 Clark.
Lampe, George, 313 Brown.

Landa, F., 27 Canalport.
Querolli, A., 457 Clark.
Raggio, A., & Son, 396 Clark.

Ice Cream Manufacturers

Duca, Peter, 359 State.

Ginocchio, Stephen, 246½ N. Clark.

Music Teachers

Cugno Bros., 421 Clark.

Musicians

De Grazia, R., rear 191 N. Halsted.
Marotta, M., 112 Dekoven.

Ruggero, Salvatore, 191 N. Halsted.
Russo, Joseph, 453 So. Canal.

Notaries

Ginocchio, John, 77 W. Madison (interpreter Italian language)
Legro, Florian, 490 So. Canal.

Painter (Sign)

Fiereo, Adelbert, 118 Randolph.

Photographer

Gentile, Chas., 3907 Cottage Grove.

Physicians

Ciolina, F., 42 Clybourn Ave.

Mauro, A., 79 W. Madison.

Plasterers—Ornamental

Bartolomei, J., & Co.

Real Estate

Ginocchio, John, 77 W. Madison

Restaurants

Barsanti, John, 470 State.
Basso, A., 199 W. Lake.
Biggio, G., 30 W. Randolph.
Biggio, L., 221 Randolph.
Cardella, J., 226 W. 12th.
Cassinelli, C., 532 State.
Castagnino, James, 3026 State.
Castellino, John, 2138 State.
Cella, Anthony, 4153 So. Halsted.
Cella, G., 20 W. Madison.
Cella, W., 365 Clark.
Del Angelica, Louis, 284 Clark.
Fabbrici, Chas., 136 Van Buren.
Gazzolo, Louis, 25 W. Kinzie.
Lagorio, Frank, 299 W. Madison.

Lagorio, Frank, 578 W. Lake.
Leoni, S., 210 State.
Leoni & Mann, 210 State.
Leoni & Ponich, 102 Randolph.
Malatesta, Louis, 1734 State.
Micheletti, P., 732 W. Madison.
Micheletti, M., 412 State.
Panasi, Joseph, 220 W. Randolph.
Raggio, A., 2262 Archer Ave.
Raggio, J., 3110 State.
Raggio, Mary, Mrs., 863 N. Clark.
Reppetto, A., 2704 State.
Sivori, A., 3908 State.
Valerga, E., 278 State.
Zatta, Antonio, 1832 State.

Saloons

Arado, A., 68 N. Franklin.
Arado, J., 491 W. Madison.
Arata, A., 346 W. Madison.
Arata, L., & Bro., 178 N. Halsted.
Bacigalupi, A., 185 Monroe.
Benzo, A., 724 Elston Ave.
Benero, John, 2872 Archer Ave.
Botto, D., 64 So. Desplaines.
Brato, A., 459 Clark.
Brignadello, A., 55 W. Indiana.
Camilla, J., 126 W. Randolph.
Caproni, A., 400 Wabash.
Casale, S., 43 N. Market.
Cassaretto, J., 360 Milwaukee Ave.
Cavana, J., 123 So. Halsted.
Cella, John, 547 W. Madison.

Cordano Bros., 44 W. Randolph.
Cordano & Cella, 115 W. Madison.
Da Costa, A., 75 Clark.
Fazzi, Pauline, Mrs., 252 Blue Island Ave.
Gazzolo, F., 79 & 82 W. Madison.
Ginocchio, John B., 89 So. Halsted.
Lagoni, P., 690 North Ave.
Malatesta & Ginocchio, 4139 So. Halsted.
Manfredi, R., 217 W. Randolph.
Minucciani, R., 135 So. Halsted.
Pascera, M., 473 So. Canal.
Petri, John, 2741 Shields Ave.
Raggio, John, 110 N. Clark.
Sbarbaro, F., 539 W. Madison.
Taraba, M., 445 So. Canal.
Toileti, Luciano, 405 W. 12th.

Vancura, Joseph, 3147 Butler.

Tailors

Persio, Anton, 63 Polk.
Fiala, A., 12 Hanover.
Ghiselli, F., 670 So. Halsted.

Lagoni, P., 216 N. Desplaines.
Menchini, A., 185 Clark.
Pesta, James, 421 W. 18th.

Sperra, L., 33 Crittenden.

Watchmakers

Alberti, Edward, 148 W. Randolph.

Marchese, Frank, 231 31st.

Wines and Liquors (Retail)
Corvini, F. A., 14 Clark.

1890

Artist
Ernesti, R., 205 Lake.

Banker
De Stefano, Emilio, 416 Clark.

Music Teachers

Altomare, Rocco, 206 N. Sangamon.
Boccabadati, Elena, 245 State.
Carati, Felice.

De Campi, Eliodoro, 241 Wabash.
De Prosse, Angelo, 241 Wabash.
Valisi, Cesare, 241 Wabash.

Valisi, Giuseppe, 241 Wabash (composer)

Physicians
Centaro, Vincent, 86 N. Wells.

Lagorio, Antonio, 79 W. Madison.

Macaroni Manufacturers
Canepa Bros., 101 Indiana.

Nardi, Luigi, 136 N. Halsted.

Uccello, Giacomo, 412 So. Canal.

Consul
Paul Bainotti, 110 La Salle.

Church
Church of the Assumption, Illinois near N. Market.
Rev. Moretti, pastor, assisted by Rev. Trussi and Rev. Moreschini.

Societies
Bersaglieri di Savoia, 228 4th Ave.
President, Luigi Spizzirri; Treasurer, G. Spizzirri; Secretary, E. G. Meli.
Societa' Cristoforo Colombo, 208 La Salle St.
President, G. Ginocchio; Vice President, Paul Basso; Secretary, E. G. Meli; Treasurer, Louis Spizzirri.
Societa' Italiana di Unione e fratellanza, 112 Randolph.
President, A. Arata; Secretary, G. Segale.

ITALIAN PHYSICIANS IN CHICAGO (1928)

Abele, L. H.
30 North Michigan Avenue
Abelio, Geo.
307 North Michigan Avenue
Abelio, J. M.
4554 Broadway
Ablaza, Avelino
3250 East Eighty-ninth Street
Adamo, Frank
4753 Broadway
Albano, Zito Galileo
3506 West Chicago Avenue
Allegretti, J. E.
1946 West Grand Avenue
Andrea, L. M.
2458 Wentworth Avenue
Aste, Geo. J.
55 East Washington Boulevard
Aurelio, Angelo
1031 South Ashland Avenue
Baratta, Fred L.
3107 Wentworth Avenue
Bellizzi, Alfredo
2600 Wallace
Benedetto, Joseph A.
6815 Sheridan Road
Berardi, James B., Jr.
3243 North Laramie
Biankini, Anton
4722 Woodlawn Avenue
Borrelli, Wm. F.
1657 West Marquette Road
Brianza, Arthur Mario
108 North State
Bruno, G. B.
812 North Dearborn
Camera, A. V.
5953 West Grand Avenue
Campione, N. L.
3037 Wentworth Avenue
Carfora, Alfonso
2451 West Adams Street
Cella, L. E.
4100 West Madison Street
Chesrow, A. J.
925 Blue Island Avenue
Chesrow, Eugene J.
925 Blue Island Avenue
Cicotte, Fred. J.
4621 Broadway
Cienciara, Felicia
1152 Milwaukee
Ciotola, Eleuterio
5001 West Chicago Avenue
Cipriani, J. B.
8 North Western Avenue
Conforti, James H.
1311 Taylor Street
Copia, Geo. H.
3658 Wentworth
Cortesi, D.
1122 West Erie Street
Crapple, William
1417 North California Avenue
Cuonzo, Peter
3655 West Chicago Avenue

Phone Monroe 6736

Dr. Peter Cutrera

Physician and Surgeon

501 North Halsted Street

Damiani, Salvator
601 West Division
De Feo, Amos
930 Blue Island Avenue
De La Garza
Damiani, J.
765 Milwaukee Avenue
9 South Kedzie Avenue
Del Beccaro, Edward
4918 West Monroe Street
De Luca, A.
1001 South Ashland Avenue
De Rosa, Rocco
1010 South Halsted Street
Di Ciro, D.
1552 West Sixty-ninth Street
Di Cosola, Frank
947 Taylor Street
Di Marca, Joseph M.
4100 Milwaukee Avenue
Dispensa, Rose
1547 West Chicago Avenue
Di Todaro, August
55 East Washington
Doretti, Peter J.
5434 West North Avenue
Drago, R. C.
3536 South Hamilton Avenue
Eterno, James
4321 West North Avenue
Eterno, John
135 Kensington Avenue
Fara, F.
3341 West Twenty-sixth Street
Farina, Joseph
433 West Division Street
Felicetti, Theresa
947 Taylor Street
Ferno, T. J.
7 West Madison Street
Ferri, N. A.
4003 West Madison Street
Filetti, Vincent
1536 West Grand Avenue
Frana, Anton O.
6254 South Kedze Avenue
Furno, Peter H.
1001 South Racine Street
Galgano, Michael
630 North Ogden Avenue

Galla, Joseph
5319 Argyle Street
Gentile, Carolina
2500 Wentworth Avenue
Geraci, Angelo
1201 West Grand Avenue
Geraci, Samuel
1201 West Grand Avenue
Gialloreti, V.
2043 Polk Street

Governale, Samuel L.
3046 Wentworth Avenue
Guca, Duro
1801 South Racine Avenue
Guido, Frank
5801 South Francisco
Indovina, Vincenzo
2546 Wentworth Avenue
Ingrao, Sebastiano
3634 West Chicago Avenue
Ladova, Rosalie M.
1619 Howard Street
Lagorio, Antonio
812 North Dearborn
Lagorio, Frank
812 North Dearborn
Larocca, Joseph
3750 Chicago Avenue
Lavieri, Jack
3635 West Chicago Avenue
LoBraico, Rocco V.
3042 Wentworth Avenue
Luria, A.
803 West Madison Street

Maltese, A. G.
319 Kensington Avenue
Marzano, Vincent
5044 Sheridan Road
Mastandrea, Lewis
2458 Wentworth Avenue
Menzalora, M.
5809 West Grand Avenue
Modica, Vincent
512 North Halsted Street
Monaco, Attilio
1000 South Paulina Street
Monaco, Donat F.
1400 West Sixty-ninth Street
Nardi, John B.
501 North Halsted Street
Nicola, Leo J.
6355 Broadway
Nicolai, J. L.
3815 North Ridgeway
Nigro, R. A.
708 Taylor Street
Nuzzo, Vincenzo
1163 West Harrison Street
Pacella, M.
5308 Fulton Street
Pagano, Aurelio
600 Blue Island Avenue
Pagano, Ralph
600 Blue Island Avenue
Palmisano, Dominic
1314 West Grand Avenue
Pape, J. A.
11441 South Michigan Avenue
Partipilo, A. V.
3363 West Chicago Avenue
Passarella, Frank A.
162 North State Street
Patera, Frank J.
1152 North Ashland Boulevard
Patera, Edw.
1809 Loomis Street
Patillo, Richard
25 East Washington Boulevard
Penchina, M.
1200 North Ashland Avenue
Pintozzi, Carmen
1010 South Halsted Street
Pisani, Vito
1154 Taylor Street
Pishotta, John
1000 Belmont Avenue
Ravasi, Angelo
11452 South Michigan Avenue
Romano, G.
1035 West Grand Avenue
Romano, John R.
1001 South Ashland Avenue
Ronga, G.
1200 McAllister Place
Rossi, Stano V.
3423 West Chicago Avenue
Scaletta, Vincent A.
1445 North Lawler Avenue
Sciarretta, Sylvio
800 West North Avenue
Serritella, M.
925 Blue Island Avenue

Sodaro, Anthony
  943 Taylor Street
Spalo, Rose
  930 Blue Island Avenue
Stranges, Giovanni
  2930 Polk Street
Suldane, John A.
  930 Blue Island Avenue
Taglia, Vito
  919 Taylor Street
Tivilini, A. C.
  522 South Kedze Avenue

Tornabene, Vincent
  5407 Hirsch Street
Tufo, Gustave F.
  104 South Michigan Boulevard
Valenta, Josephine
  190 North State Street
Vella, Salvatore
  3044 Wentworth Avenue
Vitullo, John M.
  933 South Ashland Avenue
Volini, Italo
  31 North State

ITALIAN ARCHITECTS OF CHICAGO (1928)

Capraro, A. V.
  (See photo section)
Del Campo, Scipio
  (See photo section)
Gliatto, Leonard Anthony
  343 South Dearborn Street
Gregori, Raymond
  134 North La Salle
Presto, William C.
  308 North Michigan Avenue

*Rebori, A. N.
  332 South Michigan Boulevard
Sillani, Muzio
  2511 North Clark Street
Valerio, Francis M.
  Valerio & Ullrich
  5 North La Salle Street
**Zucco, Angelo
  4241 Broadway

*Mr. Rebori is a former professor of architectural design at the Chicago Art Institute. He is considered today as one of the leading architects of Chicago. A former student at the Massachusetts Institute of Technology, Mr. Rebori spent two years abroad studying at the Fine Arts Institutes of Paris and Rome. In 1914 he was chairman of the Architects Committee of Michigan Boulevard Extension. He was associated with Holabird and Roche in the designing of the Roanoke Tower. His work includes the Studebaker and Four Cohans Theatres, the Racquet Club, the Riding Club of Chicago, the southeast corner of Wacker Drive and La Salle Street, and many other city landmarks.
**Mr. Zucco formerly was connected with the Chicago Rapid Transit Lines.

ITALIAN LAWYERS IN CHICAGO (1928)

Alfini, Anthony W.
  3927 Belden Avenue
  Born at Naples, Italy, 1900
  LL. B., De Paul University
  Admitted to bar 1922
Allegretti, Francis
  (See photo section)
Arado, Charles C.
  110 South Dearborn Street
  Born in Chicago, 1897
  LL. B., Northwestern University Law School
  Admitted to bar 1920
Barasa, Bernard P.
  (See photo section)
Bisesi, C. J.
  112 West Adams Street
  Born in Brooklyn, New York, 1903
  LL. B., Kent College of Law, 1924
Bonelli, Nuncio
  139 North Clark Street
Brizzolara, Jno. A.
  708 North Wells Street
Buoscio, Felix M.
  9130 Commercial Avenue
  Born in Chicago, 1901
  Ph. B. and J. D., University of Chicago
  Admitted to bar 1925
Caliendo, Anthony
  1201 West Harrison Street
Champagne, Anthony
Chiesa, Spiro
  160 North La Salle Street

Chisesi, Vincent
  155 North Clark Street
Clementi, Anthony
  32 West Washington Street
Chesrow, David S.
  (See photo section)
Cirese, Helen M.
  139 North Clark Street
Costabile, Michael
Covelli, D. A.
  10 North Clark Street
  Born in Chicago, 1904
  LL. B., Kent College of Law
  Admitted to bar 1926
Covello, R. R.
  7 South Dearborn Street
Crapple, Guy
  (See photo section)
Cuneo, Francis J.
  140 North Dearborn Street
  Born in Chicago, 1896
  LL. B., Northwestern Law School
  Assistant attorney general for Illinois, 1922-1927
  Former assistant corporation counsel
Cuttone, Vito
  (See photo section)
De Bartolo, Frank
  127 North Dearborn Street
  Born in Chicago in 1892
  LL. B., Chicago Kent College of Law
  Admitted to bar 1915

De Grazia, John
  155 North Clark Street
  Born in Trevigno, Italy
  LL. B., Chicago Kent College of Law
  Admitted to bar 1907
  President Justinian Society
De Stefano, Rocco
  160 North La Salle Street
Ferrari, Ettore
  901 South Ashland Avenue
Ferrio, Emil
  21 South Clark Street
Fiore, Jos. M.
  (See photo section)
Gigliotti, Cairoli
  105 West Monroe Street
Gualano, Alberto
  (See photo section)
Guidarelli, M. H.
  139 North Clark Street
Ingraffia, F.
  123 West Madison Street
Insalata, S.
  105 North Clark Street
Landise, Thomas
  (See photo section)
Lauro, Mario
  (See photo section)
Leo, Louis J.
  134 North La Salle Street
Lettiere, Louis
  6131 South Campbell Avenue
Libonati, E. M.
  155 North Clark Street
Libonati, R. V.
  (See photo section)
Lupe, John J.
  (See photo section)
Malato, Stephen A.
  155 North Clark Street
Marchello, Maurice R.
  64 West Randolph Street
  Born Coal City, Illinois, 1902
  J. D., University of Chicago Law School,
  1926
  Awarded International Institute of Educa-
  tion scholarship at University of Rome,
  Italy, 1922
Meccia, John B.
  3329 North Springfield Avenue
Mercurio, A.
  160 North La Salle Street
Mirabella, Frank
  160 North La Salle Street
Navigato, Wm.
  15 North Clark Street
Nicolai, Joseph H.
  Assistant state's attorney
  4648 Kenmore Avenue
Orrico, Joseph
  155 North Clark Street
Pace, Vincent
  11 West Washington Street
Parrillo, William
  Assistant United States district attorney
  (See photo section)

Pieruccini, H. E.
  7 South Dearborn Street
Pio, Jas. Percival
  39 South La Salle Street
Pope, Nicholas
  160 North La Salle Street
Prete, Frank
  139 North Clark Street
Quilici, G. L.
  105 West Monroe Street
Raimondi, Biagio
  1648 Polk Street
Romano, Michael
  134 North La Salle Street
Repetto, F. H.
  304 South Dearborn Street
Rinella, Sam A.
Rizzio, Donald J.
  (See photo section)
Rosinia, Michael
  (See photo section)
Russo, William J.
  Born in Chicago, 1896
  LL. B., Northwestern University
  Admitted to bar 1923
Sarley, J. F.
  208 South La Salle Street
Sasso, Henry E.
  Born in Italy, 1901
  LL. B., Kent College of Law
  Admitted to bar 1925
Sbarbaro, John A.
  (See photo section)
Schiavone, Anthony J.
  808 W. Harrison Street
Solari, J.
  332 South Michigan Avenue
  Attorney for and secretary, Peabody Coal
  Company, a corporation owning or con-
  trolling an estimated aggregate of over
  one billion (1,000,000,000) tons of coal.
  Mr. Solari is a director of several other
  large corporations.
Sorna, James
  155 North Clark Street
Spatuzza, George
  (See photo section)
Susina, Samuel
  1522 West Chicago Avenue
Taglia, J.
  77 West Washington Street
Tocco, H.
  160 North La Salle Street
Tufo, Henry
  105 West Monroe Street
Ungaro, Gerard M.
  134 North La Salle Street
  Born in Chicago, 1893
  LL. B., Northwestern University
Valens, Dominic H.
  155 North Clark Street
Viviano, Vito J.
Zaffina, Giuseppe
  127 North Dearborn Street

Illustrations

A group of members of the Justinian Society of Advocates at the annual ball given on February 16, 1928, at the Congress Hotel. First row, left to right: F. Buoscio, F. De Bartolo, Anthony Mercurio, Judge John Lupe, Judge F. Allegretti, Joseph Orrico, Secretary, John De Grazia, President, Miss Helen Cirese, President, Miss Helen Cirese, Judge F. Borrelli, ex-Judge Alberto Gualano, Rocco De Stefano. Second row, left to right: M. Constabile, Guy C. Crapple, Joseph Taglia, Vincent Chisesi, G. Zaffina, Treasurer, Chas. Arado, Salvatore Mirabella, Stefano Malato, Maurice Marchello, George Quilici, Orazio Tocco, Anthony Clementi, Nunzio Bonelli, John B. Meccia, William Russo.

Members of the Supreme Council of the Italo-American National Union. From left to right: Dr. S. Ingrao, Medical Director; Mr. V. Ferrara, Supreme Treasurer; ex-Judge Bernard P. Barasa, Supreme President; C. Vitello, First Vice President; P. Scaduto, Supreme Secretary.

FRANCIS B. ALLEGRETTI

Judge of the Municipal Court

Born in Trevigno, Potenza, Italy, on March 21, 1881. Came to America at the age of five. Educated at Hamilton College of Law. Admitted to bar in 1914. Elected Judge of the Municipal Court in 1924. One of the first truant officers in the city, from 1904 to 1914.

Member Elks Club, Knights of Columbus, Eagles, Optimist Club, Iriquois Club, Royal League, American Brotherhood, and several others. Resides at 17 So. Waller Avenue.

ARMATO, MICHELE
President Olive Can Company

Born at Sambuca, Agrigento, Italy, 1883. In America since 1897. President Olive Can Company since 1923. Resides at 2130 No. Lawler Avenue.

BAMBARA, ENRICO
Theater Owner

Born at Villa San Giovanni, Reggio Calabria, Italy, 1884. In America since 1900. In Chicago since 1910. Chairman Agricultural Committee, Italian Chamber of Commerce, 1925-1926. Member, Italian Chamber of Commerce since 1922. Venerable, Ansonia Lodge, Order Sons of Italy. Member Italo-American National Union. Member Theater Owners Association of America. Office, Avenue Theater, 306 So. Cicero Avenue.

BIGALLI, DINO
Assistant Conductor Chicago Civic Opera Company

Born at Florence, Italy. In America since 1913. American citizen. Pupil of Ildebrando Pizzetti. Formerly professor of Organ and harmony at Royal Conservatory of Music of Florence, Italy.

CANINI, ITALO EMILIO
President, Italian Chamber of Commerce

Born in Venice, Italy. In America since 1876. In Chicago since 1897. Importer of hand carved furniture.

Secretary, Italian Consulate, Philadelphia, 1878-1882. Vice-Pres. Exhibition Association California Midwinter International Exposition, San Francisco, 1894. Pres. Italian Chamber of Commerce since 1926. Chevalier of the Italian Crown. Author: "Four Hundred Years of Spanish Rule in Cuba," Chicago, 1898. Contributor to various publications. American citizen since 1884. Office 22 Quincy Street.

CAPRARO, ALEXANDER V.
Architect

Born at Pietrabbondante, Campobasso, Italy. In America since 1899. Graduate of Joseph Medill High School. Armour Institute of Technology 1912-1914. Later studied at Chicago Art Institute. Admitted to practice in 1916.

Member Illinois Society of Architects, Knights of Columbus, Italian Chamber of Commerce, Elmhurst Golf & Country Club, Frontenac Athletic Club.

Architect for the first Branch Public Library at Crawford and 27th St. Architect for Casa Bonita Apartments, one of the most handsome and most exclusive apartments in Chicago. Office, 7 So. Dearborn Street.

CASAZZA, FRANK C.
Distributor of Automobile Supplies

Born in Chicago, 1892. Graduate of Jones North Chicago Business College. President, Casazza Co., Inc., a company doing an annual business of over $200,-000 a year.

Member, Illinois Chamber of Commerce, Rotary Club, Dairymen Country Club, Mission Country Club, B. P. O. E. (Chicago) Knights of Columbus, Greater Chicago La Salle Club, etc. Office, 504-516 North Wells St.

BARASA, BERNARD P.
Attorney at Law

Born in Negaunee, Mich. April 15, 1875. Educated at University of Michigan, LLB., 1904. Chicago Kent College of Law, 1905. Admitted to Bar, 1905. Attorney for Italian Consulate, 1906-1910. Judge of the Municipal Court, 1916-1924. Special Corporation Counsel City of Chicago in Chicago, North Shore and Milwaukee case against City of Chicago. Candidate for Member of Board of Review, April 10, 1928 running ahead of ticket with over 100,000 votes. Four Minute man and member American Protective League during the war. Head of various committees. Chevalier of Italian Crown. President, Italo-American National Union since 1922. Member of Justinian Society, Lake Shore Athletic Club, Columbia Country Club, Elks and many other organizations. Member, Chicago, Illinois and American Bar Associations. Office, 123 W. Madison Street.

CHESROW, DAVID S.
Attorney at Law

Born in Chicago, 1902. Valparaiso University Law School, LLB., 1923. Chicago Kent College of Law, Master of Laws, 1925. Admitted to Bar, 1926. Appointed Committeeman for 27th ward by National Republican Party (Deneen Group) February 14, 1927. Member of Chicago Bar Association, Sigma Delta Kappa Fraternity, Masters Legal Club of Chicago, Justinian Society of Advocates, Breakers Beach Country Club, and Frontenac Athletic Club. Office 134 North LaSalle Street. West Side Office, 930 Blue Island Avenue. (Evenings only.)

CRAPPLE, GUY C.
Attorney at Law

Born in Chicago in 1888. Graduate of Northwestern University Law School, 1913. Assistant U. S. District Attorney, 1923-1925. Assistant State's Attorney, 1921. Attorney in charge, tax litigations Cook County, 1920-21. Assistant Sanitary District Attorney, 1922. Member American and Illinois Bar Associations. Member, Oak Park Elks Club, Antlers Country Club, Libertyville Golf Club, etc. Office 105 N. Clark.

CUTTONE, VITO BIANCO
Attorney at Law

Born at Partanna, Trapani, Italy, 1888. Doctor of Jurisprudence, University of Palermo, 1912. Officer in the Italian Army, 1908-1910. Lybian War, 1911. In America since 1914. Admitted to Bar, 1915. Second Lieutenant U. S. Army, 1918. Assistant State's Attorney, 1920. Grand Orator, Grand Lodge Order Sons of Italy for Illinois, since its inception in 1924. Member, Chicago and American Bar Association. Resides, Edgewater Beach Hotel. Office, 134 No. La Salle Street.

DADDI, FRANCESCO
Teacher of Singing

Born in Naples, Italy. Educated in Italy. In America since 1906. Formerly connected as Tenor with Manhattan Opera Company and Chicago Civic Opera Company (1906-1920). Member, Society of American Musicians, Cliff Dwellers, and several others. Studio, 410 So. Michigan Avenue.

DE CARLO, PASQUALE
Pastor, St. John Presbyterian Church

Born at Calitri, Avellino, Italy. In America since 1890. Studied at Collegio Torquato Tasso, Salerno, 1878, 1884. Pastor of St. John Presbyterian Church with Garibaldi Institute. Editor and Publisher, Vita Nova. Field Representative, Church Extension Board, Presbytery of Chicago. Has organized about twenty missions and churches in America. Member of Council and Chapter of Masonic Order. Member of the Columbia Commandery, Knight Templar, Carducci Lodge, Ind. Ord. Odd Fellows.

DE JEAN, H.
Manager, Foreign Department Reliance Bank

Born at Bisceglia, Bari. In America since 1906. Graduate in philosophy from the Jesuit Gregorian University Rome, Italy. Formerly professor of Italian language and literature. Married.

D'ESPOSITO, JOSHUA
Consulting Engineer, Chicago Union Station Co.

Born in Italy in 1870. Graduate of Royal Nautical Institute, Sorrento, Italy. Designing Engineer with Pittsburgh Railway Co. until 1904. Entered service of Pennsylvania Lines in 1905 and became chief draftsman in 1907. In Chicago since 1913. Assistant Chief Engineer of Chicago Union Station Company, 1914-1917. Assistant Manager, Wood Ship Division of Emergency Fleet Corporation, in charge of the installation of machinery in wooden ships. Chief Engineer, Chicago Union Station Company, 1919, in charge of all the construction and responsible for a great deal of the designing of that building. General Manager in charge of the operation of the building, as well as Chief Engineer, 1925.

At present consulting engineer for Chicago Union Station, Daily News Building, and many other important undertakings. Chairman of Architects Committee, selected by Association of Commerce to supervise the new Municipal Civic Hall of Chicago. Chairman, Building Code Committee, Western Society of Engineers, etc. Member, American Society of Civil Engineers. Member, Union League Club, Parkridge Country Club, Illinois Country Club and several others. Residence: 6963 Sheridan Road.

DE SALVIO, ALFONSO
College Professor,
Northwestern University

Born Orsara di Puglia, Italy, 1873. A. B. Trinity College, 1889. A. B. Harvard, 1902. A. M., 1903. PHD, 1904. Student, University of Paris. At Northwestern University since 1904. Member, Modern Language Association of America. Modern Language Teachers Association. Member, University Club, Evanston. Edited Tamayo's Lo Positivo. Fogazzaro's Pereat Rochus, Translated from the Spanish De Quiro's Modern Theories of Criminology. 1911—from Italian and Latin, Dealogues concerning two new sciences, by Galileo Galilei. (With Prof. H. C. Crew) 1914. Home, 1115 Davis Street, Evanston.

DE TULLIO, MARIO
Vice-President and Treasurer, Isotta
Motors of Illinois, Inc.

Born at Sepino, Campobasso, Italy, 1892. Educated in Italy. Aviation Inspector for U. S. Government during the war. Technical Expert on Caproni airplanes, with Italian Military Commission. Chicago Representative for Isotta Fraschini Automobiles, with luxurious show rooms at 846 Rush Street.

DURANTE, OSCAR
Editor

Born, Naples, 1869. Educated Istituto e Collegio Liebler, Naples. In Chicago since 1885. At age of 16 established "L' Italia." Cable Correspondent, "Chicago Tribune." Rome, Italy, 1899-1900, appointed U. S. Consul at Catania, Italy by Pres. McKinley, 1898. Member of American Commission for establishment of U. S. Postal service in Porto Rico taking first U. S. registered mail across island in two covered wagons. Official interpreter, U. S. A., assistant postmaster, San Juan Porto Rico, 1899. Special representative, Secretary of Labor at Chicago, 1923. Made survey of foreign language people in U. S. Chevalier, Italian Crown. Member, Chicago Board of Public Education. Translated De Amicis, Cuore, compiled Italian and English grammars and dictionaries. Office, 84 W. Harrison Street.

DEL CAMPO, SCIPIO
Architect in charge for Chicago Board of Local Improvements

Born in San Marco in Lamis, Foggia, Italy. In America since 1903. Architect in charge for the Board of Local Improvements since 1923. In charge of designing and supervision of the architectural work of Wacker Drive. Architect for $2,000,000 Arlington Park Race Track, at Arlington Heights, Ill. Residence, 2955 N. Kilpatrick Avenue.

EWALD, SILVIO

*General Agent for Western States
De Nobili Cigar Co.*

Born at Biella, Vercelli, Italy. In America since 1896. Educated at Royal Technical School in Italy. Married. Member, Elks Club. Resides at 2640 Coyle Avenue, Rogers Park.

FERRARA, VINCENT E.

Asst. Cashier, North Ave. State Bank

Born at Castelbuono, Palermo, 1887. In America since 1901. Student at Y. M. C. A. Business College and Northwestern University School of Commerce (1916-20). Assistant Cashier North Avenue State Bank. Vice-Pres. Italian Chamber of Commerce. Asst. Mgr. Foreign Department, Northern Trust Co., 1917-1926. Treasurer and member of Supreme Council, Italo-Amer. Nat'l Union, since 1922. Treasurer and member Executive Committee, Lower North Community Council since 1920. Member Senatorial Committee, 29th district. Chairman, 49th district State Council of Defense, 1917-1918. Member Lake Shore Athletic Club, La Salle Club, Northwestern Club, Member, Board of Directors, Italian Chamber of Commerce since 1922.

FABBRI, ALBERT H.
President, Northwestern Expanded Metal Co.

Born in Chicago, 1884. Started as messenger boy. President, Northwestern Expanded Metal Co., a corporation doing an annual business of several million dollars. President of Northwestern Steel Products Co. President Chicago Association of Credit Men, 1926-1927. President of Associated Metal Lath Manufacturers. Director, Credit Men Asso., Member, Ways and Means Committee, Chicago Asso. of Com. (Iron and steel division). Member, Knights of Columbus, Catholic Order of Foresters, Hamilton Club, Economic Club, Ridgemoor Country Club, Big Sand Lake Club, Field Museum, Art Institute, etc. Resides at 4741 No. Paulina Street.

FIORE, JOSEPH M.
Attorney at Law

Born at Montalbano D'Elicona, Messina, Italy. In America since 1905. Educated at University of Buffalo, College of Arts and Sciences,.1915-17, University of Chicago, summer sessions, 1916-1917, De Paul University Law School, 1917-1918. University of Buffalo Law School, LLB., 1920. Admitted to Illinois Bar, 1921. Member, American, Illinois State, and Chicago Bar Associations. Member, Justinian Society of Advocates and several other organizations. Office, 127 N. Dearborn Street.

FRANCO, GIUSEPPE R.
Physician and Surgeon

Born in Chicago, 1904. Doctor of Medicine University of Illinois, 1928.

LAURO, MARIO
Attorney at Law

Born in Naples, Italy, 1893. Graduate of Military College of Rome. Cadet in Royal Italian Navy. Graduate of Royal Technical Institute of Leghorn. Graduate of Royal University of Pisa (Doctor of Jurisprudence) Member of Italian Bar. Recognized as Expert of Italian Law by Great Lakes Office of U. S. Dept. of Commerce. (1927.) Organizer and Secretary, Ente Portuale di Livorno (1919-1923). Chevalier of the Italian Crown. Interstate Deputy of Fascisti League of North America for Illinois and Michigan. Organizer, Chicago "Fascio Giorgio Moriani." Contributor to newspapers, magazines, etc. Office, 155 N. Clark Street.

LIBONATI, ROLAND V.
Attorney at Law

Born in Chicago. Graduate of A. A. Lewis Institute, 1918. University of Michigan, A. B. 1921. Michigan and Northwestern Law School, J. D., 1924. Admitted to bar in 1924. First Lieut. U. S. Army during war. Attorney for West Parks, 1927. Assistant City Attorney for City of Chicago, 1928. Member, Illinois Bar and Cook County Bar Associations. Member, Fort Dearborn Athletic Club, Hamilton Club, Sportsman Club, Camels Club, etc.

GUALANO, ALBERTO N.
Attorney at Law

Born at San Vincenzo Al Volturno, Campobasso, Italy, 1868. In America since 1892. Educated at Collegio Vittorio Emanuele Naples, Italy, Northwestern University and Illinois College of Law, Chicago. Admitted to Bar, 1904. Judge of the Municipal Court, 1922. Member, Illinois Bar Association. Member, National Union, Modern Woodmen, Italo-American National Union, Arte e Professioni, Phi, Alpha, Delta fraternity, etc. Office, 145 N. Clark Street.

INGRAO, SEBASTIANO
Physician and Surgeon

Born at Grotte, Agrigento, Italy, 1890. Graduate with honors of Liceo Ruggero Settimo, Caltanissetta, 1909. Doctor of Medicine, Loyola University, 1923. On Staff of St. Ann and Jefferson Park Hospitals. Lieutenant, Italian Army, 1910. Took part in Lybian War, 1911-1912. Came to America in 1913. Returned to Italy, 1915. In Italian Army during the World War, 1915-1918. Medical Director and Member of the Supreme Council, Italo-American National Union. Office, 3634 W. Chicago Avenue.

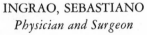

LAGORIO, FRANK A.
Physician and Surgeon

Born in Chiavari, Italy, 1884. St. Ignatius College, A. B., 1904. Northwestern University, M. D., 1911. Associate Director, Chicago Pasteur Institute. On Staff of John B. Murphy Hospital, attending physician, Columbus Hospital. Local surgeon for Chicago and Northwestern Railroad. Member, Kappa Sigma and Alpha, Kappa, Kappa fraternities. American Medical Association, Chicago and State Medical Society. Member, Lakeshore Athletic Club, Delavan Country Club, etc. Office, 812 N. Dearborn.

LANDISE, THOMAS H.
Attorney at Law

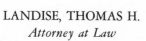

Born in New York, 1892. Graduate of Northwestern University Law School, 1917. Assistant State's Attorney, 1921-1923. Admitted to Bar, 1917. Member, American and Illinois State Bar Associations. Member, La Salle Club, Kilwinning Lodge, A. F. & A. M., 311. American Legion, etc. Member and one of founders of the Italian Club of Chicago. One of incorporators and former President, Justinian Society of Advocates. Supreme Trustee, Italo-American National Union. Office, 100 W. Monroe Street.

LAGORIO, ANTONIO
Physician and Surgeon
Grand Officer of the Italian Crown

Born in Chicago, 1857. Graduate of Rush Medical College, 1879. Post-graduate student Universities of Rome and Genoa, Italy. LLD, Loyola University. Founder and President of first Pasteur Institute in the West, in 1890. Member of Board of Directors, Chicago Public Library since 1906. President of same, 1913 and 1917. Member, Board of Trustees, House of Correction, 1904-06, Director, Cosmopolitan Bank, Life Member, Touring Club Italiano. Member, American Medical Association, Chicago Medical Society, etc. Office, 812 N. Dearborn Street. (See also Chapter on Educational Activities).

LO PRESTI, DANIEL D.
Importer of Italian Products

Born at Misilmeri, Palermo, Italy, 1896. In America since 1912. U. S. Citizen since 1917. Head of the Firm, Lo Presti Brothers importers and wholesale grocers. Member, Fort Dearborn Athletic Club, Turtle Lake Country Club and several others.

LUZZO, SAMUEL P.
President, Executive Council Hod Carriers Union

Born in Chicago, 1880. President, Executive Council Hod Carriers Building & Common Laborers Union of Chicago and Vicinity. Member of Illinois Athletic Commission. President, Track Layers Union; President, Factory yards and Mill Laborers Union. Vice President Chicago Building Trades Council. Active in the promotion of Illinois waterway. Member, Fort Dearborn Athletic Club, member of the B. P. O. E. Elks, Oak Park, Fish Fans Club, etc.

MASTROVALERIO CHEV. ALESSANDRO
Editor

Born on the Gargano, Italy, 1855. In America since 1882. On editorial staff of Progresso Italo-Americano of New York, 1883. Editor and Publisher of "Tribuna Transatlantica" since its inception in 1898. Founder of one of the first Italian agricultural colonies in U. S. (Daphne, Baldwin County, Alabama, 1886). Instrumental in the passing of the compulsory education law in Illinois. First Truant Officer in the city of Chicago. Author of a study on "The Italians in argiculture" reprinted in the volumes of the Industrial Commission. Actively interested in the affairs of Hull House ever since its foundation.

MACARINI, TITO LIVIO
Painter

Born at Lucca, Italy, 1899. In America since 1923. Graduate of Royal Institute of Fine Arts, Lucca, a branch of the Royal Institute of Florence. (Titular Professor.) Author of several mural paintings in the Church of St. Mathews. Decorator of several churches, theaters and cabarets in Chicago and other cities. Member, South Side Art Society, Illinois Art Society. Studio, 2942 Indiana Avenue.

LAVECCHA, JOHN
Official Photographer to Cardinal Mundelein and The Chicago Archdiocese

Born Paterno, Potenza, 1881. Came over in 1894. Studied at Chicago Art Institute 1898, 1899. (Miniature and Portrait painting.)

President Chicago Portrait Photographers Association, 1925. Vice President of same, 1921-1924. Official photographer for Eucharistic Congress, 1926. One of five judges of the Photographers Association of America on the Master Degree since 1926. One of three members of jury of selection, 25th Annual Exhibition of Chicago Photographers Salon, Art Institute, 1928. Studio, 612 N. Michigan Avenue.

MARIMPIETRI, A. D.
Vice-President Amalgamated Trust and Savings Bank

Born in Barete, Aquila, Italy, 1884. In America since 1905. Vice-President Amalgamated Trust and Savings Bank since 1924. Member of Board of Directors of same, since 1922. Member of General Executive Board, Amalgamated Clothing Workers of America since 1914. Manager Unemployment Insurance Fund A. C. W., Director, Employment Department Chicago Branch of A. C. W. Head of Price Department A. C. W. Chicago Branch. President local 39, coatmakers. Member City Club.

MILANI, LUIGI
Manufacturer

Born at Pietrasanta, Lucca, 1875. In America since 1904. Originator of the French Salad Dressing in America. Founder of The Milani Co., recognized as the leading firm of its kind in America. (The Milani Co. in 1928 was taken over by the Kraft Cheese Co. with salad plants in New York and San Francisco.) Member, North Shore Motor Co., Alpine Club, Chicago Art Institute, etc.

Vice President, Italian Chamber of Commerce.

MONACO, GINO
Professor of Languages

Born at Catania, Italy, 1890. In America since 1917. University of Catania, PH. D., 1912. On staff of St. Louis University, St. Louis, Mo., 1920-1921. Among Professor Monaco's pupils are the members of some of the most aristocratic families in Chicago. Studio, 410 So. Michigan Avenue.

MORINA, GIUSEPPE
Resident Manager, Chicago Agency of Banco di Napoli

Born in Naples, Italy. In America since 1926.

NAVIGATO, ROCCO D.
Artist

Born in Chicago in 1895. Educated at Chicago Academy of Fine Arts, 1910-1911; Chicago Art Institute, 1914-1915. Art director for the former Thos. Cusack Co., the largest outdoor advertising company in the world, 1920-1924. Secretary, Free Lance Artists Guild of Chicago (Branch of the Authors League of America). Member, Palette and Chisel Club. Designer of a series of posters for the Chicago Rapid Transit Lines, Field Museum, Wrigley Co., Stevens Hotel, etc. Studio, Wrigley Building.

OTTOLIN, FERNANDO H.
Vice-President, Italian Trust and Savings

Born in Venice, Italy. In America since 1907. Education: McGill University, Montreal and Northwestern University, Chicago. Director, Lake City Discount Corporation and Prudential Securities Corporation.

LUPE, JOHN J.
Judge of the Municipal Court

Born in Chicago. Graduate of John Marshall Law School. Admitted to Bar, 1909. Judge of the Municipal Court since 1923. Member, Chicago, Illinois and American Bar Associations, Lawyers Association of Illinois, Justinian Society of Advocates, Lincolnshire Golf Club, Evergreen Golf Club, Chicago Rod and Gun Club, Wisconsin Fishing Club, Elks, Frontenac Club, Moose, Knights of Pythias, American Brotherhood and several others. Resides at 901 E. 40th Street.

PARRILLO, WILLIAM
Assistant U. S. District Attorney

Born in Chicago, 1903. Graduate Kent College of Law, 1926. Admitted to Bar, 1926.

Member, Chicago Bar Association. Illinois Bar Association. Justinian Society, etc. President, 25th Ward Republican Club. Office, Federal Building.

PROVENZANO, ANGELO

Secretary and Manager, A. Lombardo & Co., Importers and Wholesalers of Italian Products.

Born in Palermo. In America since 1899. U. S. citizen since 1904. Married. Resides at 5960 Race Avenue.

PRIGNANO, A. J.
Alderman of 20th Ward

Born in Chicago, 1891. Educated at Old Polk Street and Dante Schools and at Metropolitan Business College. Started as messenger boy with Steele Wedeles & Co., wholesale grocers, rising to the position of tobacco buyer. App. Deputy clerk, Board of Election Commissioners, 1914. App. Secretary to D. J. Egan, Bailiff of Municipal Court, 1918. Appointed District Forester for the Forest Preserve of Cook County, 1924. Elected Alderman of 20th ward, 1927. Director, Public State Bank. Member of several clubs and societies. Office 1120 So. Halsted Street.

QUILICI, GEORGE L.
Attorney at Law

President, Italian Arts Club

Born in Chicago, Ill., 1897. Graduate of De Paul and Northwestern Universities. Admitted to Illinois Bar, 1920. First Lieutenant, U. S. Army (Res.) A. E. F. Member, Justinian Society of Advocates (formerly President) Chicago Bar Association. Illinois State Bar Association. American Bar Association. Phi Alpha Delta Law Fraternity. Reserve Officers Association of United States American Legion; Italian Arts Club (Pres.) Collegiate Club of Chicago. Hamilton Club, etc. Office 105 W. Monroe Street.

RIGALI, JOHN

President, Da Prato Statuary Co.
(Purveyors to the Holy See)

Born at Bagni di Lucca, Italy, 1865. In America since 1881. Former President and Member of the Board of Directors, Italian Chamber of Commerce. Chevalier of Italian Crown. Delegate of Italian Red Cross. Member, Middle West Athletic Club, Alpine Gun Club, etc. Office, 768 W. Adams Street.

RAFFAELI, JOSEPH

Manager, Chicago Civic Opera
Orchestra

Born at Lucca, Italy. In America since 1893. American Citizen. Manager of Chicago Civic Opera Orchestra since its organization in 1910. Formerly with Metropolitan Opera House of New York, and Manhattan Opera House. Graduate of Royal Conservatory of Florence, Italy.

VOLINI, ITALO F.

Professor of Medicine, Loyola University

Born in Chicago. University of Chicago, A. B. Rush Medical College, M. D. Attending physician Cook County and Mercy Hospitals. Consulting physician Columbus Hospital.

President, Loyola Historical Society, President, Italian Club, Loyola University. Member, American Medical Society, Cook County and Chicago Medical Association. Illinois State Medical Society, Italy-America Society, Lake Shore Athletic Club, Middle West Athletic Club, Phi Beta Pi, Alpha, Omega Alpha. Office, 31 No. State Street.

RIZZIO, DONALD J.

Attorney at Law

Born in Italy in 1900. In America since 1906. Educated at Lane Technical High School and De Paul University Law School. Admitted to Bar October, 1926. Member Chicago Bar Association, Justinian Society of Advocates, Italo American National Union, Art and Profession Society, and several others. Office, 110 So. Dearborn Street.

RONGA, GAETANO

Physician and Surgeon

Born at Nola, Italy, 1874. Graduate of Rush Medical College, 1900, M. D. University of Chicago, A. B., 1898. Postgraduate student, University of Strasbourg, Germany, 1901-02. Chief of Staff, Jefferson Park Hospital. Office 1200 MacAlister Place.

ROSINIA, MICHAEL L.

Assistant Corporation Counsel for the City of Chicago

Born in Chicago, 1888. Graduate of Kent College of Law, 1910. Assistant State's Attorney, 1915-1920 (in complete charge of Court of Domestic relations). Assistant Prosecuting Attorney, City of Chicago, 1922-1924. Assistant Corporation Counsel since 1924.

Secretary, Columbia Country Club. Member, Fort Dearborn Athletic Club, member of committee before U. S. Senate against Immigration Act of 1924. Office 155 N. Clark Street.

RUSSO, NUNZIO

President, A. Russo & Co. Inc.
Importers of Italian Products

Born at Termini Imerese, Italy, 1882. In America since 1884. Educated in Chicago. President and Treasurer, A. Russo and Co., importers and wholesalers of groceries, established in Chicago in 1883. Formerly Vice President, Italian Chamber of Commerce. Member of La Salle Club, Kilkare Lodge of Wisconsin, Chicago Art Institute, Italy-America Society, Chicago Association of Commerce, etc. Office 466-468 W. Chicago Avenue.

SALERNO, FRED. G.

Vice-Pres. and Gen. Mgr. Sawyer Biscuit Co.

Born at San File, Cosenza, Italy, 1877. Started with Kennedy Biscuit Works as greaser of pans and worked his way up to the present position with the Sawyer Biscuit Co. Vice-President, United Biscuit Co. Director West Side National Bank. Member, Illinois Athletic Club, Ridgemore Country Club, Elks, etc. Member, Executive Club of Chicago. Resides at 4030 Clarendon Avenue.

SACERDOTE, EDUARDO

Member of Vocal and Operatic Department, American Conservatory of Music.

Born in Asti, Piedmont, 1880. In America since 1913. Graduate of Jurisprudence and Philosophy, R. University of Turin, 1902. Bachelor of Music, Royal Conservatory of Leipzig, 1904. Director of Concerts and composition Department, Royal Conservatory of Athens, Greece, 1904-08. Orchestra Director in Italy, 1908-1910. Conductor of Melba's Opera Company in Sydney and Melbourne, Australia, 1910-11. Instructor of Singing at Chicago Musical College, 1913-1925. Substitute of Cleofonte Campanini at Chicago Opera Co., 1917-1918. Member: Romany Club, Society of American Musicians, Lincolnshire Country Club, Pro Musica, International Society of Modern Music, etc.

ZINGRONE, JOHN B.
Director, X-Ray Department, Mercy Hospital

Born in Iaccurso, Catanzaro, Italy, 1888. Started as elevator boy, in 1906, and worked his way up. Owner of J. B. Zingrone X-Ray Laboratory, one of the finest in the middle west. Instructor of Radiology at Loyola University Medical School. Lecturer for American Catholic Hospital Association. Originator of X-Ray treatment in hooping cough. Life member, Frontenac Athletic Club. Office 104 So. Michigan Avenue.

SCIONTI, SILVIO

Pianist

Silvio Scionti, one of the most brilliant pianists in this country, occupies an enviable position among the teachers of Chicago and America in general. Mr. Scionti, a native of Italy, had the good fortune to be placed under the musical guidance of such masters as Cesi, Martucci and Rossomandi, graduating with the highest honors when nineteen years old at the Conservatory of Naples.

On the staff of the American conservatory of music, since 1912. Former teacher of many of the most gifted pianists in this country. He has appeared with great success with leading Symphony Orchestras of this country, and in hundreds of recitals in all parts of the United States.

SCADUTO, PASQUALE

Secretary, Italo-American National Union

Born at Sutera, Caltanissetta, Italy, 1905. Educated at Ginnasio, Caltanissetta, and at Wheeler Business College, Birmingham, Ala. Royal Italian Consular Agent in Birmingham, 1910. Wholesaler of General Merchandise in Birmingham. Secretary and member Supreme Council Italo-American National Union, since 1926. Member, Odd Fellows and other clubs.

SERRITELLA, DANIEL A.

Inspector of Weights and Measures

Born in Chicago in 1898. Began his career selling papers and at the age of twenty was President of the News Boys Association. Elected Republican committeeman for First Ward, April 10, 1928. President, Periodical Dealers, Member Chicago Council, American Federation of Labor, and Cook County Wage earners League. Member, Knights of Columbus, and several other organizations. President San Vito Riciglianese.

SORAVIA, JOSEPH

Departmental Head, Sears Roebuck.
& Co.

Born in Venice, Italy, 1880. In America since 1897. With Sears Roebuck and Co. since 1901. In charge of four departments, both buying and selling, throughout the United States (Musical instruments, school furniture, pianos, radios, and electrical appliances).

Member, Lake Shore Athletic Club, Ithasca Country Club and others.

Resides at 526 So. Elmwood Avenue, Oak Park.

SPATUZZA, GEORGE J.

Attorney at Law

Born at Ragusa, Italy, 1896. In Chicago since 1908. Northwestern University Law School, LLB., 1917. Admitted to Bar, 1917. President, The Justinian Society of Advocates, 1925 and 1926. Grand Venerable Illinois Grand Lodge, Order Sons of Italy. Member: American Bar Association, Illinois Bar Association, Chicago Bar Association, Justinian Society, Italo-American National Union, Italian Chamber of Commerce, The Knights of Columbus and many other social and fraternal organizations. Married. Office 155 N. Clark Street.

TRINGALI, ANTONIO J.

Assistant Cashier and Mgr. Foreign Dept. Mid-City Trust & Savings Bank

Born at La Spezia. In America since 1909. With Mid-City Bank since 1917. 4th Degree Member, Knights of Columbus, member, Italian Chamber of Commerce, Order Sons of Italy, etc.

VITELLO, COSTANTINO

Wholesale Jeweler

Born, Grotte, Agrigento, Italy, 1881. In Chicago since 1907. First Vice-President, Italo-American National Union. Chairman of the Board, Italo-American National Union, 1924-1927. Four Minute Man, 1917-1918. Fourth Degree Knights of Columbus. Chairman, Finance Committee, Italian Chamber of Commerce, 1926. Office 8, So. Dearborn Street.

ZIROLI, ANGELO

Sculptor

Born at Montenero Valcocchiaro, Campobasso, Italy, 1899. In America since 1913. Graduate of Chicago Art Institute, 1923 (winner of Dunham Prize).

Awarded the Mrs. John C. Shaffer prize for an ideal conception in sculpture. (The Dancing Girl), 1924. Awarded First Prize in Sculpture, Society of Washington Artists, 1928. (The First Born.) Studio, 245 West North Avenue.

FORMUSA, VINCENT
Importer of Italian Products
One of the founders of Italian Chamber
of Commerce, and its Treasurer since
1922. Former Vice-President of same.

TONIATTI, HECTOR
Manufacturing Jeweler
Studio, Pure Oil Bldg., 35 E. Wacker
Drive.

DEL CAMPO, ANGELO RALPH
U. S. Military Academy, West Point

BORZONE, ENRICO
Commercial Artist
Born in Italy. Sculptor of the Water
Kiss Fountain in the lobby of Morrison
Hotel.

MARCHELLO, MAURICE

Attorney at Law, J. D. (cum laude)

University of Chicago Law School. Office, 64 W. Randolph Street.

GRANATA, M. O.

Photographer

Member, Chicago Portrait Association. Studio, 930 Blue Island Avenue.

BONAVENTURA, LEO

Bailiff and Deputy Sheriff

East Chicago.

In America since 1908. Member, Elks Club, Moose Club, Lincoln Political Club, McKinley Political Club, Harrison Political Club and several others.

Constable of Lake County, Indiana, for twelve years, from 1912 to 1924. Delegate to Indiana State Convention, for fourteen years.

Member, Board of Directors, Italian-American National Union Office, 227 Calumet Building.

Chicago Macaroni Company
ONE OF THE LARGEST IN THE WORLD

Capacity 125,000 lbs. a day. Located at Canalport, Sangamon and Morgan Streets, on the Chicago, Burlington and Quincy Railroad, with direct transportation facilities

F. MATALONE, Pres.   P. MORICI, Vice-Pres.   S. MATALONE, Sec.   D. CULICCHIA, Treas.

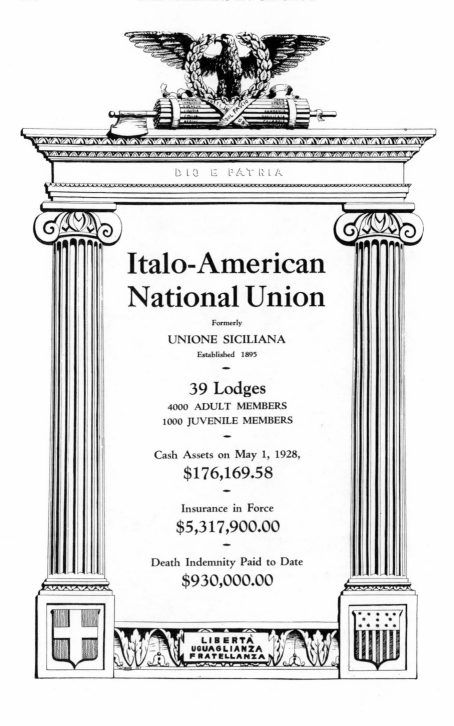

Italo-American National Union

Formerly

UNIONE SICILIANA

Established 1895

—

39 Lodges

4000 ADULT MEMBERS

1000 JUVENILE MEMBERS

—

Cash Assets on May 1, 1928,

$176,169.58

—

Insurance in Force

$5,317,900.00

—

Death Indemnity Paid to Date

$930,000.00

DIO E PATRIA

LIBERTÀ
UGUAGLIANZA
FRATELLANZA

The Italian American Experience

An Arno Press Collection

Angelo, Valenti. **Golden Gate.** 1939

Assimilation of the Italian Immigrant. 1975

Bohme, Frederick G. **A History of the Italians in New Mexico.** (Doctoral Dissertation, The University of New Mexico, 1958). 1975

Boissevain, Jeremy. **The Italians of Montreal:** Social Adjustment in a Plural Society. 1971

Churchill, Charles W. **The Italians of Newark:** A Community Study. (Doctoral Thesis, New York University, 1942). 1975

Clark, Francis E. **Our Italian Fellow Citizens in Their Old Homes and Their New.** 1919

D'Agostino, Guido. **Olives on the Apple Tree.** 1940

D'Angelo, Pascal. **Son of Italy.** 1924

Fenton, Edwin. **Immigrants and Unions,** A Case Study: Italians and American Labor, 1870-1920. (Doctoral Thesis, Harvard University, 1957). 1975

Forgione, Louis. **The River Between.** 1928

Fucilla, Joseph G. **The Teaching of Italian in the United States:** A Documentary History. 1967

Garlick, Richard C., Jr. et al. **Italy and Italians in Washington's Time.** 1933

Giovannitti, Arturo. **The Collected Poems of Arturo Giovannitti.** 1962

Istituto di Studi Americani, Università degli Studi di Firenze (Institute of American Studies, University of Florence). **Gli Italiani negli Stati Uniti** (Italians in the United States). 1972

Italians in the City: Health and Related Social Needs. 1975

Italians in the United States: A Repository of Rare Tracts and Miscellanea. 1975

Lapolla, Garibaldi M. **The Fire in the Flesh.** 1931

Lapolla, Garibaldi M. **The Grand Gennaro.** 1935

Mariano, John Horace. **The Italian Contribution to American Democracy.** 1922

Mariano, John H[orace]. **The Italian Immigrant and Our Courts.** 1925

Pagano, Jo. **Golden Wedding.** 1943

Parenti, Michael John. **Ethnic and Political Attitudes:** A Depth Study of Italian Americans. (Doctoral Dissertation, Yale University, 1962). 1975

Protestant Evangelism Among Italians in America. 1975

Radin, Paul. **The Italians of San Francisco:** Their Adjustment and Acculturation. Parts I and II. 1935

Rose, Philip M. **The Italians in America.** 1922

Ruddy, Anna C. (Christian McLeod, pseud.). **The Heart .of the Stranger:** A Story of Little Italy. 1908

Schiavo, Giovanni Ermenegildo. **Italian-American History:** Volume I. 1947

Schiavo, Giovanni [Ermenegildo]. **Italian-American History:** The Italian Contribution to the Catholic Church in America. Volume II. 1949

Schiavo, Giovanni [Ermenegildo]. **The Italians in America Before the Civil War.** 1934

Schiavo, Giovanni E[rmenegildo]. **The Italians in Chicago:** A Study in Americanization. 1928

Schiavo, Giovanni [Ermenegildo]. **The Italians in Missouri.** 1929

Schiro, George. **Americans by Choice:** History of the Italians in Utica. 1940

La Società Italiana di Fronte Alle Prime Migrazioni di Massa. (Italian Society at the Beginnings of the Mass Migrations). New Foreword (in English) by Francesco Cordasco. 1968

Speranza, Gino. **Race or Nation:** A Conflict of Divided Loyalties. 1925

Stella, Antonio. **Some Aspects of Italian Immigration to the United States:** Statistical Data and General Considerations Based Chiefly Upon the United States Censuses and Other Official Publications. 1924

Ulin, Richard Otis. **The Italo-American Student in the American Public School:** A Description and Analysis of Differential Behavior. (Doctoral Thesis, Harvard University, 1958). 1975

Valletta, Clement Lawrence. **A Study of Americanization in Carneta:** Italian-American Identity Through Three Generations. (Doctoral Dissertation, University of Pennsylvania, 1968). 1975

Villari, Luigi. **Gli Stati Uniti d'America e l'Emigrazione Italiana.** (The United States and Italian Immigration). 1912

Workers of the Writers' Program. Work Projects Administration in the State of Nebraska. **The Italians of Omaha.** 1941